Economics Revision Notes
for
Leaving Certificate

Pat Younger

Aslan

MADE IN DUBLIN

07243 522823 26

Gill & Macmillan

Gill & Macmillan Ltd
Goldenbridge
Dublin 8
with associated companies throughout the world
www.gillmacmillan.ie
© Pat Younger 1995
0 7171 2290 5
Print origination by DTP Workshop, Dublin
Printed by ColourBooks Ltd, Dublin

In memory of my Mum and Dad

CONTENTS

Preface

PREFACE

Economics is about scarcity of resources. Time is a scarce commodity for a Leaving Certificate student, particularly in second and third terms in sixth year. The key aim of this book is to help students to make the best use of their time. It will provide you with:

- a comprehensive summary of each topic,
- an assessment test on each topic,
- the solutions to each assessment test.

If you follow this method, you should find your knowledge and understanding of the course improving.

A complete summary of the key points to both the Micro and Macro elements of the course is included. This should act as a checklist to what you *should* know. You can then test yourself by answering the 100 questions which cover the entire course.

Solutions are contained to all the questions in Section A which have been asked in the Higher Level papers since 1977. You can check the key questions asked in the analysis of past papers at the beginning of the text and the text concludes with advice on how to handle the actual Leaving Certificate exam.

I have used all these materials with my own students over the years and they seem to work! If students or teachers have comments, please forward them to me.

Good luck with your studies and in your Leaving Certificate.

Pat Younger
Good Counsel College
New Ross
Co. Wexford

January 1995

Section I:
Analysis of Higher
Level Exam Papers
and Revision Notes

MICROECONOMICS

MACROECONOMICS

REVISION ECONOMICS
EXPLANATION OF TERMS

A. Introduction

defn	definition
adv	advantage
↑	increase
prodn	production
FOP	factors of production
SNPs	Super Normal Profits
CHs	charges
E/S	Economies of Scale
D/S	Diseconomies of Scale
gds/servs	goods & services
govt	government
econ	economic

B. Demand, Supply, Markets

Qd	Quantity demanded
Sub	Substitute
Comp	Complement
D/C	Demand Curve
r/ship	relationship
Qs	Quantity supplied
S/C	Supply Curve

C. Utility

behav.	behaviour
Y	income
MU	Marginal Utility
min qty	minimum quantity
LDMU	Law of Diminishing Marginal Utility
P_X	price of good X
P_Y	price of good Y
E_D^P	Price Elasticity of Demand

D. Elasticity

Δs	changes
E_D^Y	Income Elasticity of Demand
E_D^C	Cross Elasticity of Demand
wrt	with respect to

E. Costs of Production

LDMR	Law of Diminishing Marginal Returns
s/r	short run
l/r	long run
AFC	average fixed costs
AVC	average variable costs
ATC	average total costs
APC	average propensity to consume
MPC	Marginal propensity to consume
LRAC	long run average cost
diff.	different
qtys	quantities
servs	services
indv.	individual

F. Market Forms

LRS/C	long run supply curve
min.	minimum
conds	conditions
mkt	market
@	at
OAP	old age pensioners
a/c	account

G. Factors of Production

pop.	population
S_{LAB}	Supply of labour
WR	wage rate
D_{LAB}	Demand for labour
Co.	Company
govt	government
D	Demand
TU	Trade union
s/r	short run
amt	amount
cap	capital
DLF	Demand for loanable funds
r/i	rate of interest
SLF	Supply of loanable funds
MLR	Minimum lending rate
nat.	national
curr.	currency

H. Budgeting, Tax & Debt

CBS	Current budget surplus
CBD	Current budget deficit
edn	education
exp.	expenditure
rev.	revenue
ΣD	Aggregate demand
Y↑→T↑	Income↑→Tax↑
sh.	should
CPT	Corporate Profits Tax
b/e	beginning

I. Money & Banking

M^S	money supply
C^E	consumer expenditure
ΣD	Aggregate demand
Cen. Bk	Central Bank
X mkts	export markets
MP	monetary policy
info.	information
comm. bks	commercial banks
cash dep.	cash deposits
V currency	Value of currency
estb.	established
std	standard
UD	underdeveloped

J. Inflation

infl.	inflation
X	Exports
M	Imports
BOP	Balance of Payments
C_E	Consumer Expenditure
I_E	Investment Expenditure
G_E	Government Expenditure

K. Population & Employment

counts	countries
prodn	production
inds	industries
conspn	consumption
Xs	Exports
E/R	Exchange rate
MPM	Marginal propensity to import
Soc. probs	social problems

N. Economic Aims

G^E	Government Expenditure

SECTION B QUESTIONS

	1998	1997	1996	1995
Demand, Supply, Mkts		• Factors affecting Supply • Movement v. shift in D/C • Exceptions to Law of Demand		
Utility				
Elasticity	• CED & YED • PED • Knowledge of Elasticities		• YED: Defn & Formula • Inferior/Luxury Goods • Knowledge of Elasticity	• PED: Defn & Formula • Factors affecting PED • PED & Changing Prices
Costs				
Market Forms	Monopoly	Perfect Competition	Monopoly	Imperfect Competition
FOP Mkt	• Enterprise/Risks • Entrepreneurs & Profits	• Demand for Labour • Wage Differences • Labour Efficiency	• Enterprise/Types of Risk • Entrepreneurs & Profits	• S/C of Labour • Demand for Labour
Govt in Economy	• Definitions • Effects of High Taxes • Reducing Taxes	• Reasons for Nat. Debt • Nat. Debt: Problems, etc.		• Privatisation: Arguments For & Against
Banking	Savings/Investment	• M3/Credit Creation • Central Bank		• Creation of Credit • Central Bank
Inflation				
Pop & Employment	• Live Register & LFS • Unemployment	Live Register & LFS	• Overpopulation • Decline in Birth Rate • Emigration	• Live Register • Full Employment
National Income	• National Income • GDP & GNP • MPS, MPM & Multiplier	• Consumer Spending • Investment	• Factors affecting GNP • Uses/Limitations of Statistics	• Multiplier & Formula • Govt. Influence on ΣD
Inter. Trade	• Maastricht Rules • Effects of Joining Euro • Effects if UK stays out	• LOCA & TDT • Reasons for Trade	• Exchange Rate of a Curr. • Maastricht Rules/IR£	• LOCA: define & example • Assumptions of LOCA
Ec. Aims, Pols & Conflicts		Privatisation	Aims of Govt. Policies: Fiscal & Monetary	
Econ. Devel.			• Costs & Benefits of Development • Promotion of Econ. Development	
Hist. of Ec. Thought				Keynes
Intro. & EU				

SECTION A QUESTIONS

	1998	1997	1996	1995
Demand, Supply & Markets				Perpendicular S/C shows
Utility		Law of Diminishing Marginal Utility		Law of Equi-Marginal Returns ...
Elasticity				
Costs		• External Economies of Scale • Social Costs	Law of Diminishing Returns	2 Forms of Collusion ...
Market Forms	Limit Pricing ...	3 forms of Collusion	In PC, L/R equilibrium is ...	Price Discriminating Monopolist produces ...
FOP Mkt	• Supply Price ... • MPP is ...		• Economic rent is ... • A trade union is a monopoly	3 reasons why profits are important ...
Govt in Economy	• PSBR ... • The Tax Wedge is ...		• Function of NTMA • The Tax Wedge is ...	• PSBR • The Tax Wedge is ...
Banking	PLR is ...			PLR is ...
Inflation	Demand Pull Inflation			
Pop & Employment	Overpopulation is ...	Optimum population	Labour Force Survey	
National Income	• Black Economy is ... • GNP @ factor cost & GDP		MPS, MPT, MPM & Mult.	GNP @ factor cost & GDP
Inter. Trade		PPPT		
Ec. Aims, Pols & Conflicts				
Econ. Devel.	2 characteristics of land ...			
Hist. of Econ. thought		Monetarists	Monetarists or Supply Siders	
Intro. & EU				

	1994	1993	1992	1991
Demand, Supply, Mkts	FOP : Enterprise	Factors affecting S		
Utility	Def/n ; risks & importance			
Elasticity	• YED CED for sub gds. • PED: changing prices	• Normal, Giffen & inferior • PED: +/−; expl.; producer		• PED, PES & YED • Factors aff. E^P of D/S
Costs			• S/R + L/R equil. • Same as '81 Q.	
Market Forms	• Mon. are efficient? • PD: def/n + cond/ns	• SRS/C + LRS/C in PC • SR + LR Equ. in PC	PDM	Imperfect comp.
FOP Mkt	• MPP & MRP in mkts • Econ. rent + comm. rent	• Oligopoly • Price & non-price comp. • Savings & Investment	• Factors DLab • When a FOP earns ER	• Define investment • Inv.: factors affecting
Govt in Economy	Nat. Debt: problems of internal + external debt	CBD, EBR, Nat Debt ↓ CBD : how? & effects	• Char/s of a good tax • Impact v imposition	• Ireland in 1990/91 • Privatisation
Banking			• Indirect tax • Privatisation	• Creation of credit • Monetary Policy/Assets
Inflation				• How CPI is constructed • CPI : uses & limitations
Pop & Employment	• Factors : lab mobility • Causes + solns to U.	• Effects of emigration • Prob/s & remedies of unemployment	• f = S_{LAB} • Causes, effects & solns of unem.	
National Income	Define Mul. + r/ship to MPC		• Multiplier + factors • Ire -> open economy	
Inter. Trade	• Factors aff. E/R • Effects of devaluation • Why M. vary with GNP	• PPPT & ECU • Effects of IR£ deval.	• How to ↑ ΣD. • IR£ v £stg	• Loca & assumptions • Ire. sources of loca
Ec. Aims, Pols & Conflicts		Competitiveness of Ir. ind.	• EMS & SEM	
Econ. Devel.	• Define econ. devel. • Char. of UDC/s • How to ↑ development			• Ben./costs of econ. gr. • Prob/solns of UDC
Hist. of Ec. Thought	David Ricardo	Keynes	• David Ricardo • Adam Smith	
Intro. & EC				Alfred Marshal 1/3 Keynes: govt. inter.
Demand, Supply & Markets				
Utility		LDMU states		Consumer behaviour assumptions
Elasticity				
Costs	LDMR states		If MC = MR then firm is earning normal profit	
Market Forms	• Consumer surplus is • cond/ns for S/R Equil. in PC	PC firms in L/R earn normal profits. Why?	Consumer surplus is ...	• Price discrim. exists ... • MRP = MPP x P in PC
FOP Mkt		• TU is a monopoly S Lab • 2 uninsurable risks	• Liq. pref. refers to ... • Labour productivity depends on?	• Real r/i are ... • Supply price of FOP
Govt in Economy	Effective incidence of a tax depends on	• Progressive tax • A tax wedge is ...		• Incidence of a tax • PSBR
Banking	• Neutral budget is ... • M3 means		Cen. Bk re-discount rate means ...	Funding by Cen. Bk means ...
Inflation				
Pop & Employment		Over-pop. means ...	Over-pop. means ...	
National Income	R/ship between GNP and NNP	MPS, MPM & MPT	MPS is ...	
Inter. Trade			BOP capital is ...	
Ec. Aims, Pols & Conflicts	Opportunity cost of using an asset owned			
Econ. Devel.		Social Costs + 2 examples		The accelerator ...
Hist. of Ec.Thought	Malthus's theory on Pop. + food supply		Labour theory of value states ...	

	1990	1989	1988	1987
Demand, Supply, Mkts				
Utility				
Elasticity	Price & Cross		Price & Cross	
Costs		Costs & taxes		
Market Forms	Oligopoly	PDM	Oligopoly	• Oligopoly • PDM (2 Qs)
FOP Mkt		• R/ship MPP & MRP • Employment in PC/M	• Savings/investments • ↑S: effects	
Govt in Economy	• CBD, PSBR & ND • Effects of ↓ tax	Imposition & incidence of a tax (30m)	• CBD, PSBR & ND • ↓r/i : effects on above	• CBD, EBR; SLD • Econ ↓ : what to CBD?
Banking	• Causes of ↑r/i • CB: ↑s/t liquidity			• Inter. bank mkt • STF
Inflation		r/i + inflation		↓ Infl.: effects on r/i
Pop & Employment	• GDP & GNP • Δs in both (2Qs)	Emigration		• How to measure U • ↓T =>U?
National Income	Effects of Inj. into econ. (2Qs)	Multiplier prob.	• GNP v GDP • What affects GNP?	Multiplier prob.
Inter. Trade	• X : M/s + G. Borr. • F + V: E/Rs	• LOCA + assumptions • BOT + ec. growth	• Ex. value of curr. • BOT ΔMs with GNP	Devaluation : effects
Ec. Aims, Pols & Conflicts		Removal of ex. controls	• Eire: small open econ. • Fiscal policy: ↑ or ↓	
Econ. Devel.				
Hist. of Ec. Thought	Ideas of 1 school of econ. thought	Keynesian v monetarism	Smith, Malthus, Marx, Friedman	Keynes : R for Interv.? Monetarism
Intro. & EC		• EMS • Single Euro. Mkt	Competitiveness of Irish Xs	
Demand, Supply & Markets			Deductive reasoning	
Utility	Consumer equilibrium		Cond/s for consumer equilibrium	
Elasticity	Inferior good			Luxury good
Costs	To earn SNP costs must be min.		If MC > MR = no normal profit?	
Market Forms	PC: normal profit?	Equilibrium occurs:	Limit Pricing	
FOP Mkt	Speculative D money		MRP = MPP x P, where?	• Liquidity pref? • MEC • Land
Govt in economy	Neutral budget		Built-in stabiliser	Supply side econ.
Banking		• PSBR • Funding	STF	
Inflation				
Pop & Employment				
National Income		GNP @ FC / GDP @ FC:		↓ in ec. activity
Inter. Trade	Bal. of auto. trans.	Fav. Δ in our TOT	Cap. a/c BOP:	Bal. of auto trans. Common Mkt
Ec. Aims, Pols & Conflicts	Opportunity Cost: 1988 Q.		Opportunity cost:	
Econ. Devel.		• Econ. Devel. • PRI + soc. benefits of 2nd level ed.		
Hist. of Ec. thought				

A. INTRODUCTORY DEFINITIONS

ECONOMICS

is a social science which studies human behaviour & how scarce resources, which have alternative uses, are allocated to satisfy the infinite needs & wants of mankind.

So economics is concerned with reducing scarcity: whether the exchange involved money or barter.

CONSTRUCTION & TESTING OF ECONOMIC THEORIES

First a problem is seen to exist and a decision is made to try to solve it.

The next step is to examine existing information & one's own idea about the problem.

At this stage, the economist may decide to follow either the *deductive* or *inductive* method of research.

THE DEDUCTIVE METHOD

This is the most common approach to research economic problems.

It moves from a general statement to particular uses. In other words, we start with principles which are generally true, apply these principles to specific cases and arrive at conclusions which are true if, originally, the general principles were true.

e.g. All animals will die. A cat is an animal, so a cat will die.

General statement ──────▶ Particular

THE INDUCTIVE METHOD

This approach is commonly used by physical scientists. It moves from particular cases to a general statement. The economist collects data & searches this for a pattern.

From this pattern a conclusion is drawn which becomes an economic theory/law.

e.g. 20 GAA grounds examined had a 50% drop in attendance when league matches were played on Mondays. This finding leads to a general principle.

In terms of gate receipts, Mondays are bad days for league football.

DEFINITIONS

(a) **Wealth:** the total value of all assets owned by an individual or group of people. It includes tangible (land) & intangible (intelligence) assets.

(b) **Welfare:** the overall condition of well-being of an individual or group of people.
    It covers a person's material well-being as well as psychological & moral well-being.

(c) **Capital:** the total stock of wealth a community possesses at a single point in time. It consists of both fixed and working capital (stock).

(d) **Income:** this is the amount of wealth produced by a community over a period of time, i.e. a flow of wealth.

(e) **Economic laws:** these are statements that under certain conditions certain people will act in a certain way. They are *not* statements of absolute fact & do *not* have universal application.

FACTORS OF PRODUCTION

LAND:

Land is composed of those economic resources supplied by nature & not by man, e.g. land, rivers, forests etc. Each of them is economically important.

Land is unique for 2 reasons:

(i) it is fixed in supply, and

(ii) it has no cost of production.

Law of Diminishing Marginal Returns

When an increasing number of units of a variable FOP (e.g. labour) is applied to a fixed quantity of another FOP (e.g. capital), the returns per unit to the variable FOP eventually begin to diminish.

LABOUR

Definition: the application of human effort in the creation of wealth.

Division/specialisation of labour:

where each individual does *one* task to which he is best suited (e.g. Adam Smith & e.g. of pins).

The main adv. of it is: ↑ in output.

Mobility of labour: 2 types:

(a) Lateral/geographical:
    Ability of workers to move from one area to another.
    Factors which influence geographical mobility are:
    (i) existence of social relationships;
    (ii) cost of moving, e.g. housing;
    (iii) parental reluctance to disturb kids' education;
    (iv) lack of information about opportunities;
    (v) grants/social welfare available.

(b) Vertical/occupational:
    Ability of workers to move from one job to another.
    Factors which influence occupational mobility are:
    (i) age of worker;
    (ii) high costs of training & education;
    (iii) professional associations and trade union restrictions;
    (iv) social factors, e.g. address of the worker.

CAPITAL

Definition: includes all those assets which are used in the production of wealth e.g. machines etc.

(For definitions of capital widening & deepening *plus* marginal efficiency of capital: see FOP chapter.)

ENTERPRISE

Definition: is the intelligence or controlling factor in the production process. It organises the other factors to produce a good or service and it bears the risk involved in production.

It is unique for the following reasons:

1. only FOP which can earn a loss;
2. its return is residual (others must be paid first);
3. returns can vary enormously (from SNPs to losses).

SCALE OF PRODUCTION ECONOMIES & DISECONOMIES OF SCALE

As a firm grows in size it experiences certain cost advantages (economies of scale) & cost disadvantages (diseconomies of scale).

ECONOMIES

Internal

1. Specialisation of labour.
2. More efficient use of machinery.
3. Buy in bulk: discounts.
4. Large orders: transport & handling charges reduced.
5. Capital: cheaper to borrow.
6. Construction economies: cheaper to build large buildings.

External

1. Development of subsidiary trades to service the expanding industry.
2. Development of research & development industries.

DISECONOMIES

Internal

1. Slower & less effective decision-making.
2. Poor staff morale – lower productivity.
3. Communication problems.
4. Increased administration overheads.

Internal E/S

Factors which occur *within* the firm as it grows in size making the firm more efficient.

External E/S

Benefits which the firm experiences as the industry to which it belongs grows in size.

Location of a Factory: Factors to Consider

1. Proximity to markets: market oriented.
2. Proximity to raw materials.
3. Availability of skilled labour/cost of labour.
4. Govt incentives & tax concessions.
5. Availability of water & power.
6. Availability of a local infrastructure, e.g. schools, houses etc.
7. Availability of transport facilities/ communications.
8. Planning permission: any objections?/Waste disposal.
9. Closeness to similar firms.

APPLIED ECONOMICS

Concerned with the use & application of economic theories in the solution of specific economic problems, e.g. ↓ unemployment.

ECONOMIC SYSTEMS

FREE ENTERPRISE

The system decides:

1. which goods/services to produce: consumers decide;
2. who produces them: firms decide;
3. how they are produced: the most profitable;
4. who gets these goods: those who can afford them.

The govt plays no role in decision-making.

Advantages:

1. Efficiency is encouraged (hence scarce resources are efficiently allocated).
2. Individual freedom to make decisions.
3. Initiative rewarded.

Disadvantages:

1. Great inequality of wealth exists.
2. Advertising exists => ↑ costs.

CENTRALLY PLANNED

The govt decides:

1. what & how to produce the goods;
2. who gets the goods, once produced.

Advantages:

1. Possible even distribution of wealth.
2. Central control over decision-making.

Disadvantages:

1. Inefficiency may be encouraged.
2. Lack of individual freedom & choice.
3. Initiative not rewarded.

Mixed Economies

- A mixture of both the above, e.g. Ireland: 60% of econ. activity: private. 40% of econ. activity: public.
- Establishment of semi-states.
- Movement away from the degree of intervention by state now due to massive debts & ideas of monetarism prevalent.

NOTES

B. DEMAND, SUPPLY & MARKETS

DEMAND

1. **Demand Function:** This sets out the relationship between the Q_D of a good & the factors upon which it depends.

$$Q_D = f(P, P_{OG}, Y, T, E, G)$$

i.e.

P: price of the good
P_{OG}: prices of substitutes & complements
Y: income
T: taste/fashion
E: expectations
G: govt regulations

2. **Demand Schedule:** Sets out the precise relationship between Q_D & P. To do this we must assume that P_{OG}, Y, T, E & G remain unchanged as P changes. This assumption is called *ceteris paribus*.

3. **Demand Curve:** this is the graph of the demand schedule.

P	Q_D
3	15 units
6	12 units
9	9 units
12	6 units
15	3 units

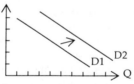

is downward sloping from L → R, indicating an inverse relationship between P & Q_D, i.e. as $P \uparrow \to Q_D \downarrow$

4. **Movement along the D/C** is caused by a change in P_n, i.e. the price of the good. This leads to a change in the Q_D of that good.

5. **Shift of the D/C.** This is caused by a change in P_{OG}, Y, T, E and G.

If: [A]
price of sub. ↑
price of comp.: ↓
income: increases
taste: becomes
stronger,

then D/C shifts to right.

SUPPLY

1. **Supply Function:** This sets out the relationship between the Q_S of a good & the factors upon which it depends.

$$Q_S = f(P, P_{OG}, T, C, G, D)$$

i.e.P: price of the good
P_{OG}: prices of subs & comp.
T: technology, state of
C: costs of production
G: government taxation etc.
D: durability/obsolescence.

2. **Supply Schedule:** Sets out the precise relationship between Q_S & P. To do this we must assume that P_{OG}, T, C, G and D remain *unchanged* as P changes. This assumption is called *ceteris paribus*.

3. **Supply Curve:** this is the graph of the supply schedule.

P	Q_S
3	3 units
6	6 units
9	9 units
12	12 units
15	15 units

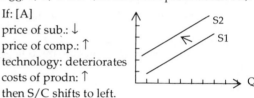

is upward sloping from L → R, indicating a positive r/ship between P & Q_S, i.e. as $P \uparrow \to Q_S \uparrow$.

4. **Movement along the S/C** is caused by a change in P_n, i.e. the price of the good. This leads to a change in the Q_S of that good.

5. **Shift of the S/C.** This is caused by a change in P_{OG}, T, C, G & D (assume max. profit doesn't Δ).

If: [A]
price of sub.: ↓
price of comp.: ↑
technology: deteriorates
costs of prodn: ↑
then S/C shifts to left.

MARKETS

FREE MARKETS

Equilibrium: occurs @ P_e where D = S.

AT P_1: surplus

i.e. $Q_S > Q_D$: suppliers must ↓ price to eliminate surplus.

AT P_2: shortage

i.e. $Q_D > Q_S$: consumers push prices up.

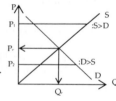

GOVT INTERVENTION

Allocation of available supply
A.   On sellers' preferences

e.g.
(i)   first come – 1st served
(ii) rationing
(iii) on basis of colour,
      religion or sex.
B.   Black mkt situation may develop, with P_B existing.

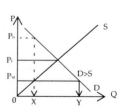

P_M: max price for this service

EFFECTS OF CHANGES OF D & S ON PRICES

e.g.

A. Tariff on imported raw material reduced.

B. Successful adv. campaign introduced.

In a Q. like this, ask does it affect D or S.

A. Affects S :   Costs of prodn are reduced.
                  Hence S/C shifts to right.
                  So P_e & Q_e should change.

B. Affects D: Taste/pref. of consumer is
                  strengthened.
                  D/C shifts to right.
                  P_e & Q_e change.

C. UTILITY

1. ASSUMPTIONS MADE ABOUT A CONSUMER'S BEHAVIOUR

(i) **He acts rationally,** i.e. if he has to choose between 2 goods of equal quality, he will pick the cheapest.

(ii) **He has limited income** with which to satisfy his needs.

(iii) **He wishes to maximise his utility** from this Y.

(iv) **He is subject to the Law of Diminishing MU.**

2. CHARACTERISTICS OF AN ECONOMIC GOOD

(i) It must be scarce in relation to demand.

(ii) It must command a price.

(iii) It must be capable of being transferred from one person to another. Beauty or intelligence (think of *yourself*) cannot be transferred.

(iv) It must provide utility.

3. UTILITY

This is the satisfaction which a person gets from consuming a good/service.
It is assumed that we can measure this – in utils.

A. Total Utility
This is the total satisfaction which we get from consuming a bundle of a good/service.

B. Marginal Utility
This is the extra or additional utility got from consuming an extra/additional unit of a good.

4. LAW OF DIMINISHING MARGINAL UTILITY

This states that as a person consumes additional units of a commodity, marginal utility eventually diminishes.

Assumptions on which LDMU Is based

1. That sufficient time has not elapsed for circumstances to change.

2. That it only applies to non-addictive goods, e.g. drugs etc. would not apply.

3. That LDMU only applies after a certain min. qty of the good is consumed: the *origin*.

4. That it doesn't allow for changes in *tastes/fashions*

5. CONSUMER EQUILIBRIUM

(or: How does a consumer allocate his income?)
A consumer will allocate his limited income so as to achieve maximum utility until the last penny spent on each good will bring him the same marginal utility, i.e.

$$\frac{MU_X}{P_X} = \frac{MU_Y}{P_Y} \text{ (and for all gds bought)}$$

called: Equi-Marginal Principle of Consumer Behaviour

6. WHY DOES A D/C SLOPE DOWNWARDS FROM LEFT TO RIGHT?

(i) At equilibrium: $\dfrac{MU_A}{P_A} = \dfrac{MU_B}{P_B}$

(ii) Assume P_A falls, what will happen Q_A^D?

(iii) If $P_A\downarrow$ then

$$\left(\frac{MU_A}{P_A}\right) \text{ will be greater than } \left(\frac{MU_B}{P_B}\right)$$

To restore equilibrium he should *buy more A.*

(iv) Hence as $P\downarrow \rightarrow \left(\dfrac{MU_A}{P_A}\right)\uparrow \rightarrow Q_A^D \uparrow$

Inverse r/ship 'tween P & Q!

(v) Hence the equi-marginal principle explains why a D/C slopes downwards from L $\rightarrow$ R.

7. EXCEPTIONS TO THE LAW OF DEMAND

(a) **Exclusive/snob value/goods of conspicuous consumption** which are demanded for their exclusive price, e.g. Rolls Royce cars etc.

(b) **Commodities whose prices are affected by expectations,** e.g. shares, land & property speculation. When their prices $\uparrow \rightarrow$ demand may also rise.

(c) **Giffen Goods** (see Elasticity) i.e. $+ E_D^P$

8. DEFINITIONS

A. Effective Demand
This is a person's desire for a commodity supported by purchasing power. (If you haven't got the money then it remains a desire – you can't demand it!)

B. Joint Demand
exists where demand for 2 gds is linked, e.g. egg cups & eggs. Such goods are called *complementary*

C. Composite Demand
exists where a single product is wanted for a number of uses, e.g. sugar.

D. Joint Supply
gds produced together, e.g. mutton & wool.

E. Consumer Surplus
This is the difference between what a consumer *actually pays* for a commodity and the max. price he *would have been willing to pay,* rather than do without it.

F. Goods: Examples

		Examples
Consumer	provide direct utility over a limited period of time to consumer	bread, crisps!
Consumer durables	provide utility to consumer over a long period of time.	T.V., fridges
Capital	gds needed to produce consumer gds & consumer durables	factories, machines

PRICE ELASTICITY OF DEMAND

1. Definition
This measures the responsiveness of Q_D to Δs in P.

2. Formula: $\dfrac{\Delta Q}{\Delta P} \times \dfrac{P_1 + P_2}{Q_1 + Q_2}$

3. Sign:
Normal goods: as $P\uparrow \to Q_D \downarrow$ i.e. *minus* –
Giffen goods: as $P\uparrow \to Q_D \uparrow$ i.e. *plus* +
e.g. potatoes in Ireland during the famine: if $P \uparrow$ they could buy less 'other' goods & so the Q_D of potatoes $\uparrow$.

4. Values

Value	e.g.	What it means	Definition
>1	–1.8 –2.4 +1.3	Good X: $E_D^P = -2.4$. If P $\uparrow$ 10%: $Q_D \downarrow$ 24%	Elastic good (luxuries)
<1	–0.02 –0.90 + 0.01	Good Y: $E_D^P = -0.2$ If P $\downarrow$ 10%: $Q_D \uparrow$ 2%	Inelastic good (necessities)
= 1	+ 1.0 – 1.0	Good Z: $E_D^P = -1.0$ if P $\downarrow$ 10%: $Q_D \uparrow$ 10%	Unit elasticity

5. E_D^P & Total Revenue

P	Q	TR = (P x Q)	E_D^P: $\dfrac{\Delta Q}{\Delta P} \times \dfrac{P_1 + P_2}{Q_1 + Q_2}$
25p	200	£50	1. P$\downarrow$ 25p to 20p = –1·8
20p	300	£60	2. P$\downarrow$ 20p to 15p = –1·0
15p	400	£60	3. P$\downarrow$ 15p to 10p = –0·5
10p	500	£50	

Note:
1. When good is elastic: a $\downarrow$ P => a $\uparrow$ in TR.
2. When good is unitary elastic: a $\downarrow$ P => no change in TR.
3. When good is inelastic: a $\downarrow$ P => a $\downarrow$ in TR.

Hence:
For elastic gds: Δ P in the opposite way to TR (i.e. to $\uparrow$ TR $\to \downarrow$ P).

For inelastic gds: Δ P in same way to TR (to $\uparrow$ TR $\to \uparrow$ P).

6. Factors on which E_D^P depend:
(a) No. of substitutes available:
   if high – highly elastic
   if low – inelastic.
(b) Durability/obsolescence of the product: the more durable the good, the higher its price elasticity.
(c) % of income spent on the good:
   if it's high, then good will have a high E_D^P.
(d) Necessity or luxury?
   If necessity: relatively inelastic
   If luxury: relatively elastic.

(e) The no. of alternative uses the good has: e.g. sugar is used in many things (industrial & domestic); a small Δ P might lead to a small Δ in D in each area, but the overall $\downarrow$ might be significant.
(f) Degree of importance of the good.

INCOME ELASTICITY OF DEMAND

Definition:
This measures the responsiveness of Q_D to Δs in Y.

Formula: $\dfrac{\Delta Q}{\Delta Y} \times \dfrac{Y_1 + Y_2}{Q_1 + Q_2}$

Sign:
Normal goods: as $Y \uparrow \to Q_D \uparrow$ i.e. *plus* +
Inferior goods: as $Y \uparrow \to Q_D \downarrow$ i.e. *minus* –
e.g. white sugar, white bread & potatoes are inferior gds.
N.B. The term inferior does not mean that the good is inferior in quality, but that it has a $- E_D^Y$.

Values:

$E_D^Y > 1$	income elastic, generally luxuries
$E_D^Y < 1$	income inelastic, generally necessities

CROSS ELASTICITY OF DEMAND

Substitutes: $(P_B \uparrow \to \overset{\text{Margarine}}{Q_D^M \uparrow})$ i.e. $+ E_D^C$.
Complementary: $(\overset{\text{Butter}}{P_P} \uparrow \to Q^D \downarrow)$ i.e. $- E_D^C$
$\qquad\qquad\qquad$ Petrol $\quad$ Cars

> This is a complex area. You will only understand it fully by answering questions.

PRICE = SUBSTITUTION + INCOME EFFECTS

i.e. if the P good changes it gives rise to both a *substitution effect*, i.e. more of the cheaper good will always be bought, and an

income effect, i.e. because of the increased purchasing power, the demand for both goods can change.

Explanation:

Case	Δ P =	Substitution + Income	= Overall ΔQ_D
A	P$\downarrow$	$Q_A^D \uparrow$ by 5 units + $Q_A^D \uparrow$ by 5	=> $Q_D \uparrow 10$

This gd is normal with respect to both price and income

B	P$\downarrow$	$Q_B^D \uparrow$ by 5 + $Q_B^D \downarrow 2$ => $Q_B^D \uparrow 3$ Negative income effect

While this gd is inferior with respect to income overall, it behaves normally with respect to price Δs.

C	$P\downarrow$	$Q_C^D \uparrow$ by 3 + $Q_C^D \downarrow$ 5 => $Q_C^D \downarrow$ 2
		Negative income effect Positive income effect
		Inferior Gd Giffen Gd

Therefore in Case C, this is a Giffen good. It is also inferior. So *all Giffen goods are inferior goods*. But *not all inferior goods are Giffen* – as can be seen in Case B, where the inferior good is *normal*.

To summarise:

> A Giffen good must be Inferior,
> but an inferior good can be Giffen or normal.

Can a normal good be a Giffen good?

Looking at the Table above, particularly Case A: For a normal good, the substitution effect is *always* positive.

The income effect will also be positive.

Hence if $P\downarrow \rightarrow$ overall Q_D will $\uparrow$.

For a Giffen good, however, the income effect is negative (it's inferior). So a normal gd cannot be Giffen.

E. COSTS OF PRODUCTION

PRODUCTION PERIODS

The costs which a firm faces depends on whether it is operating in the *short run* or *long run*.

Short run: this is a period of time over which all the FOP remain fixed in supply except 1. So to ↑ output, only 1 FOP can be ↑. (However, this is subject to the LDMR.)

Long run: this is a period of time over which all the FOP are variable. So to ↑ output, any of the FOP can be increased.

In the s/r some costs are *fixed*, some *variable*. In the l/r *all costs are variable*.

COSTS

1. **Fixed:** costs which remain fixed as output varies, e.g. rates of premises, management salaries etc.

AFC: is the FC per unit produced, i.e. $\frac{FC}{Quantity\ Produced}$

 These decline rapidly over the early stages of prodn and then fall slowly as prodn increases.

2. **Variable:** costs which do change as output changes, e.g. raw materials, labour.

AVC: is the VC per unit produced, i.e. $\frac{FC}{Quantity\ Produced}$

 After point X, AVC rise rapidly. Why? Because to produce extra output it takes increasing qtys of the variable FOP Why? This is due to the LDMR.

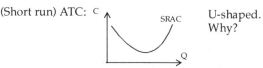

LDMR: As increasing qtys of 1 FOP are applied to a fixed qty of another FOP, the returns per unit to the first factor eventually begin to diminish.

3. **Total cost:** TC = FC + VC (ATC = AFC + AVC)

(Short run) ATC: U-shaped. Why?

Downward sloping: due to AFC declining rapidly.
Upward sloping: due to AVC rising rapidly due to the LDMR.

4. Marginal Cost: MC

This is the additional cost of producing an additional unit of output.

e.g. in order to increase his labour force from 10 to 11 an entrepreneur is obliged to raise the weekly wage from £100 to £105. What is the MC?

Ans.: the total cost of 10 men: £100 × 10 = £1,000

the total cost of 11 men: £105 × 11 = £1,155

∴ The MC of the 11th man is: £155

Relationship between SRAC and MC

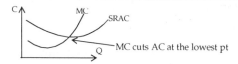

MC cuts AC at the lowest pt

When MC is above AC: AC is *rising*
When MC is below AC: AC is *falling*
When MC equals/cuts AC: AC is *at a minimum*

(Think of the av. age of the class as 17. If a new student enters aged 20, the marginal age is 20; the av. age of the class rises & vice versa.

DERIVING THE LRAC CURVE

In the LR output can be ↑ by varying *all* the FOP. So costs vary as follows:

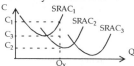

Each SRAC represents a diff. factory size & so a diff. cost structure.

If he wishes to produce Q_X then the lowest cost of production is C_2 (SRAC$_2$).

We can continue this & derive a whole series of SRAC facing the firm.

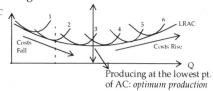

Producing at the lowest pt.
of AC: *optimum production*

The firm is a profit miximiser & will try to produce at minimum costs, i.e. the lowest pts of all SRACs. If we join the lowest pts of all these SRACs we get the LRAC curve: shallow L-shaped. Why?
Costs ↓ in LR due to: *economies of scale*.
Costs ↑ in LR due to *diseconomies of scale*.

Refer to Economies & Diseconomies of Scale in Section A, p. 7.

Profit

This is the return to the FOP enterprise & it's unique for 3 reasons:
1. Its return is residual, i.e. it gets what's left after all other factors have been paid.
2. Its return can vary from large profits to large losses.
3. It's the only factor that can earn a loss.

Normal profit: the return which sufficiently rewards the risk-taking of the entrepreneur. It is incl. in the firm's AC curve.

SNP: anything which is earned in excess of normal profit, i.e. if a firm sells a good above AC.

Opportunity costs:

this is the cost of the foregone alternatives.

F. MARKET FORMS

PERFECT COMPETITION

ASSUMPTIONS

1. Product is homogeneous: no need for advertising.
2. Large no. of buyers & sellers: no indv. buyer or seller can affect prices.
3. Perfect knowledge of profits & prices.
4. Free entry & exit from the industry: no barriers to entry.
5. No collusion between the producers.

IMPLICATIONS OF ASSUMPTIONS: FIRM IS A PRICE TAKER

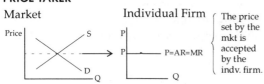

Market   Individual Firm   The price set by the mkt is accepted by the indv. firm.

SHORT RUN

Equilibrium condns	Equilibrium diagram	Supply curve
1. MC = MR. 2. MC increasing as it cuts MR from below. 3. AVC covered.	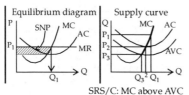	

SRS/C: MC above AVC

S/R TO L/R ADJUSTMENT

If SNP exist, then because of assumptions 3 & 4 above, new firms enter the industry & the market S/C expands, i.e. shifts to the right.

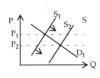 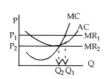

Here AR>AC & so SNP exist. So S/C₁ shifts to SC₂ & P↓ until SNP eroded.

LONG RUN

Equilibrium condns	Equilibrium diagram	Supply curve & advantages
1. MC = MR. 2. MC cuts MR from below & is increasing. 3. ATC covered.		LRS/C: MC above ATC Advantages 1. Max. efficiency: the firm produces at the lowest point of AC. 2. Consumers face min. prices because no SNP exist in the LR.

IMPERFECT COMPETITION

ASSUMPTIONS

1. Products are *not* homogeneous but are *close substitutes*.
2. Large no. of buyers & sellers.
3. Freedom of entry & exit: *no barriers*.
4. Perfect knowledge of profits & prices.

DEMAND FACING FIRM

Because the firm sells a close substitute, the firm can affect the qty it sells, e.g. if it cuts P then the Q_D ↑ & vice versa. The firm faces a downward-sloping D_C.

So if the firm ↓ price (it gets less AR for its sales). Hence to ↑ sales it must cut the prices for all goods. So MR lies beneath AR.

SHORT-RUN EQUILIBRIUM (same condns as PC)

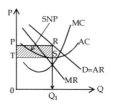

Where MC = MR the firm produces Q1. To get the P we go up to the AR/P lines. So the price is P. AR exceeds AC: so SNP exist of RS per unit produced or RSTP: total profits. With SNPs new firms enter the industry.

So each indv. firm's share of the mkt declines, i.e. D/C shifts to left.

LONG-RUN EQUILIBRIUM

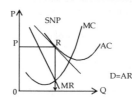

The D/C has shifted in until the SNPs are eroded, i.e. at point X: AR=AC: *No SNPs*. Notice that the firm is *not* producing at the lowest point of AC. Called *excess capacity*.

ADVS & DISADVS OF IC

Advantages:

great choice of goods available to the consumer.

Disadvantages:

Inefficient use of resources: a firm is *not* producing @ the lowest pt of AC.

Competitive advertising: because the products are close substitutes, firms must advertise to ↑ sales. Because *all* firms engage in adv. no single firm gains an advantage. Thus the effect is to ↑ prices to the consumer. Why is adv. not necessary in PC or monopoly?

MONOPOLY

ASSUMPTIONS

1. Only *one* seller in the industry producing the product or selling the service, e.g. ESB, Smurfit, Telecom Éireann etc.
2. The firm can either determine the price or the output.
3. There is *no* freedom of entry/exit: barriers to entry exist.

SOURCES OF MONOPOLY POWER: BARRIERS TO ENTRY

1. State monopolies: the state doesn't allow competition, e.g. ESB.
2. Sole control of *one* of the FOP, e.g. a mining operation.
3. Ownership of a patent, e.g. Waterford Glass, Dolby noise reduction.
4. Capital required is too large to allow competition, e.g. aircraft manuf.

IMPLICATIONS OF ASSUMPTIONS

1. Because there is only one firm in the industry, the industry's D/C is the firm's D/C so the firm can ↑ sales by ↓ price.
2. We'll assume he faces the same cost structure as a PC firm. (How accurate is this?)
3. Same condns of equilibrium as before.

EQUILIBRIUM

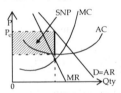

- it produces where MC=MR; price is P_e.
- it earns SNP & this can continue into LR because barriers to entry exist.
- if costs ↑ then the level of SNPs ↓

ADVANTAGES OF MONOPOLY

1. Costs may decrease due to economies of scale & passed on in the form of lower prices to consumers.
2. The size of the market may *not* justify more than 1 firm.
3. State monopolies may be non-profit making providing essential services.

DISADVANTAGES

1. Not producing @ lowest pt of AC: inefficient use of resources.
2. High prices (∵ of SNPs) & less produced.
3. Consumer may be exploited.

PC & M COMPARED

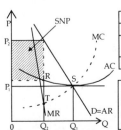

	PC	M
Output	Q1	Q2 smaller
Price	P1	P2 higher
Lowest pt of av. cost	Yes	No: RT waste of res.
SNPs	No	Yes

Dominant Firms

A firm which is not a pure monopolist dominates the industry and acts in a monopolistic manner, e.g. Waterford Glass.

PRICE DISCRIMINATING MONOPOLY

DEFINITION:

When goods or services are sold to different consumers at varying ratios between MC and price.

CONDITIONS NECESSARY FOR PRICE DISCR.

1. Monopoly power, i.e. the seller must have control over price or quantity.
2. Separation of mkts: otherwise gds could be bought cheap & sold in another mkt @ a higher price.
3. Consumers must have different price elasticities of demand: people with high E_D^P: low prices/ people with low E_D^P: high prices.
4. Consumer indifference.
5. Lack of knowledge on the part of consumers.

TYPES OF PRICE DISCRIMINATION

First degree: occurs when the seller can get from each buyer the highest price which he is willing to pay, i.e. eliminate his cons. surplus.

2nd degree: i.e. price concessions or quantity discounts *not* related to a reduction in the unit cost of production.

3rd degree: consumers divided into different classes depending on E_D^P and charged different prices accordingly.

Examples: 1. Students, OAPs etc. charged lower prices for some services.

2. Lower admission charges to some things for women.

EQUILIBRIUM: CONDITIONS & DIAGRAM

A. Conditions for maximising TR:

$$MR(d) = MR(e)$$

B. Conditions for maximising profit:

1. MC = MR.
2. MC increasing and cuts MR from below
3. MC = MR(d) = MR(e)

Helps decide how to allocate output.

i.e. assume monopolist at home; PC in foreign mkts.

When MR at home *falls* below MR in foreign mkt: output switched.

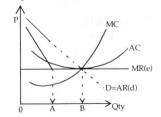

- Overall output: OB
- Domestic sales: OA
- Export Sales: AB

OLIGOPOLY

KINKED D/C

DEFN:
Mkt with few sellers, selling closely competing gds; trying to maximise their share of the mkt & taking into a/c the likely reactions of other sellers.

ASSUMPTIONS:
1. Few sellers who are dependent on each other.
2. No perfect knowledge of profits.
3. Product differentiation exists.
4. SNPs can be earned in the l/r.
5. Price leaders may exist.
6. Cartels may exist, e.g. OPEC.

EXAMPLES.
1. Cars: Ford, Nissan, Opel.
2. Food: Kellogg's, Quaker.
3. Detergents: Lever, Proctor & Gamble.

Price Rigidity
exists in oligopolistic markets where prices tend to be inflexible, due to the fact that if you ↓ price your rivals will follow you (inelastic D/C) & if you ↑ price they leave theirs alone (elastic D/C).

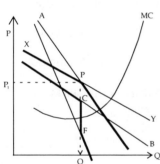

1. AB is the D/C when *all* sellers move prices together. (Inelastic D/C)
2. XY is the D/C if 1 firm *alone* changes its price & loses sales to rivals.
3. Below P, as others ↓ their Ps, AB prevails. Above P, others don't Δ Ps, XY prevails.
4. The total D/C is XPB. This caused a 'kink' in the D/C and a split in the MR curve between C & F.

In other words, if this firm:

↑ P above P (to try to ↑ profits), rivals will *not* follow suit. Hence this firm will lose sales. It operates on the *elastic* D/C, i.e. XY. If it ↓ P (to ↑ sales) rivals will follow suit. So this firm won't benefit: it's operating on the *inelastic* D/C: AB. So a firm will tend *not* to change prices at all: price rigidity.

HOW DO OLIGOPOLISTS COMPETE?

They engage in *non-price competition*: free gift schemes, special offers, trading stamps. Possibly also with more attractive packaging and improved after-sales service etc.

The most important form of course is advertising.

COURNOT MODEL

Assumptions
1. Two sellers produce an identical product at constant identical unit costs.
2. Both wish to maximise profit.
3. Both have *full* details of total demand & the D/C is linear.
4. Each assumes that the other will continue to produce the same amount in the next period.
5. Both adjust their level of output (but not their prices) in pursuit of their aim of max. profit.

Oligopoly, Monopoly & Perfect Competition Compared
This is *most important* to understand.
- Output in a *monopoly* is ½ that of a PC firm.
- In an *oligopoly* with 2 firms output is ⅔ that of a PC.
- In an *oligopoly* with 3 firms output is ¾ that of a PC.
- In an *oligopoly* with 4 firms output is ⅘ that of a PC,

and so on.

Example of Determining Equilibrium
An oligopoly with 2 firms reaches equilibrium producing 12,000 units.

Show how it's reached.

Stage	Firm 1	Firm 2	Explanation
1	9,000	—	Only 1 firm in industry: ½ PC
2	—	4,500	Firm 2 enters into the monopoly, produces ½ of 18,000 = 9,000
3	6,750	—	Firm 1 reacts; demand = 18,000 - 4,500 = 13,500 x ½
4	–	5,625	Firm 2 reacts; demand = 18,000 - 6,750 = 11,250 x ½ = 5,625
5	6,000	6,000	Adjustment continues until together they produce ⅔ of 18,000 = 12,000 and each produces half of this.

An oligopoly with 2 firms produces ⅔ the output of a PC firm. Hence in stage 1, with only 1 firm, output: 12,000 = ⅔ ∴ ³⁄₃ = 18,000.

G. FACTORS OF PRODUCTION

INTRODUCTION

1. The demand for any FOP is a *derived demand*, i.e. they are demanded *not* for the utility they provide but rather for their contribution to the production process.
2. Extra FOP employed will produce extra output. The extra output produced by employing an extra unit of a FOP is called the *Marginal Physical Productivity* – MPP (Remember: MPP declines due to the LDMR.)
3. The extra output produced above is then sold in the market place. This extra revenue received (from the addition of an extra FOP) is called *Marginal Revenue Productivity* – MRP.
4. MRP = MPP x MR
   But in PC, MR = P, so in PC only:
   MRP = MPP x P (because he faces a horizontal D/C)
5. The D/C_{FOP} = MRP curve.
6. **MRP Theory of Wages:** this states that each unit is paid the equivalent of the value that the *last* unit contributes when other FOP are constant.
7. **Difficulty of Measuring MRP**
   (i) It is sometimes difficult to separate the MRP of an extra unit of labour if extra capital is used, e.g. when new machinery is used workers look for higher pay due to increased responsibility.
   (ii) Recall:

   MRP = MPP   x   MR (=P IN PC)
   $\downarrow$ $\downarrow$
   extra output   price got in mkt
   $\downarrow$ $\downarrow$
   not all jobs produce   In the public sector,
   output, e.g. all the   if output is
   services area.   produced it
                              may not be sold.

   (iii) How can we determine pay?
   Pay comparability; qualifications; length of service

ECONOMIC RENT & TRANSFER EARNINGS: see later.

LABOUR

DEFINITION:
Labour is all human activity used in the prodn of wealth.

SUPPLY OF LABOUR IN THE ECONOMY:

(a) *Population size* : as pop. $\uparrow \rightarrow S_{LAB} \uparrow$
(b) *Wage rate:* generally as $W^R \uparrow \rightarrow S_{LAB} \uparrow$ (except 1 case)
(c) *Participation rate:* those between 16–65. Factors affecting this are:
   state of economy; level of social welfare; tax rates; pension levels; married women; wage rates.

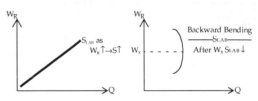

DEMAND FOR LABOUR

(i) D_{Lab}: is its MRP curve & downward sloping L→R
(ii) Factors affecting the Q^D_{Lab} by an indiv. firm:
   (a) *productivity*: how much extra revenue does he generate compared to his cost?
   (b) *tax on co. profits*: if $\uparrow \rightarrow \downarrow Q^D_{Lab}$
   (c) *payroll taxes*: as above
   (d) *govt subsidies*: if available, $\uparrow Q^D_{Lab}$
   (e) *demand for firm's output*: if it $\uparrow \rightarrow Q^D_{Lab}$
   (f) *availability of new technology*
   (g) *trade union involvement*.
(iii) Wage determination:

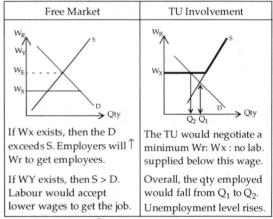

Free Market	TU Involvement
If Wx exists, then the D exceeds S. Employers will $\uparrow$ Wr to get employees.	The TU would negotiate a minimum Wr: Wx : no lab. supplied below this wage.
If WY exists, then S > D. Labour would accept lower wages to get the job.	Overall, the qty employed would fall from Q_1 to Q_2. Unemployment level rises.

REASONS FOR W^R DIFFERENCES

(a) *TU strength*: a strong TU can get workers their MRP.
(b) *Skill*: if you have a rare skill you can command high pay, i.e. a brain surgeon.
(c) *Training*: extra training $\uparrow$ your productivity, hence possibility of extra pay $\uparrow$.
(d) *Tradition*: may be used to determine pay where MRP is difficult to calculate particularly in services sector, i.e. teachers/gardai. Their pay is set by pay in Civil Service – reflects what people with similar ability can earn in private sector.
(e) *Nature & Conditions of Job*: e.g. dangerous work; shift work; seasonal work.
(f) *Monetary Benefits*: e.g. pension rights; VHI; subsidised loans & housing.

(g) *Non-Monetary Benefits:* helps to cut pay rates, e.g. social hours, length of holidays.

WAGE DRIFT

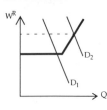

If D_{LAB} was to ↑ beyond the S_{LAB} available at the negotiated rate in the SR, W^R would ↑ above the negotiated rate & then TU would negotiate a new minimum W^R. If firms are banned from ↑ W^R they may offer other benefits like overtime.

> If D ↓ would Wr ↓? No. As wages & prices tend not to fall in an economy when demand falls. This is called a RATCHET ECONOMY.

DEFINITIONS

Transfer earnings: the amount a FOP can earn in the next best available employment.

Economic rent: anything which a FOP earns above its supply price. If it's short term it's called *Quasi Rent*, e.g. say there's a shortage of electricians. To get more, wages are ↑ and existing electricians earn these until S ↑ and they are eliminated.

CAPITAL

DEFINITIONS

(i) **Capital:** is man-made wealth used in the prodn of gds & servs.
(ii) **Cap. goods:** gds used in the prodn of other gds, e.g. factories, plant & machinery.
(iii) **Consumer gds:** gds which people demand for utility.
(iv) **Consumer durables:** consumer gds. which have a long life span, e.g. house/videos.

WHY ARE CAPITAL GDS DEMANDED?

(i) Because they help ↑ productivity.
(ii) Because capital gds ↑ productivity they ↑ profitability. The increase in profitability due to employing an extra unit of capital is called the *Marginal Efficiency of Capital:* MEC. It is the MRP of additional capital *minus* their costs.
(iii) **Investment:** is the prodn of capital gds. (capital formation).
(iv) **Capital widening:** when a ↑ in capital leaves the capital/labour ratio unchanged, i.e. both capital & labour ↑ but their ratio is unchanged.
(v) **Capital deepening:** if the capital stock ↑ at a faster rate than labour, then the amount of capital per worker will ↑.

SAVINGS

(i) **Definition:** savings is non-consumption.
(ii) Generally it was thought that the higher the r/i → the supply of savings (loanable funds LF) ↑. The D_{LF} depended on the MEC & this was sloping downwards from left to right. This loanable fund theory (that the r/i was set where $D_{LF} = S_{LF}$) is now considered too simplistic.
(iii) This theory also said that *all* savings were available for investment. This is *not* the case as people save for diff. reasons: precautionary, speculative, old age etc.
(iv) **Who saves?**

Individuals	Businesses	The State
↓	↓	↓
not spending	keeping profits	budget surplus

(v) **Types of savings:**
Compulsory: i.e. compulsory deductions from income.
Forced: where people can't get the gds they want.

FACTORS AFFECTING THE R/I

(i) **Bank rate/MLR/re-discount rate:**
all other r/i must be higher than this.'
(ii) **'Pure' r/i:** i.e. 'riskless' r/i which is 2.5% on govt consols with no redemption date.
(iii) **Degree of lender's risk:**
The greater the risk, the higher the return which the lender will require if he is to be enticed to lend.
(iv) **Length of time for repaying the loan:**
The longer the time period, the higher the r/i which must be paid.
(v) **Rate of inflation:**
If inflation is high, savers will want to be compensated thro' high r/i & the bank will ↑ r/i to try to ↓ spending.
(vi) **Demand for funds:** If D ↑ → r/i ↑.
(vii) **International factors:**

> **REAL R/I = NOMINAL R/I – INFLATION RATE**

e.g. I have a bond on 1/1/95 valued £1,000 @ 5%. If new bonds are issued at a r/i of 4%, how much could I sell my bond for? Less - Why? Because the new bond would get only £40, while my bond would get £50.

So 4% = £50 then 1% = £12.50 x 100 = £1,250: selling price of my bond.

If r/i are rising: possible effects:
Savings encouraged; *Borrowing* discouraged; *Investment* discouraged; *Mortgages* more expensive; *Imports* reduced; *Spending* reduced & inflation ↓ *Servicing* nat. debt ↑; *Curr. value* rises.

KEYNES'S LIQUIDITY PREFERENCE

The desire of people to hold wealth in money form.
3 reasons:

Transactionary: for daily expenses; depends mostly on income; little on r/i.

Precautionary: for irregular expenses; depends on income & r/i.

Speculative: for profitability opportunities; depends on r/i (opportunity cost).

LAND

DEFINITION:

that provided by nature for the construction of buildings &/or cultivation.

LAND IS UNIQUE FOR 2 REASONS:

It is fixed in supply to the country (but for individual uses it obviously can change).

It has no cost to society as a whole as it is provided by nature. Hence all its earnings are economic rent.

ENTERPRISE

DEFINITION

This is the controlling factor in the production process.

It supplies the 'ideas' and organises the other factors of production into producing a good/service.

It bears all the risk involved in production in the hope of making profit.

WHAT PRICE IS PAID FOR ENTERPRISE?

Normal profit is what is required to encourage entrepreneurs to set up businesses. It is included in the *average cost of production*.

Anything earned above normal profit is called *super normal profit*–SNP.

(*Rent of ability*: the extra profit which an entrepreneur earns because of his/her extra business acumen.)

ENTERPRISE IS UNIQUE FOR THE FOLLOWING REASONS:

1. It is the only factor which can earn a loss.
2. The return to enterprise is residual, i.e. it gets what is left after all the other FOP are paid.
3. The return to enterprise can vary enormously: from SNPs to losses.

RISKS FACED BY THE ENTREPRENEUR

The risks can be divided between insurable & non-insurable risks:

Insurable	Uninsurable
1. Theft by people	1. Loss of profits
2. Fire to buildings	2. Bad decision-making
3. Injuries to workers/customers	3. Strikes
	4. Changes in taste or fashions
	5. Entry of new firms into industry
	6. Changes in competitive conditions, e.g. new legislation

WHY ARE ENTREPRENEURS IMPORTANT TO AN ECONOMY?

1. They help create jobs by organising the FOPs into production units.
2. They decide *what* goods & services will be produced & *how much*.
3. They decide the *prices* that will be charged for goods & services.
4. They help achieve economic growth within a country.
5. If successful they encourage investment by other people.

WHAT IS THE ROLE OF PROFITS IN A FREE ENTERPRISE ECONOMY?

1. Normal profit encourages people to take risks & set up a business.
2. A firm needs profit in order to expand.
3. SNPs are the rewards to those firms which are most efficient/innovative.
4. Profits provide revenue for the government through taxation.
5. Profits are an indication to producers what goods & services consumers want.
6. If resources are scarce, those firms with the highest profits can get the scarce FOP by paying higher prices.

INVESTMENT: WHAT IS IT AND WHY IS IT IMPORTANT?

Definition: investment is the production of capital goods, i.e. those which help in the production of other goods, e.g. factories, machinery.

Why is it important?

1. Capital is essential to make our economy more productive.
2. The use of capital goods by workers makes their work more efficient.
3. By having capital goods it might help young people find employment.

WHAT FACTORS AFFECT THE LEVEL OF INVESTMENT IN THE ECONOMY?

1. What interest rates are being charged to acquire the capital?
2. What is the marginal efficiency of capital, i.e. how profitable will it be?
3. How buoyant is the economy?
   e.g. if GNP is high there is more demand & possibly more opportunities.
4. What type of economic policy is the government following? If expansionary, then investment may increase.
5. What are the businessmen's expectations about the future? If positive, entrepreneurs will invest.

NOTES

1. **Money wages:** the amount of money you get: your nominal wages.
2. **Real wages:** the purchasing power of your money wages.
3. **Labour cost per unit:** money wages *plus* PRSI divided by the no. of units produced.

THE FACTORS OF PRODUCTION MARKET

INTRODUCTION

1. D_{FOP} is a derived demand.
2. Each extra unit of an FOP employed creates additional output, called MPP.
3. This output is sold for a price.
4. The price obtained depends on PC or IC/M. So MRP = MPP x MR (but in PC because MR=P, then MRP=MPP x P).
5. The D/C$_{FOP}$ is its MRP curve (telling us the qty to employ at various prices).
6. MRP theory of wages:
   (a) Workers are paid what the *last* worker contributes to MRP, *not* what each worker contr.
   (b) Can you give each worker his MRP? No because: (i) he might not produce output; and/or (ii) it may not be sold in the market place.
7. Definitions: Supply Price, Transfer Earnings, Economic Rent; Quasi Rent.

LABOUR

1. Defn: human effort in the prodn of gds/servs.
2. D_{LAB} = MRP$_{LAB}$.
3. S_{LAB} = f(pop. size; participation rate; wage rate $\rightarrow$ as $W^R \uparrow$: Q^s_{LAB}?).
4. Wage Determination: (a) Free market: S & D for LAB (b) Trade union intervention: min. wage level *but* less people employed.
5. Reasons for Wage Differences: (a) MRP; (b) Skill, training, education; (c) TU strength; (d) Inflation; (e) Tradition; (f) Monetary & non-monetary benefits.
6. What Factors Affect the Q^D_{LAB} by a firm?
   (a) MRP; (b) Payroll taxes; (c) Tax on co. profits; (d) Govt subsidies; (e) Demand for firm's output; (f) Technology available.

7. Wage Drift: occurs when the D_{LAB} rises & wage rates tend to rise above the min. negotiated wage rate.

CAPITAL:

1. Defn: man-made wealth used in production.
2. Types of Goods: *capital* (produce other gds), *consumer* (provide utility), *consumer durables*.
3. D_{CAP} = MEC (= MRP *minus* the MC):
   What might cause the MEC to decline? (Productivity declines or cost increases.)
4. Capital Widening: amount of cap. goods per worker *hasn't changed*; Capital deepening: it *has* changed.
5. Savings: income *minus* consumption; investment: the prodn of capital goods. What factors affect savings/investment?
6. Classical School Theory: r/i are determined by the D_{LF} and S_{LF}.
7. Keynes's Liquidity Preference Theory: the desire of people to hold their wealth in money form. Depends on 3 factors: *transactionary*: day-to-day expenses/depends on income; *precautionary*: unforeseen events/depends on income & r/i; *speculative*: to invest in speculative opportunities/ depends on r/i.
8. Rates of Interest:
   (a) Real r/i = nominal r/i - inflation rate.
   (b) Determinants of r/i : bank rate; inflation; pure r/i; risk involved; repayment period; international factors.
   (c) Effects of changing r/i: savings, borrowing, investment, inflation, mortgages, imports, nat. debt, value of IR£.

LAND

1. Defn: gift of nature.
2. Unique for 2 reasons:
   (a) Fixed in supply;
   (b) No cost of production to society as a whole.
3. High prices cause high rents $\rightarrow$ exclusive shopping areas in Dublin can charge high prices, so rent paid increases.
4. Location of Industry: markets, raw materials, tax concessions, grants, labour, infrastructure, facilities, cost of land, planning permission.

ENTERPRISE

1. Defn: person willing to bear the uninsurable risks inherent in running a business.
2. Unique.
   (a) return is residual;
   (b) return may be negative;
   (c) returns can vary a lot.
3. Rent of Ability: earning in excess of N. profit.
4. Uninsurable v Insurable risks.
5. Role of Profits in a Free Enterprise Economy.

H. GOVT BUDGETING, TAXATION & THE NATIONAL DEBT

1. There are 3 types of economic systems: *Free enterprise* (capitalist) v *centrally planned* & between the two: *mixed economy*.
2. No 'pure' free enterprise or centrally planned economy exists as all are mixed - it's just the extent of the intervention of the state which varies.
3. • Why does the state intervene in the running of the economy?
   • Are there any disadvantages to its involvement?
   • How does it become involved?
   These are some of the questions this topic answers.

STATE INVOLVEMENT

Arguments for:
(i)   It provides grants as an incentive for companies to establish in Ireland.
(ii)   The state stops the development of private monopolies.
(iii) It provides employment.
(iv)   It develops industry which individuals couldn't or wouldn't provide.
(v)   It is more interested in the provision of services rather than making profit.
(vi)   There is a need for social welfare benefits.
(vii) It provides essential services which otherwise wouldn't be provided.
(viii) It provides public/social goods.

Public Goods
These are gds where the quantity available to one person is not affected by the quantity consumed by another, e.g. public parks.

Arguments against:
(i)   Too much state involvement reduces initiative/enterprise.
(ii)   It tends to mess up everything it gets involved in, i.e. too much bureaucracy.
(iii) State services tend to be inefficient.
(iv)   Effort is not rewarded.
(v)   A reduction in its involvement would generally lower taxes.
(vi)   Public sector employees tend to be safeguarded from competition.

HOW DOES THE STATE BECOME INVOLVED?

1. levying *taxation*: (& giving benefits);
2. giving *social welfare & subsidies*;
3. operating *govt departments directly*;
4. running *semi-state companies*;
5. by passing *legislation*.

To become involved the state requires finance (*taxation*) which it then spends (*expenditure*). This is called *budgeting*.

BUDGETING : THE STEPS INVOLVED:
Step 1: Each govt dept will meet in Aug. - Nov. & prepare estimates of expenditure. The Cabinet will meet & discuss these estimates, i.e. should expenditure be reduced further? If so, all Ministers will go away & come up with alternatives.

Step 2: When the Cabinet has eventually agreed on its planned expenditure for the forthcoming year, they will publish these in late Nov./Dec. of the year in a book called : *Estimates of Receipts & Expenditure*.

Step 3: In the 3rd week of January the Minister for Finance will present in the Dáil:
(i) the *current budget*: dealing with expenditure & revenue on a yearly basis; &
(ii) the *capital budget*: dealing with expenditure & revenue over a number of years.

Step 4: In April of each year the provisions of the budget will be implemented by passing the *Finance Act* (allowing increases in taxation etc.).

CURRENT BUDGET

A. Tax revenue	1. Central fund charges
B. Non- tax revenue Opening budget deficit	2. Supply services
Add: C. ↑ in tax rev.	*Add:* 3. ↑ in expenditure
Deduct: D. tax allowances	*Deduct* 4. savings in spending
Closing budget deficit	

CAPITAL BUDGET

• CBS	or	• CBD
• Borrowing (selling govt bonds)		• Loan repayments
• Loans from international sources		• Govt expenditure on roads, schools, hospitals etc.

1. *Central fund charges:*
   This is a prior charge on the state's expenditure; it cannot be debated by the Dáil, e.g. salary of President, interest repayment on national debt.
2. *Supply services:*
   The cost of running the Civil Service; providing education, health etc.

TYPES OF BUDGET POLICY

Budget Deficit

- Govt curr. exp. exceeds govt curr. rev. Prices tend to rise:
  inflationary effect.
  ↑ need to borrow.

Balanced/Neutral Budget

- Govt curr. exp. equals govt curr. rev.
- it is neither inflationary nor deflationary. No effect on our level of borrowing.

Surplus Budget

- Govt curr. exps are less than govt curr. rev.
- Means govt is spending less money than it's receiving.
- prices tend to fall: *deflationary effect.*
  ↓ need to borrow.

TRYING TO REDUCE A CURR. BUDGET DEFICIT

A. ↑ tax revenue

either direct or indirect. In 1989/90 the govt began the process of:

(i)   reducing direct tax rates, e.g. PAYE rates ↓
(ii)   harmonising VAT rates prior to 1992. So the top VAT rates are being reduced while the lower rates are being ↑.

B. ↓ expenditure

The govt has been trying to reduce expenditure in the last few years. How?

(i)   by limiting pay increases in the public sector;
(ii)   by reducing the nos in the public sector;
(iii)   ↓ curr. expenditure in health, education, environ. (i.e. the cutbacks).

ECONOMIC EFFECTS OF REDUCING THE CBD

A. ↑ tax revenue:

- Not much scope for this in income taxes or indirect taxes.
- ↑ indirect taxes would lead to ↑ smuggling.
- ↑ indirect taxes would also lead to ↑ inflation and its consequent effects.
- ↑ PAYE: unwilling to take a bigger burden.

B. ↓ expenditure:

- immediately would lead to lower ΣD and more unemployment.
- It's difficult to ↓ the wage costs of public sector.

EFFECT OF DOWNTURN IN LEVEL OF ECONOMIC ACTIVITY ON TRYING TO REDUCE THE CBD (i.e. higher unemployment/less spending power)

Expenditure:

higher unemployment resulting in more social welfare payments, so ↑ expenditure.

Revenue

Direct tax: ↑ unemployment → less income tax collected.

Indirect tax: less incomes → less spending → less VAT collected.

TAXATION

The Canons of Taxation
(Adam Smith: classical school of economics)

Equity: A person's ability to pay the tax should be taken into account as ↑ → T↑.

Economy: Cost of collection & assessment should be low.

Certainty: The taxpayer (& govt) should know *when* & *how much* tax must be paid.

Convenience: The tax should be collected in a way and at a time convenient to the taxpayer.

Functions of taxation

(a)   It should not act as a disincentive to work or invest.
(b)   Taxation should be progressive, i.e. take a larger % of income from a richer person.
(c)   Taxation should assist the govt to achieve its other economic objectives, i.e. create employment, achieve economic growth etc.
(d)   It should act as a *built-in stabiliser*.
      This is anything which ↑ govt deficits during slumps & ↑ govt surpluses during booms without requiring policy decisions.
      Examples:
      1.   Taxation (VAT or income tax) e.g. if employment ↑ → tax ↑ & vice versa.
      2.   Welfare payments

TYPES OF TAXES

Direct

(i)   This is a tax paid directly to the exchequer.
(ii)   It's a tax on incomes/profits.

Examples: income tax; CPT etc. Generally they are *progressive*.

Advantages

1. Related to ability to pay
2. Cost of collection: low
3. Convenient
4. Stabilises the economy
5. Liability is known.

Disadvantages

1. Disincentive to effort
2. May ↓ savings
3. Encourages black economy
4. May cause an ↑ in wage demands

Black economy: refers to people that do not declare their income for tax purposes.

Indirect

(i)   This is paid directly to a shopkeeper/trader.
(ii)   It's a tax on goods/services.
       VAT/excise duties

Generally they are *regressive*.

Advantages

1. Produces revenue
2. Cheap to collect
3. Convenient for payers
4. Stabilises economy
5. No disincentive to work.

Disadvantages

1. May be regressive
2. May be inflationary
3. Discriminates between people on the same economic standing
4. May affect employment.

IMPACT/INCIDENCE OF TAXATION

- **Impact:** refers to the individual, firm, good or service on which the tax is levied.
- **Incidence:** refers to the individual who actually pays the tax.
- Whether the impact & incidence are the same or different depends on the *relative price elasticity of demand & supply.*
- **Impact/incidence the same:** the good has an inelastic S or D, e.g. VAT on cigarettes.

DEFINITIONS

(a) **Revenue buoyancy:** describes a situation where the actual tax revenue collected is greater than the amount estimated in the current budget @ beginning of the year.

(b) **Fiscal drag:** in a time of revenue buoyancy when rev. is greater than expected, govt exp. may remain at the same level. Thus rev. > exp., causing a decrease in income & a deflationary effect on the economy.

(c) **Regressive tax:** a tax which takes a larger % of income from a poorer person.

PRIVATISATION

The sale of a semi-state body into public ownership either by an issue of shares or directly into a publicly quoted company's hands.

Examples

- Irish Life plc
- Greencore plc
- B & I

Case For

1. Increased efficiency/competition
2. Possibly cheaper prices
3. Reward for initiative
4. Revenue for govt
5. ↓ need for govt borrowing.

Case Against

1. Possible loss of jobs → ↑ unemployment levels
2. Maybe higher prices or discontinued services
3. Might be sold too cheaply
4. Loss of a valuable publicly owned asset.

BORROWING AND THE NATIONAL DEBT

This state borrows for the following reasons:

1. To finance the Current Budget Deficit.
2. To finance borrowing for Capital Purposes.

Combined this is called the EBR: Exchequer Borrowing Requirement.

3. For State-sponsored Bodies & Local Authorities.

> EBR + No. 3 = Public Sector Borrowing Requirement (PSBR)

THE PSBR AND DOMESTIC CREDIT EXPANSION (DCE)

1. EBR = CBD + Borrowing for capital purposes
2. PSBR = EBR + Borrowing by State-sponsored Bodies + Local Authorities.

Where does the money come from?

Financed by:

Non-Monetary Means

(a) Money saved in the P.O. Savings Bank;
(b) Govt bonds bought by Irish investors.

Both are savings by the public & so there is no increase in the money supply due to this type of borrowing.

Monetary Means

(a) Govt borrowing from domestic banks.
(b) Govt borrowing from abroad.
(c) Sale of govt bonds to non-Irish residents.

Each of these ↑ the domestic money supply.

3. Domestic Credit Expansion (DCE) = Monetary financing of the PSBR + ↑ in bank lending to private sector.

THE NATIONAL DEBT

Definition: It is the total outstanding debt owed by the nation. It consists of 2 parts: internal (owed to Irish citizens) & external (owed to non-nationals).

Repayments: consist of both interest & capital repayments.

When repaying Foreign Debt, account must be taken of:

(a) Exchange rate fluctuations, and
(b) Our inability to tax non-nationals (unlike internal lenders).

What is the only reason acceptable for borrowing & increasing the national debt?

In today's economic climate it is only considered acceptable to borrow for what is termed:

self-liquidating debt, i.e. if the return on the investment of the money borrowed is greater than the cost of servicing the debt.

Measures taken to Reduce the Cost of the National Debt

An independent agency now exists with responsibility for managing our national debt.

It is called the National Treasury Management Agency: NTMA.

It has been quite successful since it was established. It replaces existing (dear) debts with new loans which carry lower interest rates.

Problems Caused by our National Debt

1. It is difficult to decrease due to the fact that we continue to have current budget deficits.
2. In the future taxation must rise to repay our debt.
3. If domestic borrowing ↑ it may put pressure on domestic interest rates to rise.
4. If the govt ↑ domestic borrowing it leaves less funds available for use by the private sector.
5. When repaying the domestic debt taxpayers' funds are given to the lenders as repayments.
6. The lenders may be able to dictate to the govt the type of economic policies it should follow.
7. If our exchange rate deteriorates the cost of our external debt rises.
8. At the moment our debt is approx. £25 bn which means a high debt per head of population.

I. MONEY & BANKING

SECTION A: MONEY

BARTER
is the swapping of one good for another good.
The difficulties attached to barter are:
(a) establishing the relative value of things;
(b) it relies on a *double coincidence of wants*;
(c) it stops *specialisation* & the *division of labour*.

MONEY

A. FUNCTIONS
Medium of exchange money allows the process of exchange to be broken into 2 separate activities: buying and selling. The double coincidence of wants need not exist. It helps in the exchange process.

Measure of value money serves as a common denominator in which the relative values of diff. commodities can be expressed.

Store of wealth: money allows people to save wealth for the future by depositing it in financial institutions & gaining interest.

Standard for deferred payment: money is capable of measuring value for a future date reducing the risk of credit trading.

B. QUALITIES OF EFFICIENT MONEY
Confidence: in that it will perform its functions.

Portable: light & be capable of being carried around.

Divisible: into small units to help buy cheap items.

Durable: tough & durable to withstand handling.

Homogeneous: items of the same value must be identical.

Recognisable: it should be easily recognisable, giving confidence & making counterfeit money difficult to produce.

Scarce: so that it maintains its value.

Malleable: made from metal to withstand the handling it receives.

SECTION B: CREDIT CREATION & MONEY

Banks' power to create credit
Banks accept cash from depositors. Only a small % of this will be demanded back in cash, as most customers use cheques. So if the banks keep enough cash to meet customers' demands, they can give credit far in excess of their cash reserves. It can be calculated by:

$$\uparrow \text{Money Supply} = \uparrow \frac{\text{Cash}}{\text{Deposits}} \times \frac{1}{\text{Bank's Reserve Ratio}}$$

Is this power of credit creation important?
Yes as $\uparrow M^S$ can
(a) $\uparrow$ consumer spending and so boost aggregate demand, hence *employment*; and/or
(b) boost *inflation* & *imports*.

Limitations on banks' power to create credit
(a) The amount of its *cash deposits*: depends on their ability to offer attractive interest rates.
(b) The availability of creditworthy customers: in recent years bad debts have risen sharply.
(c) The % of its deposits it must keep to meet customers' cash demands. Can be divided into:
   I. **Primary liquidity ratio/cash ratio–PLR**
      The ratio of holdings by a bank of notes, coins & balances with the Cen. Bk to its current & deposit a/c liabilities, usually 3%, i.e. £3 of each £100 deposit must be in cash form.
   II. **Second liquidity ratio–SLR**
      The ratio of holdings by a bank of govt paper: exchequer bills & govt bonds, to its deposit a/c liabilities, usually 25%, i.e. £25 of each £100 deposit must be in liquid assets.
(d) It is restricted by the Cen. Bk monetary policy (see below).

A bank wishes to be as profitable as possible, yet it must retain enough funds to meet its customers' demands for cash. How does it attempt to reconcile these conflicting objectives?

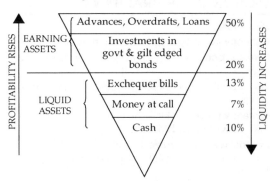

A bank must have enough cash to meet its depositors' demands. But keeping all its assets in cash form isn't on–they wouldn't earn interest & profits would fall.

The *more* liquid the form in which assets are held → less profit

The *less* liquid the form in which assets are held → more profit

Banks must strike a balance between these two objectives. Hence banks structure their assets in the above portfolio.

(Note: Both the PLR & SLR are satisfied.)

IF A BANK RUNS SHORT OF CASH : WHAT TO DO?

A. Dublin–Inter-bank market

When Ireland joined the EMS in '79 access to the London inter-bank market was broken. The DIBM developed.

> It is the means by which banks that have surplus funds lend to banks which require liquidity.

e.g. If there's an ↑ in credit creation, banks must borrow to maintain their PLR & SLR. If the demand for money exceeds supply, pressure on r/i to ↑ will develop. So will the DIBM r/i. All other r/i will ↑.

B. Use the short-term credit facility (STF) of the Central Bank

If a bank cannot satisfy its cash demands in DIBM

> It may borrow from the Cen. Bk using approved securities as collateral.

There is a limit to the amount which a bank can borrow: it can use it only once every fortnight.

Also, if a commercial bank has surplus funds it can lodge such funds with the Central Bank & earn interest. The r/i on STF is set by the Cen. Bk.

SECTION C : CENTRAL BANK

FUNCTIONS

Currency issue: sole right to issue notes & coins

Bankers' bank: acts as a *clearing house* & *lender of last resort*.

Govt's Bank: keeper of all govt funds; *drawee* of govt cheques.

Currency value: protects the value of the IR£ on X mkts & within the EMS.

External reserves: protects their value by having *stable currencies* & ↑ r/i to stop money leaving Ireland.

International institutions: represents Ireland on IMF & World Bank.

Monetary policy: implements MP on behalf of govt (see below).

Consumer information: provides consumers with inf. on X mkts, r/i etc.

MONETARY POLICY

> Defn: any action by Cen. Bk which affects (i) r/i; (ii) money supply; (iii) availability of credit.

Open mkt operations:

(a) ↑ M^S → buy govt bonds → comm. bks cash ↑ → credit ↑

(b) ↓ M^S → sell govt bonds → comm. bks cash ↓ → credit ↓.

Special deposits of comm. bks with Cen. Bk: if they ↑ → cash dep. ↓ → credit ↓.

Advice/directives: issue advice to ↓ credit. If disobeyed: issue a directive.

Alter PLR & SLR: to ↓ M^S : ↑ both.

Alter bank rate/MLR/re-discount rate:

The r/i charged by the Cen. Bk for re-discounting first class bills of exchange, i.e. acting as *lender of last resort*.

Funding

When banks based their credit creation on their holdings of cash, the Central Bank, by selling exchequer bills to the banks through open mkt operation, ↓ the cash holdings of the comm. banks & so also the amount of loans which they could loan.

The Cen. Bank then noticed that the comm. banks were basing the amount of loans which they could make on their total liquid assets rather than on their cash holdings alone.

When the Cen. Bank was selling exchequer bills to the comm. bks in return for cash, the comm. bks were merely exchanging one form of liquid asset for another & their credit-creating ability was not being significantly affected.

Hence it became necessary for the Cen. Bank to sell to them medium or long-term loans other than short-term exchequer bills. This is called funding: the exchange of s/t loans for l/t loans.

MONETARY POLICY PRIOR TO 1971

Control of the banking system by the Cen. Bk was not strong, due to:

1. Because of the small scale of operations of the Irish Stock Exchange, the Cen.Bank was limited in its ability to sell shares, e.g. if they issued large quantities of govt stock their price could fall. This would make them less saleable & cause uncertainty in the market place.

2. If interest rates were higher here than in the UK → people would transfer their funds here, disrupting Irish money markets. Hence altering the bank rate had implications for the Irish economy.

3. Irish comm. banks had external assets in the UK. If the Irish Cen. Bank sought special deposits from the comm. bks, these comm. bks could bring back some of these assets from the UK rather than use their assets at home & so they did not cut back on their ability to create credit.

SECTION D: DEFINITIONS

Modern Forms of Money: (a) Currency: notes & coins; (b) Plastic money: credit cards; (c) Cheques; and (d) Bank balances: current & deposit accounts.

Narrow M^S: M1: Currency & current account balances in the associated banks.

Wide M^S: M3: Currency & current & deposit account balances in both the associated & non-associated banks less inter-bank balances.

Legal Tender: anything which must be accepted in payment of a debt.

Token Money: the coin's *face value* is greater than its *intrinsic value*.

Fiduciary issue/Fiat currency: that % of a country's currency which is not backed by gold but by foreign currencies.

SECTION E: INTERNATIONAL FINANCIAL INSTITUTIONS

THE WORLD BANK

- Estb. in 1944 at the Bretton Woods Conference, along with the IMF. The W. Bank:
  1. uses its finance to give capital gds and technical knowledge to UDCs.
  2. encourages trade by members so as to ↓ poverty in UDCs.
- It gets its funds from:
  1. Each member govt pays according to its GNP + IMF quota.
  2. It borrows from rich countries.
- Uses of its funds:
  1. for infrastructural development, i.e. water transport, communications.
  2. to help agr., education, health sectors.
- Ireland has used funds from the World Bank for community schools & Turlough Hill.

THE INTERNATIONAL MONETARY FUND–IMF

- **Aim:** to prevent fluctuations in the E/Rs of currencies & so encourage trade.
- **Funds:** it receives a quota from each member govt, used when BOP difficulties arise.
- e.g. if a country has a BOP deficit it puts downward pressure on the V currency. To prevent this a country borrows from the IMF to support its currency.
- When the IMF gives loans it insists that the borrowing country take corrective active measures to cure its BOP problems, e.g. credit squeeze etc. so as to stop further borrowings.

THE EUROPEAN INVESTMENT BANK

- Estb. under the Treaty of Rome & belongs to the EU member states.
- It lends funds & gives financial guarantees for:
  - (a) creating jobs where the reduction in barriers & ↑ competition has resulted in ↓ jobs.
  - (b) projects to ↑ std of living in underdeveloped parts of EU.
  - (c) projects of common interest in EU.

J. INFLATION

Inflation: is the continuing rise in the prices of gds/servs as measured by the Consumer Price Index.

PRICE INDICES

An index is a statistical table constructed to measure changes in price levels. There are two types: *simple* & *composite* price indices.

A. SIMPLE PRICE INDEX/SPI

Measures changes in the price of *one gd*, over a time period. 2 Steps:

Step 1: Choose a *base year* & let prices = 100 (%).

Step 2: Express all subsequent prices as a % of this price,

i.e. $\dfrac{\text{P current year}}{\text{P Base year}} \times \dfrac{100}{1}\%$

B. COMPOSITE PRICE INDEX

Measures changes in the prices of a *bundle of goods*.

Step 1: Choose a base year & let prices = 100.

Step 2: Construct a SPI for each good: $\dfrac{P_c}{P_B} \times 100\%$.

Step 3: Multiply the SPI by the 'weight' of each good,
i.e. the proportion of income spent on that good.

Step 4: *Add*, to get the final composite price index.

Example: 1980 HLC

Item	P_{BASE}	P_{CURR}	SPI	x Weight
Food	£4.00	£5.00	$\frac{5}{4} \times 100 =$	$125.0 \times 30\% = 37.5$
C & F	£30.00	£33.00	$\frac{33}{30} \times 100 =$	$110.0 \times 10\% = 11.0$
T	£0.50	£0.75	$\frac{75}{50} \times 100 =$	$150.0 \times 20\% = 30.0$
Other	£1.00	£1.40	$\frac{140}{100} \times 100 =$	$140.0 \times 40\% = 56.0$

Composite Price Index → | 134.5 |

C. LIMITATIONS OF ALL PRICE INDICES

1. Expenditure patterns are based on *samples*. These samples may be unrepresentative of the pop.
2. Old products become outdated & are still included in the index while new gds are not included.
3. The 'weighting' attached to items may change.
4. An index does *not* take account of changes in the quality of commodities.

THE CONSUMER PRICE INDEX

Defn: this is an index which measures changes in the cost of living.

CONSTRUCTION OF THE CONSUMER PRICE INDEX

1. Based on the 'National Average Family Shopping Basket', i.e. those items which a family buys in large quantities & regularly.
2. 10 categories are included: food, drink, tobacco, clothing & footwear, fuel & light, housing, transport, banking etc.
3. A base year is selected and the average cost of these items is taken to = 100.
4. Calculate the 'weight', i.e. the proportion of income spent on the goods.
5. Find the change in the price of each good. The Household Budget Surveys are used for this.
6. Apply the weights to the prices to get the weighted average & the resulting CPI.

USES OF THE CONSUMER PRICE INDEX

1. Trade unions use it as a basis for wage increases.
2. It tells us the prevailing official rate of inflation.
3. It allows us to compare Ireland's competitiveness as against our competitors.

ARE CHANGES IN THE CPI AN ACCURATE MEASUREMENT OF CHANGES IN COST OF LIVING?

1. It relates to a *fixed* basket of goods (cost of updating might be prohibitive).
2. It does not take into account *switching* by consumers, i.e. moving from one good to another.
3. It does not reflect changes in *quality*.
4. The base year might not be representative.
5. Plus the problems listed in C, over.

PROBLEMS CAUSED BY HIGH INFLATION

1. **Savings discouraged:**
   If r/i < inflation rate, money loses its purchasing power.
2. **Exports dearer:** & so less competitive → less jobs.
3. **Imports cheaper:** & so possibly ↑ D imports.
4. **↑ in wage demands by trade unions:** to maintain their standard of living.
5. **Borrowing encouraged:** because the cost of repayments falls.
6. **Speculation encouraged:** in land/property because they are increasing in value, unlike investments in a bank.
7. **Weaker sections of society suffer most:** because the cost of living rises and their incomes do not ↑ by the same rate. Hence their purchasing power falls, e.g. dole, social welfare recipients.
8. **Pressure on the value of our currency:** with X ↓ & M ↑ → BOP problems & hence downward pressure on the value of our £.

IS IT DESIRABLE TO HAVE A LOW INFLATION RATE?

1. Exports become cheaper & more competitive abroad, while imports become less competitive.
2. ↑ D for Irish goods → ↑ employment.
3. With lower prices → ↑ demand → ↑ jobs → ↑ both direct & indirect taxes.
4. Workers will moderate their wage demand ↑s → lower costs → higher investment.
5. BOP position improving → our currency becomes stronger.
6. People on fixed incomes can cope better.
7. Savings are encouraged (due to better real r/i's) & speculation is less attractive.

INFLATION: CAUSES & REMEDIES

A. DEMAND-PULL INFLATION

Aggregate demand exceeds aggregate supply
Too much money chasing too few goods $\Big\}$ So ↓ Σ D

↓ C_E:
- ↑ direct taxation:
  unlikely due to high rates.
- Credit squeeze: ↑ r/i & ↓ borrowing.
- Link income ↑ to ↑ Ps.

↓ I_E: Highly unlikely as ↓ I would reduce the ability of the country to generate future wealth in the country.

↓ G_E:
- ↓ No. of public sector employees.
- ↓ Volume of services provided.
- ↓ Social welfare spending.
- ↓ Govt capital spending.

(Demand-Pull inflation is not a serious problem in Ireland because we're an open economy → which means if ΣD > ΣS → ↑ imports.)

B. COST-PUSH INFLATION

i.e. rising prices are caused by rises in the costs of production.

Hence cuts in costs required.

Cut wage costs

PCW : *Programme for Competitiveness & Work:* an agreement between the govt and other social partners to limit pay increases so as to help curb cost-push inflation

Prices & incomes policy: where on the one hand the govt agrees to control price increases and in return the unions agree to limit wage increases.

Statutory wage controls: where the govt passes a law banning wage increases above certain minimum percentages (not used in Ireland).

Productivity increases: Wage ↑ do not always cause cost-push inflation. If output (= productivity) increases at the same rate as wages, cost-push inflation does *not* occur. What we are concerned with is the *wage cost per unit* of output *produced.* If output ↑ by the same % as wages, then unit labour costs remain unchanged.

It is very difficult to do the above because of the following reasons:

(i) Employees may resist the concept of greater work effort for ↑ in pay.
(ii) It's easy to measure productivity when physical goods are involved, i.e. cars etc., but in services such as medical, teaching etc., their productivity cannot be measured.
(iii) Many people would say that they are overworked as it is, e.g. nurses etc. Consequently they say an ↑ in productivity is unrealistic.
(iv) ↑ productivity & output is of no benefit to an employer who cannot sell more, i.e. may be unable to sell extra output due to market situation.

REDUCE INTEREST RATES:

It is difficult for the govt to contract r/i as Irish r/i are subject mostly to international factors.

REDUCING OTHER COSTS

Costs of imported oil; cost of electricity; communications costs; indirect taxes.

Irish communication costs are among the highest in the EC. This makes our goods less competitive abroad.

Energy costs are also high, due primarily to the price of imported oil, but also due to higher labour costs in the ESB.

High indirect taxes: the scope for reducing indirect taxes is very limited.

K. POPULATION & EMPLOYMENT

WORLD POP. – TRENDS & IMPLICATIONS

Generally world pop. is growing due to:
(a) rising birth rates and (b) falling death rates.
However this growth is unbalanced between:
developed nations & developing nations. Growth is highest in the developing nations (due to using children as an insurance in old age) with some nations in western Europe experiencing a decline.

PROBLEMS CAUSED BY THIS POP. EXPLOSION

1. Inadequate food supply, e.g. southern African countries.
2. Inadequate infrastructure & capital in UDCs to cope with pop. pressure.
3. UDCs demand additional aid.
4. Because of ↑ pop., average GNP per head is ↓, making survival more difficult.
5. Lack of education facilities & employment.

Rev. Thomas Malthus (classical economist)

Pop. grows geometrically; food supply grows arithmetically. Pop. ↑ will be greater than ↑ food S. Pop. is kept in check by things such as disease, famine etc. – called 'population checks'.

TRENDS IN IRISH POPULATION

Up to 1841: 8.1 m.   After 1841: rapid decline
The Famine: (1843-1845) resulted in this decline & precipitated an ↑ in emigration.

Push Factors	Pull Factors
1. The Famine	1. Availability of
2. Inadequate resources in Ireland to support pop.	employment
	2. High real wage levels in London, N. York, etc.
3. Lack of available employment in Ireland	3. Strong family ties in other countries.

EMIGRATION

Effects on economy	↓ Pop: econ. implications
1. ↑ dependency ratio.	1. Size of domestic mkt ↓.
2. We lose skilled/ educated workers.	2. Under-utilisation of servs.
3. Size of domestic mkt ↓.	3. Lack of mobility of labour in country.
4. Loss of return on govt investment in education.	4. Changing pattern of demand.
5. Need to ↑ domestic wages.	

1991 CENSUS

1. Pop. has fallen since 1986 census of population.
2. Pop. had decreased in all regions except the east.
3. Trend of movement from rural to urban areas continued.
4. The marriage rate had declined.
5. Fall in both birth rates and death rates.
6. Ratio of males to females still declining.
7. In urban areas the city centres and even town centres suffered pop. decline at the expense of suburban development.

UNEMPLOYMENT

Causes	Remedies
1. Worldwide economic recession (↓ aggregate demand).	1. Reduction in PRSI/ payroll taxes/real wage rates.
2. Rapid pop. growth.	2. Encourage entrepreneurs to set up businesses.
3. Payroll taxes: ↑labour costs.	3. Stop subsidising capital.
4. Less foreign cos due to increased mobility: towards low wage countries.	4. Encourage labour intensive industries.
5. ↑ no. of participants in the workforce.	5. Stimulate investment.
6. Mechanisation in prodn process/ reduction of nos in agriculture.	6. ↑ consumption of Irish-made gds (e.g. encourage Xs; E/R control).
7. Slowdown in Irish emigration.	7. Reduced tax levels/ r/i.
	8. Govt schemes/ agencies.

MEASURING UNEMPLOYMENT

(a) From records of the nos registering for social welfare/signing on the dole each week (called the 'Live Register').
(b) Is it accurate?
    (i) It includes those who work also (i.e. in 'nixers').
    (ii) It excludes those who have emigrated; in education; in training schemes; (women who would work if it were available).

TYPES OF UNEMPLOYMENT

Type	Explanation
Cyclical	U. brought about by swings in the pendulum of business activity, i.e. during a recession.
Frictional	Reduction in the D for LAB in a particular job, though jobs are available in other occupations or areas, but people are unaware.
Institutional	U. which arises because of obstacles to the mobility of lab., i.e. lack of housing, refusal of a foreign govt to give work permits.
Seasonal	Those who are unemployed due to the fact that their job depends on the climate, e.g. hotel workers.
Structural	People who become unemployed because their skills are no longer in demand caused by technical progress/competition.

WORKSHARING (SHARING OF JOBS)

Effects on economy:

1. Less people on social welfare.
2. Less absenteeism due to flexitime?
3. Lower tax rev. to govt due to lower marginal tax rates.
4. Less imports due to $\downarrow$ MPM.
5. Lower unit costs of prodn because higher productivity.
6. $\uparrow$ staff admin. costs etc.
7. $\uparrow$ training costs.
8. $\downarrow$ vandalism & social problems.

$\downarrow$ PAYE - ITS EFFECT ON UNEMPLOYMENT

(a) Might encourage people to seek work as their take home pay $\uparrow$.
(b) It might result in lower wages having to be paid by employers which would $\uparrow$ D. for workers.
(c) Agg. demand would $\uparrow$ => $\uparrow D_{LAB}$.

How will $\downarrow$ tax affect emigration?

DEFINITIONS

Overpop.: when $\uparrow$ pop. => $\downarrow$ GNP per head.

Underpop.: when an $\uparrow$ pop. => $\uparrow$ GNP per head.

Full employment: all those willing to work are working at existing wage levels.

L. NATIONAL INCOME

SECTION A: MEASUREMENT OF NATIONAL INCOME

There are three ways of measuring national income: income, output and expenditure. There are similarities between each. To try to summarise each it is best if you think of the economy in sectors, i.e. agriculture, industry, services (public and private). Next consider that each sector uses each of the factors of production: land, labour, capital and enterprise. Each factor will provide itself, produce output or provide a service, receive an income in return, and this income will then be spent on the goods and services in the economy.

What is national income?

It is the <u>income</u> which accrues to the permanent <u>residents</u> of a country from current <u>economic activity</u> during a specified period of time.

Look at the words underlined and go back to the introduction: you should see why this is so.

The methods and how they are inter-related.*

Income	Output	Expenditure
These are the incomes to each of the 4 FOPs, i.e. land, labour, capital & enterprise. They are earned in each of the sectors: agr., industry and services.	The output produced in the agricultural, industrial and services sectors is calculated. Note: because the output in govt depts is not sold to the public the value of it is calculated in terms of the incomes paid to the FOPs.	Here the expenditure on goods and services is added up, i.e. Consumption expenditure Investment expenditure Government expenditure Exports expenditure *less* Imports expenditure.
Adjustments needed. 1. Stock appreciation: the increase in stock value due to inflation and *not* because anything was produced. Hence the increase must be *deducted*. 2. Financial services: an amount deducted equal to the excess of interest received by the banks over interest paid to depositors.		
Net Domestic Product at Factor Cost	Net Domestic product at Factor Cost	Gross Domestic Product at Market Price
add: Net Factor Income from the rest of the world (see below for explanation)		
Net National Product at Factor Cost (Nat. Income)	Net National product *at Factor Cost *plus*: Provision for Capital Depreciation	Gross National Product at Market Price
	GNP at Factor Cost *add:* Indirect Taxes *less:* Subsidies	Defined as: the value, at current mkt prices, of the gds & servs produced in the economy in a year.
	GNP at market prices	
1. Transfer payments like the dole, OAPs etc. must be excluded as they are not received because they supplied a FOP. 2. Payments in kind, like the use of a company car, board and lodging, should be included. 3. Contributory workers' pensions are included as they are payment for work done in the past.	Precautions 1. Only goods & services for which payment is made are included, e.g. housewives' work is omitted. 2. Only the value added by each firm is calculated, *not* the total output, as this would be double counting.	1. The purchase of second-hand goods, originally included in GNP when new, is *not* included. 2. The incomes of an Irish band abroad should be included.
	Why are three methods used to calculate nat. income? 1. To ensure that the figures are accurate. 2. So that they can act as a cross-check on each other.	

Now look again at the similarities between each of the methods.

Income	Output	Expenditure
Having added up each you arrive at:		
Net Domestic Product at Factor Cost		GDP at Market Prices
Add: Net Factor Income from the rest of the world.		
= Net National Product at Factor Cost		GNP at Market Prices
to go from NNP at Factor Cost to GNP at market prices:		

NNP at Factor Cost *add*: Depreciation
GNP at Factor Cost *add*: Indirect Taxes *less*: Subsidies
= GNP at market prices

Aslan

Net Domestic Product is the income earned by Irish FOP in Ireland, while Net National Product is the income earned by Irish FOP *in* Ireland and *outside* it. The relationship between the two is: *Net Factor Income from Abroad*.

Net Factor Income from the rest of the world

This is the difference between income earned by Irish factors abroad and sent home, and income earned by foreign factors in Ireland and sent back to their own country.

Examples	
Incomes earned by Irish factors returned home	Incomes earned by foreign factors sent back abroad
Bord Telecom personnel working in the UK and the profit earned is returned to Ireland. Cement Roadstone earns profit abroad and returns it here.	Profits earned by foreign cos operating here which they return back to their home countries. In Nov. '89 it was declared that this amounted to £730 m. approx.

To summarise:

The relationship between *Domestic* and *National* is: *Net Factor Income*.

The relationship between *Gross & Net* is: *Depreciation.*

Try to remember this.

Rather than wasting your time with material adequately covered in the textbooks, I'll summarise the problems which may occur when interpreting national income statistics. You will have these explained in any textbook.

Importance of GNP statistics	Shortcomings of GNP Statistics
1. Indicates changes in the level of economic growth. 2. Employment: if GNP is high, then there should be a beneficial effect in jobs. 3. We can compare our performance with other countries (GNP per head). 4. The figs give a *broad* indication of how income is distributed, e.g. between the different sectors. 5. They indicate the contribution which the govt makes to the economy each year and its trend. 6. Indicates changes in the standard of living. 7. Can be used in wage negotiations by the social partners.	1. GNP at market prices: to eliminate the effect which rising prices have on the stats we need to keep prices constant, i.e. look at GNP at constant market prices. 2. They only include goods exchanged for money & so they exclude the work done by housewives and social/charity organisations. 3. They do *not* tell us how much is each person's income. They only give us an average figure. 4. Rising GNP might have been achieved by increased overtime, more arms production etc. 5. Rising populations mean falling GNP per head.

SECTION B: WHAT DETERMINES THE SIZE OF A COUNTRY'S GNP? SHOE SIZE

Look back at the expenditure method of calculating national income. This is the key to this section. It is called 'Keynesian Determination of Income'.

Simply: national income/GNP/aggregate demand depend on: consumption, investment and government expenditure *plus* exports *minus* imports.

i.e. | GNP / Y / Demand = C + I + G + X - M |

What does each of these components depend on?

Consumption expenditure : C

depends on :

(i) *the size of your income.* As income increases, so does your spending. But do you spend all your income? No. It depends on the size of your Marginal Propensity to Consume – MPC.

(ii) MPC: this is the percentage of each additional unit of income which you spend,

i.e. $\dfrac{\uparrow C}{\uparrow Y} \times 100\%$

Investment Expenditure:

depends on:

(i) the prevailing rates of interest; and

(ii) businessmen's expectations about the future, e.g. is the economy improving? What is the level of demand in the country? What is the probability of making profit? What are the rates of taxes it will pay? What is the government doing re the economy?

Hence investment does not depend on the level of nat. income.

Government expenditure: G

This simply depends on a political decision made by the Cabinet at budget time. It does not depend directly on the level of national income.

Exports: X

The level of exports from Ireland depends on the level of national incomes in our foreign markets, *not* on our domestic level of national income. They do of course depend on our level of international competitiveness.

Imports: M

behaves similarly to consumption expenditure, i.e. depends on:

(i) the size of your income; and

(ii) your marginal propensity to import: MPM. This is the percentage of each additional unit of income which you spend on imports,

i.e. $\dfrac{\uparrow M}{\uparrow Y} \times 100$

To recap:

C	Size of income MPC
I	rate of interest expectations of businessmen
G	govt political decision
X	level of GNP in our export markets
M	size of income MPM

Represented on a diagram:

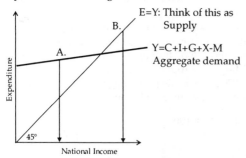

E=Y: Think of this as Supply

Y=C+I+G+X-M Aggregate demand

Questions:

- If the level of income needed to have full employment is that at point B, what needs to be done?

- The level of demand needs to be increased. By increasing C or I or G or X or cutting M.
- The amount needed depends on the *multiplier*, (see below).
- If supply exceeds demand, prices may fall. This is called a *Deflationary Gap*.

• Can you work out what happens at point A?

> If the level of national income at the moment is £6,000 m. and that required to generate full employment is £7,000 m., must an extra £1,000 m. be pumped into the economy?

No. Because each additional £1 spent will generate more than this single £1 due to the *multiplier effect*.

This simply means that if I spend an extra £100 on clothes, this £100 is additional income for the clothes shop.

Recall: people spend a percentage of this extra income (called the MPC). Let's say it is 80%. The shop will spend £80. This is extra income for someone else. They spend 80% of the £80, i.e. £64, and so it goes on. Keynes called this the multiplier and gave the following formula:

$$\frac{1}{1-(MPC)}$$

However, the size/magnitude of this multiplier is decreased if the economy engages in foreign trade. This is because some of the money will leak out of Ireland and into foreign countries because of our imports (see below).

Hence in an open economy the formula is:

$$\frac{1}{1-(MPC-MPM-MPT)}$$

> If you have read the Leaving Cert. Papers you will see that many questions appear in the Leaving Cert. based on this. The following formulas might help.

1. Multiplier: $\dfrac{1}{1-MPC}$ (Closed)

   $\dfrac{1}{1-(MPC-MPM-MPT)}$ (Open)

2. MPC: the % of each extra unit of income spent on goods and services

   $= \dfrac{\uparrow C}{\uparrow Y} \times 100$

3. MPS: the % of each extra unit of income saved

   $\dfrac{\uparrow S}{\uparrow Y} \times 100$

4. MPM: the % of each extra unit of income spent on imports $\dfrac{\uparrow M}{\uparrow Y} \times 100$

5. Given MPC, MPM or MPS, how to find the $\uparrow$ in GNP:

   (a) $\uparrow$ in GNP = Injection × Multiplier

   (b) $\downarrow$ in GNP = Withdrawal × Multiplier

6. With the ↑ in GNP calculated, how to find the ↑ in C, ↑ M or ↑ C domestic gds.
   (a) ↑ in C = ↑ GNP × MPC
   (b) ↑ in M = GNP × MPM
   (c) ↑ in C domestic gds = (a) *minus* (b) i.e.
   $$\begin{array}{c}\uparrow \text{ in C}\\ \uparrow \text{ in M}\\ \hline \uparrow \text{ in C domestic gds}\end{array}$$
7. MPT: the % of each extra unit of income taken in tax.

SECTION C: CIRCULAR FLOW OF INCOME

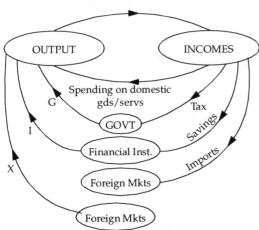

Injections	Leakages
Will increase GNP	Will decrease GNP
Govt expenditure Investment expen. Exports	Taxation Savings Imports

Effects on GNP of Injections/Leakages
(a) If injections > leakages, then GNP will ↑
(b) If leakages > injections, then GNP will ↓
(c) •If leakages = injections, then GNP will *not* change, in equilibrium.
The 1980 question on Honours (Q. 5) asks simply for this.

NATIONAL INCOME QUESTIONS

Q. 1

Year	Y	=	C	+	I	+	X	-	M	S
1	2,200	=	1,750	+	500	+	500	-	550	
2	2,600	=	2,050	+	600	+	600	-		
Changes										
3										
					Injections		?		Leakages	

Steps
1. Always check to see if Y does equal C + I + X - M.
2. Calculate: Savings (S = Y − C).

3. Complete the 'changes' line.
4. Now compare the ↑ C, ↑ M and ↑ S to the ↑ Y to calculate MPC, MPM & MPS.
5. As a check on your answers calculate the multiplier using 'Method 2', i.e.
   (i) What's the total ↑ Y 'tween Yr 1 & 2?
   _____
   (ii) What's the total ↑ in injection 'tween Yr 1 & 2? _____
So the mul. must be _____

Q. 2
If the level of investment remains unchanged at 600, what would be the level of imports when X = 1,000? Show how you arrived at your answer. (20)

Steps:
1. Put the new level of Xs (£1,000) into the table above in Year 3.
2. By how much has Xs ↑ between Yr 2 & 3? _____ Is it an injection or leakage?
3. Now by how much will GNP ↑? (Rem: Inj. × mul.): _____
4. How much of this ↑ in GNP will be spent on M^S? (Rem: ↑ GNP × MPM): _____

Q. 3
If the level of investment remains unchanged at 600 at what level of GNP would our Balance of Trade be at equilibrium?

Yr	Y	=	C	+	I	+	X	-	M	S
3										

Steps:
1. Put in the level of investment.
2. Now if the economy is in equilibrium the _____ must equal _____ .
3. If this is the case, then savings must equal _____ Why? Because [I + X] must equal [M + S].
4. Now if MPS = _____, and between Yr 2 & Yr 3 savings have ↑ by £ _____, then GNP must have ↑ by _____ × _____ = £ _____
5. Now of this ↑ in GNP, how much is spent on M^S (Rem: ↑ GNP × MPM): _____
6. Hence calculate the value of Xs: _____

1984
In a particular economy it is known that the AVERAGE propensity to save is 0.15 and the AVERAGE propensity to import is 0.25; it is also known that the AVERAGE propensity to save and the AVERAGE propensity to import both increase as the economy expands. If there is an injection of IR£1 m. into this economy would you expect the multiplier to be:
(i) less than 0.4,
(ii) 0.4,
(iii) between 0.4 and 2.5,
(iv) 2.5,
(v) between 2.5 and 4.0? •
Explain your answer. (20)

NATIONAL INCOME: (RELATIONSHIPS BETWEEN MPC AND APC)

1. The *multiplier* was developed by John Maynard Keynes to define the fraction by which any initial increase in expenditure is multiplied to give the eventual total increase in GNP resulting from that initial injection.

2. In a closed economy: In an open economy:

$$\frac{1}{1\text{-MPC}} \text{ or } \frac{1}{\text{MPS}} \qquad \frac{1}{1\text{-(MPC-MPM-MPT)}}$$

3. (i)   MPC: the proportion of each additional unit of income spent.
    (ii)   APC: the proportion of *total* income spent.
    (iii) MPS: the proportion of each additional unit of income saved.
    (iv) APS: the proportion of *total* income saved.

4.

	Income	Consumption	Savings	Investment
Period 1	£3,000	£2,800	£200	£200
There is an ↑ in investment of £100, so new equilibrium is:				
Period 2	£3,500	£3,200	£300	£300

In Period 1:

$$*APC = \frac{2,800}{3,000} = 0.933$$

$$APS = \frac{200}{3,000} = 0.067;$$

$$APC + APS = 1$$

$$* MPC = \frac{400}{500} \times 100 = 0.8$$

$$MPS = \frac{100}{500} \times 100 = 0.2 ;$$

$$MPC + MPS = 1$$

In Period 2:

$$APC = \frac{3,200}{3,500} = 0.914$$

then APS must be increasing.

So APC is declining. $APS = \frac{300}{3,500} = 0.086$ (i.e. ↑)

5.   Relationship between 'averages' & 'marginal'

Take, for example, the 6th year Economics class. Let us assume the average age is 17. Now suppose Johnny Baby joins the class and his age is 21.

The marginal age is 21 (& is greater than the av. age), hence the av. age rises.

Now suppose Eddie Ready rejoins the class and his age is 15.

The marginal age is 15 (& is less than the av. age), hence the average age falls.

So if the average is falling, then the marginal must be lower than it.

Now attempt the 1984 question here.

SECTION A: REASONS FOR TRADE

MAIN REASONS

1. Lack of essential raw materials.
2. Small size of domestic market.
3. Soil/climate unsuitable for prodn of certain crops.
4. Not as cost efficient as other countries.
5. Lack of tradition in workforce.
6. Higher standard of living.
7. Higher Xs: more jobs.
8. Law of Absolute Advantage:
'Where one country has an abs. adv. in the prodn of one commodity - it should produce that good.'

e.g.

Country	Beef		Tomatoes
Ireland	400	or	600 kg
Holland	200	or	2,400 kg

Ireland produces beef; Holland tomatoes.

9. Law of Comparative Advantage - LOCA
'Where one country is more efficient in producing all gds, it should concentrate in producing that gd in which it has the greatest comparative advantage.'

Country	Beef	Tomatoes	Opportunity Costs
Ireland	400	or 600 kg	B for T: 600/400 so 1B = $1\frac{1}{2}$T T for B: 400/600 so 1T = $1\frac{2}{3}$B
Holland	800	or 2,400 kg	B for T: 2400/800 so 1B = 3T T for B: 800/2400 so 1T = $\frac{1}{3}$B

(i) LOCA applied because Holland is more efficient in both,

it is $\frac{800}{400}$ (twice) more efficient in beef,

it is $\frac{2,400}{600}$ (four times) more efficient in tomatoes.

Holland sh. produce tomatoes; Ireland, beef.

(ii) Possible terms of trade:
In Ireland: 1 unit of beef is worth $1\frac{1}{2}$ kg tomatoes.
In Holland 1 unit of beef is worth 3 kg tomatoes
For beef the possible TOT are 'tween $1\frac{1}{2}$ & 3 kg tomatoes.

(iii) Assumptions of LOCA:
1. Free trade exists.
2. No transport costs.
3. Perfect mobility of FOP.
4. Alternative employment possible.
5. Equal distribution of benefits.
6. LDMR does not apply.

IMPORTANCE OF FOREIGN TRADE

Exports
1. By exporting, Irish firms can ↑ sales & profits.
2. Xs earn foreign currency which help pay for Ms.
3. Xs help ↑ the value of IR£.
4. ↑ Xs ⟹ ↑ jobs.
5. ↑ Xs ⟹ ↑ GNP & ec. growth.
6. Healthy export trade encourages investment.

Imports
1. Ms are essential for prodn.
2. By Ms jobs are created in distribution.
3. More Ms ⟹ greater choice.
4. Unsuitable climate means we *must* import some gds.
5. Some gds need large investment, e.g. car manuf.

REASONS FOR TRADE PROTECTION
1. To protect domestic *employment*.
2. To prevent (unfair) *competition for low wage producers*, e.g. Korea: textiles.
3. To correct a *trade imbalance* which might cause the value of the currency to drop.
4. To *protect industries* which the govt fears might be wiped out by foreign competition, e.g. air transport.
5. To protect *infant industry*: such that it can grow & expand & be able to withstand international competition.
6. To prevent *dumping*: when gds are sold at an uneconomic price in a foreign market.

METHODS OF TRADE PROTECTION

	Tariffs	Quotas	Embargo	Exchange Control
Defn	Tax on gds imported into country	a limit on the quantity of gds imported	a total ban on importatn of gds	limiting amt of foreign curr. to imps
Main adv.	Brings in revenue for the govt	Does not interfere with prices	Can keep harmful gds out of country	Govt can keep a check on qtys imported
Main disadv.	Push up the cost of prodn ⟹ ↑ in price of exports	Don't bring in revenue for the govt		Importer must plan yr ahead v. carefully

SECTION B: BALANCE OF PAYMENTS

BOP: defn: the record of economic transactions with rest of world

CURRENT A/C

Physical Xs + Invisible Xs	Physical Ms = Balance + of trade Invisible Ms
(a) Foreign tourists in Ireland (b) Emigrants' remittances (c) Aer Lingus servicing aircraft	(a) Irish tourists abroad (b) Use of foreign consultancy firms (c) Irish people using foreign banks
Current A/C Deficit or	Current A/C Surplus

PROBLEMS CAUSED BY A BOP DEFICIT

1. *Circular flow of income*: falls as more money is spent on imports.
2. *Jobs* may be lost if people buy imported gds. instead of Irish gds.
3. *The value of the IR£ falls*: as the S IR£ exceeds the D IR£.
4. If the Pm's rise, then *inflation will rise*.
5. We might pay for Ms by using our *external reserves* or ↑ *borrowing*.

CORRECTING A BOP DEFICIT

(Recall: Ms > Xs)

1. Cut Ms: trade protection.
2. ↑ Xs, e.g. tax incentives & subsidies.
3. Deflation, i.e. ↓ ΣD by:
   (i) reducing incomes through extra taxes;
   (ii) cut govt spending;
   (iii) ↑ interest rates & make borrowing more expensive.
4. Devalue the currency: Reduce the foreign exchange value of our currency & make Xs cheaper & Ms dearer (see below).

CAPITAL A/C

Definition: It is an a/c of a country's inflow & outflow of capital which gives rise to a rise/fall in our external reserves.

Composition:

BOP current a/c Surplus or + Long-term K. Inflows	BOP Curr. a/c Deficit + l/t K. Outflows
• Loans rec. from abroad • Foreign firms investing • EC grants/aid/loans • Rec. of dividends on for. inv. • ↓ in for. curr. reserves	• Irish firms investing abroad • Loans to 3rd world countries ↑ in for. curr. reserves

Definitions

(a) Balance of autonomous transactions:
This is the balance on the current a/c section of the BOP *plus* long-term capital inflows.

(b) Accommodating transactions:
Any official transaction in the cap. a/c which maintains the E/R between the domestic & foreign curr. at a desired level.

Inter-r/ships between Transactions

There are inter-r/ships 'tween transactions appearing on the bal. of trade & capital transfers, e.g.

(a) Funds transferred by a multinat. to its Irish subsidiary.
This is a l/t K. inflow. The money could be used to buy foreign capital equipment: appears as a physical import in the bal. of trade.

(b) A loan negotiated in a for. country to buy K. gds in that country.
A l/t K. inflow to buy a physical M. (in the bal. of trade).

(c) Foreign cos resident in Ireland exporting gds.
Exporting gds has a beneficial effect on our bal. of trade. They might then send back their profits to their home country (repatriation). This is a l/t K. outflow.

$$\text{Terms of Trade} = \frac{\text{Index of Export Prices}}{\text{Index of Import Prices}}$$

If our TOT improve, then for each unit of exports we can buy more units of imports. TOT improve when:

(i) P_x ↑ while P_m remain the same;
(ii) P_x ↑ faster than the ↑ P_m;
(iii) P_m ↓ while P_x stay same.

Devaluation

• This is a reduction in the foreign exchange value of our currency.
• It tries to make P_x cheaper & P_m dearer.
• It suffers from these shortcomings:

(i) Price elasticity of demand for Xs: must be >1
If inelastic the ↓ P_x will not lead to a sufficient ↑ D & in export earnings.

(ii) Price elasticity of demand for Ms: must be > 1
otherwise the ↓ P would not lead to a ↓ in Q_D.

Known as MARSHALL - LERNER Condition.

(iii) ↑ in P_m could lead to a subsequent rise in P_x
(iv) ↑ in P_m ⇒ ↑ in cost of living ⇒ ↑ in wage demands.
(v) Deval. leads to instability in E/Rs.

SECTION C: EXCHANGE RATES

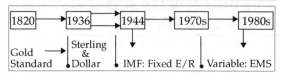

```
1820 ──► 1936 ──► 1944 ──► 1970s ──► 1980s
           Sterling     │        │         │
Gold  ──►     &         ▼        ▼         ▼
Standard    Dollar   IMF: Fixed E/R  Variable: EMS
```

Gold standard:

(i) M^S directly related to S gold;
(ii) Each curr. directly convertible into gold;
(iii) Self-adjusting mechanism, e.g.
      BOP deficit $\rightarrow$ gold given $\rightarrow$ Ms $\downarrow \rightarrow$ Ps $\downarrow \rightarrow$ Xs $\uparrow$;
(iv) Abandoned due to:
      (a)   severe deflationary adjustment;
      (b)   surplus wouldn't allow inflation.

Sterling area:

(i)   Fixed E/R maintained 'tween domestic curr. & sterling;
(ii) Significant % of reserves held in sterling;
(iii) Sterling was important curr. because of Commonwealth and London being the financial capital.

EXCHANGE RATES

	Fixed	Variable
Defn	When one curr. has a fixed value in terms of another.	When the price of one curr. in terms of another is determined by S & D, without official interference.
What sets value?	1. Imports & Exports. $\downarrow$ $\downarrow$ S: IR£ D: IR£ 2. Central Bank official intervention: support buying.	1. Imports &Exports. 2. Speculation. 3. Capital transactions.
How to correct BOP deficit	Must maintain fixed value so if deficit exists must reduce ΣD by: $\downarrow$ incomes; $\uparrow$ interest rates; $\downarrow$ imports; $\uparrow$ exports.	If deficit exists, then the S curr. > D curr., so the value of the currency will fall making Xs cheaper & Ms dearer.
Main adv.	Stability in E/R encouraged trade.	No govt interference reqd to correct deficit.
Main disadv.	Govt intervention required to correct a BOP deficit.	Instability in E/Rs discourages trade. Exchange risk!

DETERMINANTS OF EXCHANGE RATES

Supply of our currency:

1. To pay for our visible/invisible imports.
2. To repay capital borrowed.
3. Repatriation of profits to for. countries by cos resident in Ireland.
4. Govt intervention to protect value of curr.
5. Speculation.

Demand for our currency:

1. Others must pay for our visible & invisible exports.
2. Foreign investment in Ireland by non-Irish cos.
3. Emigrants remittances.
4. Foreign aid, i.e. EU structural funds.
5. Speculation.
6. Govt intervention.

PURCHASING POWER PARITY THEORY:

The E/R of a curr. will settle @ that level where the purchasing power of a single unit of currency is the same regardless of where spent. Defective due to:

1. E/Rs determined by many factors: pt 3, above.
2. Prices don't equate due to transport costs; tariffs.
3. Certain gds/servs cannot be easily exported.

EUROPEAN MONETARY SYSTEM: EMS

- Each currency is given a fixed value in terms of ECUs.
- It expects that each country must keep its currency within 2.25% of its fixed value.
- If it does fluctuate by more than 2.25%, then the Central Bank must act (i.e. 'support buying').
- The EMS is backed by £27,000 m. which is used for support buying by the central banks to prevent the curr. falling in value.
- It is an attempt by EU states to return to a fixed E/R system.
- In the run-up to 1992 full European Monetary Union – EMU – is being sought. Along with the EMS – a common Central Bank with a single currency.

N. ECONOMIC AIMS, POLICIES & CONFLICTS

ECONOMIC AIMS

Full employment
A very important objective of any govt, total employment depends on total aggregate demand in the economy (which depends on G_E in a big way). Both fiscal & monetary policies can affect the total no. of jobs in the country.

Stable prices
To curb inflation it is necessary to find the causes, i.e. demand-pull or cost-push; and once discovered, they can be tackled.

BOP equilibrium
This is necessary in order to avoid the problems associated with BOP deficits:
- currency weakness;
- fall in external reserves;
- increased borrowing.

Economic growth
This is achieving an annual growth in a country's GNP.

Controlling govt borrowing (as a % of GNP)
This is a major problem in Ireland presently caused by the govt $\uparrow G_E$ to stimulate growth & prevent job losses. Since 1982 attempts have been made to control it.

Protect the value of our currency

Achieve a fair distribution of national income
through taxation, social welfare, education & health policies.

Miscellaneous
tax reform; provide essential services.

ECONOMIC POLICIES

Fiscal policy
The use of changes in the level of govt spending or revenue in order to achieve its economic objectives, e.g.

$\uparrow G_E$ to stimulate ΣD.
$\downarrow$ VAT rates to stimulate the economy.

Monetary policy
The use of changes in the level of interest rates; the money supply & the availability of credit in order to achieve its economic objectives,

e.g. $\downarrow$ r/i to encourage borrowing.

Monetarist policy
Monetarists believed that $\uparrow G_E$ leads to $\uparrow \Sigma D$ & so inflation. So they want to $\downarrow G_E$ to $\downarrow$ inflation. This will cause s/t unemployment. In the l/t, a fall in inflation will boost business confidence, demand & investment, leading to an $\uparrow$ in jobs in the long run.

CONFLICTS BETWEEN ECONOMIC AIMS & ECONOMIC POLICIES

The solution of one economic problem can lead to another, i.e. achieving 2 econ. aims simultaneously can be impossible.

Examples:

Full employment & BOP equilibrium (Phillips curve)
When (in Ireland) full employment exists there is a large demand for gds/servs & because of our high MPM we tend to import a lot of goods & $\uparrow$ total Ms, BOP equilibrium is difficult to achieve.

Full employment & price stability
When full employment exists, there is – as said above – high levels of spending & thus high demand for gds/servs. This tends to cause demand-pull inflation. Professor Phillips indicated this by the 'Phillips curve', which showed the inverse r/ship between unemployment and inflation.

Economic growth & BOP equilibrium
When an economy is experiencing growth, demand is buoyant. This causes $\uparrow$ demand for imports in an open economy like Ireland. So while achieving economic growth, steps must be taken to avoid BOP deficits.

Economic growth & social policy
When econ. growth is taking place, the returns to the 4 FOP are generally increasing. However, nothing ensures that the benefits of this growth are equitably distributed throughout the economy. Generally they accrue to the better-off, i.e. landowners, investors. So with higher GNP this may be unevenly distributed. To redistribute the benefits the govt can change its taxation, social welfare, education policies etc.

SOCIAL COSTS & PRIVATE COSTS
Private cost: is the cost to an individual or firm of using or producing a certain product or service.

Social cost: is the cost to society, as a whole, of using or producing a certain product or service.

Where there is a difference between private & social cost, the difference may be any of the following:

1. External economies of consumption:
occurs when an action taken by a consumer results in a *benefit* to 3rd parties for which the consumer is not recompensed,

e.g. A person maintains his house & garden in good condition: it benefits his neighbours.

A person educates his kids to be good citizens: it benefits society. (How?)

Hence there are *social benefits*.

2. External economies of production:

occurs when an action taken by a producer results in a *benefit* to 3rd parties for which the producer is not compensated,

e.g. a producer who trains his staff even though they leave & work for others.

3. External diseconomies of consumption:

occurs when an action taken by a consumer imposes a *cost* on 3rd parties for which the 3rd party is not compensated,

e.g. a person using a ghetto-blaster in a public park: causes a nuisance.

4. External diseconomies of production:

occurs when an action taken by a producer imposes a *cost* on 3rd parties for which the 3rd party is not compensated,

e.g. pollution from factory chimneys; disposing of nuclear waste.

Externalities are actions taken by producers/consumers which result in a benefit/cost to a 3rd party, for which the person conferring the benefit is not rewarded & the person suffering the cost is not compensated.

THE EQUALISATION OF SOCIAL & PRIVATE COST

Society would obviously wish to equalise social cost and private cost.

The government can attempt to equalise the private & social cost by:

1. prohibiting the action, or
2. imposing a charge of some form until the two are equalised.

Methods available are for:

(a) **External diseconomies of production**
   (i) impose a tax or levy;
   (ii) the local authority could ↑ the rateable valuation in order to get extra funds to compensate those who suffer from the producer's action;
   (iii) prohibit the production of the good thro' planning permission.

(b) **External diseconomies of consumption**
   introduce laws to prohibit those actions which are a nuisance, e.g. the new smoking laws: 1 May '90

(c) **External economies of production:**
   (i) provide grants for premises (IDA) & training (FÁS);
   (ii) export tax relief;
   (iii) provide services through CTT, Bord Fáilte etc.

(d) **External economies of consumption:**
   (i) encourage tidy towns competitions;
   (ii) free medical treatment for contagious diseases.

O. ECONOMIC GROWTH & DEVELOPMENT

MAIN CHARACTERISTICS/PROBLEMS OF UDCS
1. Rapid population growth: high birth rates.
2. Very low GNP per head.
3. High dependency on one crop: hence open to low terms of trade.
4. Inequality in the distribution of wealth.
5. Lack of capital for investment.
6. Depends mostly on primary industries: agriculture.
7. Large & crippling foreign debts.
8. Poor infrastructure & hence very poor living conditions, e.g. no water.
9. Very little education.
10. Corruption/political strife.

HOW CAN THESE PROBLEMS BE OVERCOME?
Economic development can be helped both by the countries themselves and by foreign means.

Own Countries
1. ↓ population growth.
2. Diversify agricultural production/land reform.
3. Try to promote capital investment in the economy.
4. Restructure debt repayments.
5. Develop the infrastructure: water, sanitation, roads.
6. Promote education: start with primary.
7. Eliminate corruption within the state: try to provide efficient state services.

Foreign Countries
1. Provide aid.
2. Provide better terms of trade & remove barriers to trade.
3. Allow UDCs to reschedule their national debts.
4. Foreign companies might locate in UDCs & provide jobs.
5. Allow UDCs to get the available technology from the West.

BENEFITS & COSTS OF ECONOMIC GROWTH/ DEVELOPMENT

Benefits
1. Improved standard of living.
2. Increased employment.
3. Improved infrastructure.
4. More state services including education.
5. Less poverty.
6. Lower population growth.

Costs
1. Pollution.
2. Landscape disfigured.
3. Displacement of population: increased urbanisation.
4. Possibly greater inequality in wealth distribution.
5. World's resources scarcer.

EC FOOD SURPLUSES – THEIR ROLE

A. The Cost to Ireland of CAP
1. £90 m. cost of storing the EU butter mountain.
2. Value of food surpluses in EU: £6,500 m.
3. Massive accumulation of intervention stocks of beef, butter, wheat, wine & other products, while thousands die in the 3rd world.
4. Cost to Ireland is £10 m. - £13 m. per annum for butter & £96,000 for skim milk powder.
5. Cost of CAP (& keeping up farmers' incomes) is astronomical – so it is being reformed thro' devices such as the Milk Super Levy & the McSharry Proposals/Plans.

B. Arguments Against Food Aid
1. Aid agencies regard food aid as being a substitute solution to the problem of famine & underdevelopment.
2. Indefinite food aid to recipient countries encourages passivity, disrupts local mkts & creates tastes in urban dwellers that can't be satisfied internally.
3. CAP should be reformed so no surpluses exist & UDCs should be guided to self-sufficiency.
4. There should be structural food aid linked to development, e.g. 'food-for-work programmes'.

C. Arguments For Food Aid
1. Emergency food aid keeps people alive.
2. Emergency reserve stocks should be established.
3. Reduce food aid now & fund a general rehabilitation programme, i.e. irrigation programmes, feeds, fertilisers, restoration of animal herds.
4. Establish an independent famine relief unit in the EU to help the famine relief programme.

ROSTOW'S THEORY OF ECON. DEVELOPMENT

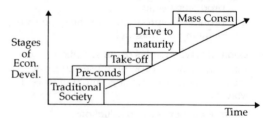

1. Traditional Society
Large % in subsistence agr. No industry. Poor infrastructure. Power in hands of landowners.

2. Pre-conditions for Take-off
Increased awareness of the benefits of econ. devel. Social climate now encourages econ. & social change. Investment ↑, infrastructure improves & industrialisation commences.

3. Take-off

Rapid growth in manu. industry. Infrastructure improves further.

$\Sigma D \uparrow$ as incomes $\uparrow$. This leads to $\uparrow$ investment & economic growth. $\downarrow$ in nos in agr.

Pop. changes from rural to an urban-based society.

4. Drive to Maturity

Incomes continue to $\uparrow$. Industry diversifies. Import substitution commences. $\uparrow$ state inter. $\rightarrow$ social welfare. About 50/60 yrs after take-off, the economy reaches maturity.

5. Mass Consumption Age

$\uparrow$ urbanisation & $\uparrow$ demand for consumer goods. Continued improvement in public services & soc. welfare.

CRITICISMS OF THEORY

1. Too generalised: each economy must overcome its own particular problems.
2. Little factual evidence to support this theory.
3. Countries may make the same mistakes as the economy develops.

ECONOMIC GROWTH & DEVELOPMENT: KEY POINTS

ECON. GROWTH:

is defined as $\uparrow$ GNP without changing the structure of society.

ECON. DEVEL.:

rising GNP accompanied by changes in the structure of society.

DEVELOPMENT TERMS COMMONLY USED:

(a) **Poverty belts:** those parts of the world which contain the greatest proportion of the world's poor.

(b) **Underdeveloped country:** (UDC): one whose level of development is not sufficiently advanced to generate savings needed for further econ. growth. (The term 'Third World' is often used to describe these.)

AID FOR THE THIRD WORLD

- Aid is defined as grants & loans undertaken by govts for the promotion of economic welfare & at concessional terms.
- The UN set 1% of GNP of developed countries as a target for transfer of resources to UDCs. Of this 0.7% was to be official aid.
- This commitment is not being fulfilled. Ireland's contribution of £35 m. (1989) is only 0.17% of GNP. (We also contribute thro' voluntary organisations.)

Capital

- Capital increases output per head (it helps to $\uparrow$ the productivity of labour).
- Large amounts of investment are needed to make up for depreciation & to expand the capital stock.

- The capital/output ratio* is the ratio of net investment to changes in output. If it's 4, then £1 m. of net investment $\Rightarrow \uparrow$ GNP by £250,000 per annum.

* The quantity of capital in money terms which is required in order to produce an extra unit of output in money terms.

- Investment in many types of capital is required:
  (a) land improvement (land ownership needs changing: S. George Text)
  (b) infrastructure
  (c) education
  (d) health.
- Where do UDCs get their capital from?
  (a) Export earnings: fairly limited.
  (b) Internal taxation: again little possibility of this.
  (c) Foreign borrowing: expensive.
  (d) Foreign aid: may be wasted.
- With this additional capital it must try to $\uparrow$ demand ($\uparrow$ demand thro' $\uparrow$ exports is called export-led growth).
- This $\uparrow$ in demand should lead to a *balanced growth*, i.e.

> that as economic growth takes place, the $\uparrow$ demand should be met by an $\uparrow$ in production and not by an $\uparrow$ inflation or excessive supply. Thus ΣD & ΣS should increase at the *same* rate.

FACTORS AFFECTING DEVELOPMENT & GROWTH

How society awards & esteems effort

1. *Religious beliefs & social attitudes*: manual work was associated with slavery in Roman times. If work is not esteemed by society, econ. growth is retarded.
2. *Social mobility*: econ. growth is helped if it's possible for indvs to move up the social scale as a result of effort.
3. *People who work hard must benefit from it*: high tax rates discourage effort.

Quantity of Labour

1. It's possible to achieve econ. growth by $\uparrow$ increasing labour productivity.
2. More labour can be obtained by extending workforce participation, e.g. among women.
3. In the l/t, the qty of lab. can be $\uparrow$ by $\uparrow$ in pop.

Quality of Labour: Education & Training

1. Education makes people adaptable to change. (There are notable exceptions.)
2. Educational requirements change with econ. development.
3. Education is necessary but an educated workforce does not guarantee econ. growth.
4. Expenditure on educ. grows as a country develops.

P. DEVELOPMENT OF ECONOMIC THOUGHT

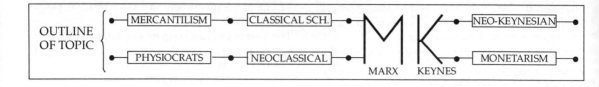

OUTLINE OF TOPIC

MERCANTILISM — CLASSICAL SCH. — M K — NEO-KEYNESIAN

PHYSIOCRATS — NEOCLASSICAL — MARX KEYNES — MONETARISM

MERCANTILISM 1500–1780

- Wealth consists of gold & silver.
- Money supply is most important.
- Countries with little gold & silver could get these by exporting.
- Countries should strive for a favourable trade balance by ↓ imports & ↑ exports.
- Countries should acquire colonies to export to and acquire gold/silver.
- Self-sufficiency: aim for this by pursuing trade protection policies.

THOMAS MUN (1571–1641)

- English. A merchant. Director of the East India Co.
- Wrote: *England's Treasure by Foreign Trade*.
- England: export more than import.
- Limit consumption of imports.
- Encouraged development of domestic industries.
- Charge high prices for necessities & low prices for non-essentials.

SIR JAMES STEUART (1712–1780)

- Wrote: *Inquiry into the Principles of Political Economy*.
- A favourable trade balance helped a nation acquire wealth.
- In the national interest he urged government intervention to regulate economic activity. Because of this English people did not accept his views.

PHYSIOCRATS (1750–1800)

- Agriculture was the key source of a country's wealth.
- They favoured a *laissez-faire* system.
- State interference should be limited.
- Free competition should be encouraged.
- The right to private ownership of property is most important.

FRANÇOIS QUESNAY (1694–1774)

- Doctor to the court of Louis XV.
- Wrote: *Tableau Economique*.
- A country generated wealth from the surplus created by agriculture. This surplus he called: *Produit Net*.

- He showed in his book how the surplus from agr. spread throughout the country.
- Society consisted of 3 classes: productive workers; those in agr.; & landowners & traders.

ANNE ROBERT JACQUES TURGOT (1727–1781)

- Min. for Finance in France prior to French Revolution.
- Did not favour govt interference in the economy.
- The value of an item depends on its *utility* to the buyer. This utility varies from time to time & from person to person.
- Stated law of diminishing returns as it applied to agriculture.

CLASSICAL SCHOOL (1780–1880)

- Favoured a *laissez-faire* policy of no interference by the govt in economic matters.
- Favoured *free international trade*.
- Stated that labour determined the value of items.
- Believed interest rates settled when savings equalled investment.

ADAM SMITH (1723–1790)

- Born in Scotland. Father a customs official. Lived in France and returned to Glasgow to become professor of philosophy.
- Labour was the source of a country's wealth.
- Wealth could be ↑ by the division of labour. (Showed this by observing the manufacture of straight pins.)
- Developed a *labour theory of value*: the value of an item is equal to the quantity of labour which it can demand in exchange for itself.
- Free competition ensured that prices were set freely.
- Encouraged free international trade.
- Role of government: defence, justice and education.
- Favoured taxation of rent to fund govt and developed *canons of tax: equity, economy, convenience & certainty*.
- Wrote: *Wealth of Nations*, 1776.

ROBERT THOMAS MALTHUS (1766–1834)

- English. Clergyman. Member of a large family. Professor of economics at Haileybury Staff College of East India Co.
- Wrote: *'Essay on the principle of Population & Principles of Political Economy'*.

- *Theory of Population & Food Supply.*
  Pop. $\uparrow$ geometrically 1, 2, 4, 8, 16 ...) while food supply $\uparrow$ arithmetically (1, 2, 3, 4 ...) Pop. must be kept in check: disease, famine. The green revolution helped avert predictions.
- *Iron Law of Wages/Subsistence Wages.*
  If Wages $\uparrow$ above subsistence level the pop. will $\uparrow$. This $\uparrow$ pop. $\rightarrow \uparrow S_{LAB}$ and would $\downarrow W_R$. This would $\downarrow$ pop. and force wages up to subsistence level.

DAVID RICARDO (1772–1823)
- English. Wealthy stockbroker. MP.
- Wrote: *Principles of Political Economy & Taxation.*
- Favoured free trade: developed the 'Law of Comparative Advantage' to show this.
- Developed a 'Theory of Rent' and extended this to a theory of Economic Rent.
- The charging of rent resulted in a transfer of wealth from industrialists to landowners.
- Accepted Malthus's 'Iron Law of Wages'.

JEAN BAPTISTE SAY (1767–1832)
- French.
- Wrote: *A Treatise on Political Economy.*
- *Say's Law:*
  Economic crises & overproduction could *not* exist because production created demand. However they *did* occur and he explained this by the restrictions imposed on free markets.
- Enterprise: said this was the 4th FOP: the return being profit or loss.

JOHN STUART MILL (1806–1873)
- English
- Head of the East India Co., MP.
- Wrote: *Principles of Political Economy.*
- *Wage Fund Theory:* Wages come from a fund. More workers mean lower wages. So the only way to $\uparrow$ wages is to $\downarrow$ population.
- Viewed the law of diminishing returns as most important.
- Favoured: free trade, *laissez-faire*, perfect competition etc.

NEOCLASSICAL SCHOOL

ALFRED MARSHALL (1842–1924)
- English
- Professor of economics in Cambridge Uni.
- Wrote: *Principles of Economics.*
- *Utility theory of value:* In the s/r the value of an item is determined by its utility and in the l/r it is determined by its costs of production.
- *Marginal revenue productivity:* The return to each FOP is determined by its MPP, i.e. the productivity of the last unit of FOP used to produce output.

- *Competition:* regulated economic activity as well as some govt intervention.
- *Growth of monopolies:* could be prevented by: govt intervention; consumer information.
- *Quasi rent:* i.e. s/r economic rent.

JOHN BATES CLARK (1847–1938)
- American.
- Professor of economics in US.
- Developed: marginal productivity theory of wages: the price of labour is determined by its use to the employer. Each extra unit hired contributes less.
- He will stop hiring workers when the contr of the last worker = the wages paid.

SOCIALISM

KARL MARX (1818–1883)
Personal Life
1. Was born in Germany. He studied at the Universities of Bonn & Berlin & obtained a doctorate, but because of radical ideas he was not appointed to the university post he desired.
2. In Paris he met Friedrich Engels, a wealthy textile manufacturer with whom he developed a lifelong friendship.
3. After returning to Germany in 1848 to join in the Revolution he was re-exiled and spent the remainder of his life in London. There he suffered hunger, hardship and poverty – his wife and two of his five daughters dying from malnutrition.
4. From his student days until 30 he was an active rebel.
   From 30 onwards he was a poor reclusive scholar writing in the British Museum. His two most famous works were: *The Communist Manifesto* and *Das Kapital* (Vols I, II, III and IV).

His View of History
He interpreted history materialistically as a sequence of conflicts between classes in which the proletariat or working classes merely exchanged one oppressor for another. Eventually through struggle the workers would control the means of production and the destiny of society.

Labour Theory of Value:
- The value of a good was the labour cost needed to produce the good.
- Labour was paid just enough to rear a family but workers were required to work a no. of hours in excess of this.
- For this he was producing value/profit for his employer.
- This excess value was called 'surplus value' and represented the exploitation of the workers by the capitalist.

- Marx said that the only 2 sources of income, value and surplus value, were created by the workers and should be kept by workers.

Distribution of Capitalist Profits

Capitalists try to max. profits. So they reinvest in new machinery which lessens the demand for labour. *This results in unemployment.* A recession sets in due to unemployment: falling demand and smaller profits. Smaller businesses fail and bigger businesses take control of the markets. The introduction of machinery de-skills labour and competition between workers for jobs allows capitalists to worsen working conditions by speeding up machines and lengthening working hours.

Evolution of Communism

The depression ends only when surplus stock is sold off and demand grows again. The process repeats itself as crisis follows crisis in a spiral of cycles. Employers become fewer and bigger. The unemployed grow. These now organise themselves. Revolution occurs and the workers take control of society in an ideal socialist state where unlimited economic growth is possible.

Criticisms of Marx

1. The labour theory of value has been discarded: labour is useless without land and capital.
2. Contrary to what Marx believed, the lot of workers was considerably improved by trade unions.

THE FABIAN SOCIALISTS

- George Bernard Shaw, H.G. Wells, Beatrice Webb, among others.
- They played an important role in the founding of the British Labour Party.
- They believed it was impossible to separate the contribution made to production by one individual or any of the 4 FOP. Hence the wealth created belonged to all.

ROBERT OWEN, MP (1771–1858)

- Scot, owned New Larark – a compassionate workplace, i.e.
- lectures for adults
- singing for orphans
- pubs closed & alcohol banned
- kids under 12: no work
- kids work ↓ (from 13 to 10½ hours).

KEYNESIAN SCHOOL

JOHN MAYNARD KEYNES (1883–1946)

- English. Studied at Eton and Cambridge. Editor of *Economic Journal*. Represented UK's Dept of Treasury at Versailles Peace Conference. Became very wealthy. Married UK's chief adviser at the Bretton Woods Conference.
- Wrote: *Treatise on Money and General Theory of Employment, Interest & Money.*

- *National income could be in equilibrium at less than full employment* (i.e. the opposite to Say's law). He believed that wage cuts did not finish depression, but rather makes them worse by reducing demand and hence ↑ unemployment.
- *Favoured govt intervention to create demand.* A major change from classical economics. He said that any initial increase in govt expenditure would generate a much greater increase in GNP through the *multiplier effect.*
- *Investment*: he believed that people invest with the hope of making a capital gain, not because of the interest rate received.
- *Interest rates:* he felt, were determined by the demand for cash. He developed a *Liquidity Preference Theory.*
- *Savings & investment*: The classical economists held that the interest rate ensured that all savings were invested. Keynes did not agree. Entrepreneurs invested depending on their expectations more so than the rate of interest. Hence investment could be less than savings resulting in a leakage & so a drop in demand and more unemployment.
- Today Keynes's policies of reducing unemployment are out of fashion:
  1. due to the large increases in govt borrowing; and
  2. in small open economies like Ireland, some of the injections could leak out on imports.

MONETARISM

- Concentrates on monetary policy: believes that the supply of money determines the level of economic activity.
- Favoured a reduction of money supply. This would:
  1. reduce demand-pull inflation;
  2. restrict govt and firms' ability to pay higher wages.
- A reduction in prices makes a country's exports cheaper and so in the long run exports should rise, creating jobs.
- Stable prices would make the economic climate more favourable for investors.
- In the short term a reduction in money supply would cause a loss of jobs.
- Did not favour government intervention, but rather the *privatisation* of state firms.

MILTON FRIEDMAN (1912–)

- American.
- University of Chicago School of Economics.
- Considered the main proponent of monetarism.
- Wrote: *A Modern History of the United States; Free to Choose.*
- Favours deregulation of all markets; *laissez-faire;* privatisation and strict control of government expenditure.

MODERN ECONOMISTS

SUPPLY SIDERS

- Favour policies which will improve economic performance by improving economic incentives and competitive market forces.

Examples:

- Reduce taxes: encourage workers to work and businesses.

  Employment will rise. Govt revenue will rise.

- Deregulate markets: privatise state bodies.

KEYNESIAN VIEWS:

JOHN KENNETH GALBRAITH (1908–)

- Canadian.
- Professor of economics in Harvard.
- Economic adviser to President J. F. Kennedy.
- US Ambassador to India.
- Wrote: *The Affluent Society; The New industrial State.*
- Favours govt intervention: tax incomes and create public wealth, e.g. better education, better public transport etc.
- Favours state control of big business to eliminate wasteful expenditure.

INTRODUCTION

Free Trade Area: gds are allowed to move freely without tariffs between members.

Customs Area: consists of a

(i) Free Trade Area, plus a

(ii) Common External Tariff against non-members.

Common Market: consists of

(i) Free Trade Area,

(ii) A common External Tariff,

(iii) Free movement of Labour & Capital.

> • EC was set up under the Treaty of Rome in 1957.
> • Ireland joined with the UK and Denmark in 1973.
> • Greece joined in 1981; Spain & Portugal in 1986.
> • Turkey has applied for membership.
> • Finland, Sweden & Austria joined on 1/1/95.

AGRICULTURE & THE EU

The Common Agricultural Policy (CAP) provides the following:

1. Guaranteed Prices: for agricultural produce to help increase farmers' incomes.

2. Intervention: Because the prices are high it encourages ↑ prodn. This must be stored so as to stop prices (& therefore) incomes falling.

3. Mechanisation: i.e. to establish viable farm units, grants are provided to help farmers mechanise, i.e. use more machinery. This results in ↑ unemployment.

4. Farm Structures: i.e. create viable farm units by

(i) encouraging specialisation of production; and

(ii) increasing farm size (above 40 acres)

5. The Green Pound

> This is an agral exchange rate system introduced to immunise the agral sector from the effects of changes in exchange rates.

e.g. If the Irish £ is devalued (to make exports cheaper & imports dearer), then this also makes agral Xs cheaper. This however is against EU policy.

So to stop our agral Xs becoming more competitive, a tax is placed on them (equal to the price advantage gained). These taxes are known as Monetary Compensatory Amounts – MCAs.

6. EU Membership: Irish Agr.

Advantages:

1. Higher Guaranteed Prices than in a 'Free World Market'.
2. Access to a much larger EU market.
3. Fall in dependence on UK mkt (cheap food policy).
4. Massive financial Aid. £8,400 m. (73-89).

Disadvantages:

1. Payment of MCAs on our agral exports.
2. Operation of the 'PRICE COST' Squeeze.
3. Increased competition for Irish produce.
4. Higher food prices.
5. Cost of Intervention.

INDUSTRY & THE EU

1. **Competition:** EU membership resulted in the closure of traditional industries i.e. textiles, clothing & footwear. Ireland also became a favourable location for foreign industry, i.e. electronics & chemicals -> we're very good at attracting the 'pollutant' industries.

2. Access to a wider market for our indal exports. But our industry must (& has) become more competitive.

3. **Financial Aid**

   (a) European Social Fund: £1,500 m. – makes employment easier thro' FÁS courses.

   (b) Euro Regional Devel. Fund: £1,200 m. – for developing the 'poor' areas of the EU, e.g. developing the local infrastructure & promoting industry.

   (c) Euro Investment Bank: gives loans for projects in underdevel. regions; developing industry. (See notes on banking)

ENLARGEMENT OF THE EU

Problems caused by this:

1. ↑ Agricultural Food Mountains *plus* ↑ costs of the CAP. Britain is the prime agent behind moves to central agral expansion.
2. Problems of overspending by EU, given the restrictive budgeting policies by member govts.
3. ↑ structural problems with the admission of Spain & Portugal, with very poor regions.
4. Because of enlargement, the amount available to distribute to members is reduced.
5. Administrative problems.

DEVELOPMENTS

EMU: European Monetary Union: essentially means a Single Currency (with a fixed E/R system). Econ. union requires the Community to have common econ. objectives & also common budgetary policies.

EMS: see handout on Banking.

1992 Single European Mkt: No Barriers:

• Free entry of foreign gds/servs to our market

• Easier access to EU & free movement of Lab & Cap.

• Harmonisation of VAT & Income Tax Rates

• Non-EU countries invest in Ire. To gain access to EU.

EUROPEAN MONETARY UNION EMU

DEFN:
Where the EU states have a single integrated mkt., a common currency & a common central bank; such that all economic policies become standardised.

NECESSARY STEPS:
1. Completion of the int. mkt. by Dec. '92. } ERM
   Participation of all countries in the EMS.
2. Setting up a single European Central Bank
3. Setting up a single European Currency

IRELAND HOPES/FEARS:

Hopes:
(a) Lower r/i
(b) Financial stability
(c) $\uparrow I_E$ & Jobs

Fears:
(a) Lack of funds to improve the economy;
(b) Loss due to being a peripheral region.

THE ECU:
1. Is a basket consisting of specified amts of the 12 EU currencies
2. Each specified amt is determined by ref. to each country's GNP & its participation in the EU's external trade.

THE IMPLICATIONS OF 1992 – SINGLE EUROPEAN MARKET

The existence of pure free trade will benefit consumers, industry, workers and the economy. These benefits will include the following:
1. There will be an internal market for 320 million consumers in 12 member countries. The size of this market will give opportunities for everyone in business.
2. Industrial firms will be able to reduce production costs due to economies of scale. This will enable them to be competitive with foreign competition and be able to avail of the benefits of a big market.
3. All trading barriers will be removed so pure free trading between Member Countries will be allowed.
4. Irish firms will have access to foreign Government contracts.
5. Increased opportunities for Irish exporters due to greater access to a single market of 320 million consumers. In 1973 Ireland had a trade deficit of £160 m. with the other EU countries. In 1988 there was a trade surplus of £190 m. These figures clearly show the potential for Irish exporters after 1992.

6. Foreign banks, building societies, insurance companies, market research and advertising agencies, i.e. service firms will set up in Ireland. This will provide competition for Irish service firms and of course give a wider choice to consumers. Consumers should now receive a better service at a lower cost.
7. The harmonisation of tax rates will result in a decrease in Ireland's VAT rates.
8. Hectic competition will force firms to improve the quality of their products.
9. There will be no Exchange Control so there will be free movement of capital. This will allow Irish investors to buy foreign shares, i.e. people will have a wider choice when deciding on an investment portfolio.
10. The free movement of labour will allow Irish people to work in any member country without restrictions, e.g. work permits.
11. It is hoped that there will be a big increase in foreign investment from America and Japan as industrialists from those countries strive for a share of the European market. Between 1973 and 1988 over 1,000 foreign firms set up in Ireland. They provide 100,000 jobs, so it is easy to see how the economy benefits from foreign investment.
12. Ireland will have access to larger grants from the European Regional Fund, European Social Fund and European Farm Fund. Likewise it will be possible to borrow more from the European Investment Bank.

THE COMMON AGRICULTURAL POLICY – CAP

OBJECTIVES
1. To increase agricultural productivity by promoting technical progress and the best use of labour.
2. To ensure a fair standard of living for farming communities.
3. To stabilise markets.
4. To guarantee regular supplies.
5. To ensure reasonable prices for consumers.

SUCCESS
1. Price support and financial aid for modernisation (fertiliser, machinery) have resulted in increased levels of production and productivity.
2. Average farm incomes have increased, especially for the progressive, large-scale farmers.
3. Food production has increased, and fluctuation in price levels has been reduced.
4. Self-sufficiency for many farm products has been achieved.

5. Dependency upon imports reduced. Competitiveness also increased by greater specialisation. Farms and regions have concentrated increasingly on producing products for which they have a comparative advantage, e.g. cereals in south-east England, dairy and beef in Ireland.

FAILURE

1. Although the number of small farms declined (e.g. 570,000 fewer farms less than 5 ha 1970-85), there are still too many uneconomic holdings. Structural reform has been especially less than effective in peripheral regions.
2. Farm incomes lag behind the non-farm sector. Low standards of living in marginal regions.
3. Price support policy has created a massive and expensive surplus problem. This has caused political tension between governments that support the CAP (e.g. Ireland, France) and those that want major changes (e.g. Britain).
4. Larger farmers and the most productive regions have benefited most. This emphasises a division between farmers and regions.
5. Costs still higher than world food prices. To protect European farmers, trade disputes with other countries have occurred, e.g. USA.

Section II:

Assessment Tests

TEST YOURSELF

TOPIC BY TOPIC

TEST: INTRODUCTORY ECONOMICS

SECTION A

1. Economics is _____
    _____
    _____

2. The *deductive method* of economic analysis involves _____
    _____
    _____

3. The *inductive method* of economic analysis involves _____
    _____
    _____

4. Define *land* as a factor of production: _____
    _____
    It is unique for two reasons: (a)_____(b)_____

5. State the *Law of Diminishing Marginal Returns*: _____
    _____
    _____
    _____

6. Define *capital* _____
    _____

7. Define *enterprise* as a factor of production: _____
    _____
    It is unique for *three* reasons: (a) _____
    (b)_____   (c) _____

8. Explain: *economies of scale*_____
    _____
    _____

    Give *two* examples of internal and external economies of scale.

Internal	External

SECTION B

(a) Define labour as a factor of production.
(b) Explain what is meant by the term 'the division/specialisation of labour'.
(c) Explain what is meant by the terms 'geographical' & 'occupational' mobility of labour.
    Set out the factors which influence both types of mobility of labour.

1. State the *four* characteristics of an economic good.

   1. _Scarce_
   2. _provides utility_
   3. _capable of transfer_
   4. _command a price_

2. (a) $Q^D = f(\underline{P, T, E, G})$ (b) $Q^S = f(\underline{P, P_{oy}, T, C, P})$.

3. Equilibrium Price refers to: _that price at which Qp_
   ses quantity demanded = supply

4. State *two* developments which would cause a S/C to shift inwards to the origin.
   - _increase in of P_
   - _price of sub ↑_

5. Give *two* examples of commodities which would *not* be considered as *economic* goods. Justify each choice by a very brief explanation.
   BEAUTY
   INTELLIGENCE , cant be transferred.

6. State the Law of Diminishing Marginal Utility
   As extra units of a good are consumed
   the marginal utility will eventually
   decrease.

7. For a utility maximising consumer in equilibrium the marginal utility of each good purchased would be the same. True/False (Circle your choice & explain your answer).
   CONSUMER   EQUILIBRIUM

8. When the *price* of a good changes it gives rise to both a _____effect (and this is always _____i.e. you will always buy _____of the_____ good) and an _____effect. (This may be _____or _____.) If the negative income effect is greater than the positive substitution effect, then this good is called a _____ good.

9. Explain what is meant by the term Price Elasticity of Demand.

10. For PED if the sign is *negative* it means _normal_
    If the sign is *positive* then this means _giffen_
    The formula for measuring PED is:
    $$\frac{\Delta Q}{\Delta P} \times \frac{P_1 + P_2}{Q + Q_2}$$

You have £10. You buy *two* goods A & B. You buy 10 of A @ 50p and 5 of B @ £1.

The MU of the 10th unit of A is 10 utils and the MU of the 5th unit of B is 20 utils.

1. In this case is the $\dfrac{MU_A}{P_A} = \dfrac{MU_B}{P_B}$? Yes/No

Prove it. _____ = _____

2. This is the principle on which a consumer allocates his income.

    What is it called?_____

    What does it state? That the consumer will spend his income in such a way that s/he gets:

    _____

3. Suppose the P_B falls to 50p each.

    How much extra income/purchasing power have you? _____

4. Now put in the *new* prices: $\dfrac{MU_A}{P_A}$? $\dfrac{MU_B}{P_B}$

_____ ? _____

    (i) Which good gives the most MU per penny spent?_____

    (ii) So what good should you buy more of? _____ Why?_____

    (iii) What good should you buy less of? _____ Why? _____

    (iv) To summarise, what's happened to the Q_A^D? _____ and the Q_B^D? _____

5. What 'effect' is this called? The _____ effect.

We will now consider the effect of this extra income/purchasing power.

6. Do you think you will buy more/less of one or both goods?
    (Think back to $Q^D = f(\_\_,\_\_, Y,\_\_)$).
    ▶You will buy more/less of one good or both goods.◀ Circle the appropriate words.
    So as your Y ↑ what has happened to the Q^D of both? _____

7. What 'effect' is this called? The_____ effect.

8. Suppose the extra purchasing power was taken in tax. What would the only effect *now* be
    when the P_B falls? The _____ effect.

And (return to point 4) what happens the Q_A^D? _____ and the Q_B^D? _____ .

9.

Summary	Substitution Effect		Income Effect	
	Q_A^D	Q_B^D	Q_A^D	Q_B^D
When P_B ↓ & you've extra Y ▶				
When P_B ↓ & you've *no* extra income ▶				

1. $Q_N^D = f\left(\dfrac{1\underline{\hspace{2cm}} \quad 2\underline{\hspace{2cm}}}{3\underline{\hspace{2cm}} \quad 4\underline{\hspace{2cm}}} \right)$

2. Prices of many gds have ↑ in recent years, yet the demand for them has also increased. Is the Law of Demand obsolete (as $P \uparrow \rightarrow Q_D \downarrow$?)
   Yes/No   Why? _____

3. **(1984 Q.1(b))**

Income	%Y Spent	Actual Amt	Is this good inferior?
£200	50% →		Yes/No
If ↑ £400	40% →		

4. **(1982 Q.1(a))**

Good	PED	Normal/Giffen	YED	Normal/Inferior
X	– 1.6		+ 2.21	
Y	– 0.6		– 0.42	

   Are any of these goods X or Y, Giffen? Yes/No

5. **(1984 Q.1(c))**
   Given:

Good	Price	Q_D	Marginal Utility
A	6p	12	30 utils
B	3p	9	15 utils

   - P_A falls to 4p & P_B stays the same.

     A price change gives rise to two effects:

     _____and _____

   - Equi-Marginal Principle states: _____

     _____

     _____

   - Because $P_A\downarrow$, how much is his additional purchasing power?_____

Substitution Effect

We assume the additional p.p. of _____ is _____ by the govt.

Now which good gives the most MU per p. spent_____ .

So Q_A^D _____ and Q_B^D _____ until _____

INCOME EFFECT

With the extra p.p. because $P_A\downarrow$ he will now buy more of good _____ and _____ of good _____.

Do the above *two* effects have to be the same for all goods? Yes/No

1. An economic good is:

    (i) _____

    (ii) _____

    (iii) _____

    (iv) _____

2. The main assumptions made about a consumer's behaviour are:

    (i) _____

    (ii) _____

    (iii) _____

    (iv) _____

3. $Q_N^S = f\left(\begin{array}{ccc} 1\underline{\quad\quad} & 2\underline{\quad\quad} & 3\underline{\quad\quad} \\ 4\underline{\quad\quad} & 5\underline{\quad\quad} \end{array} \right)$

4. What causes a movement along a S/C?

    _____

    and a shift in the S/C?

    _____

    _____

5. Explain what is meant by the expression: 'The market is in equilibrium.'

    _____

    _____

    _____

6. A person who seeks to maximise his utility is at long-run equilibrium buying good A which costs £8 and good B which costs £3. Would you expect each of these goods to provide the same utility to him? Explain.

    _____

    _____

    _____

    _____

    _____

    _____

    _____

    _____

ELASTICITY (1)

	Price Elasticity of Demand		Income Elasticity of Demand		Cross Elasticity	
1. Definition: what is it?						
2. Formula	▲					
3. Signs	Positive	Negative	Positive	Negative	Positive	Negative
	as P↑ → Q_D ?	as P↑ → Q_D ?	as Y↑ → Q_D ?	as Y↑ → Q_D ?	if P_{butter} ↑ what happens to the Q_D margarine?	if P_{cars} ↑ what happens to the Q_D petrol?
	▲ Complete ▲ These goods are called				So E_D^C for substitute goods is:	So E_D^C for complementary goods is:
4. Values	• Elastic: > 1 • Inelastic: < 1 • Unit elasticity: = 1					
	1. if P↑ by 10% then Q_D___ by ___ 2. if P↑ by 10% then Q_D___ by ___ 3. if P↑ by 10% then Q_D___ by ___		1. if Y↑ by 10% then Q_D___ by ___ 2. if Y↑ by 10% then Q_D___ by ___			
5. What factors determine the E_D^P for a good?	1. ___ 2. ___ 3. ___ 4. ___ 5. ___ 6. ___		Luxury goods are:			
6. Price changes & their effects on TR	For elastic goods For inelastic goods For unit elastic goods					

1. Income elasticity of demand for a good is 1.5 and sales in year 1 are 10,000 units. If the level of income is expected to rise by 10% in the following year, what level of sales is likely in year 2? ___

2. 100 items are sold when the selling price is £1. When the price is increased to £1.25 the quantity sold falls to 78. Is demand for this good elastic or inelastic with respect to changes in its price? (Give a one sentence explanation of your answer.) ___

3. A woman spends 50% of her income in purchasing a certain quantity of good X. The woman's income is doubled (everything else remaining unchanged) and she now spends only 35% of her income on good X. In this example is good X an inferior good? Explain your answer. (20)

TEST: ELASTICITY (2)

1. 100 items are sold when the selling price is £1. When the price is increased to £1.25 the quantity sold falls to 78. Is demand for this good elastic or inelastic with respect to changes in its price? (Give a one sentence explanation of your answer.) _____

   _____

   _____

2. An increase in supply will decrease price most, when:
   (a) Demand is relatively inelastic and supply is relatively inelastic. ☐
   (b) Demand is relatively inelastic and supply is relatively elastic. ☐
   (c) Demand is relatively elastic and supply is relatively elastic. ☐
            (Tick the correct answer.)

3. Which of the following do you think is the closer estimate of price elasticity of demand for meat (i) + 3.2   (ii) – 0.45?   Give a very brief explanation of your choice.

   _____

   _____

4. Is the elasticity along a demand curve constant? Yes/No (Circle your choice.)

5. Demand is inelastic if:
   (a) the proportionate change in demand is > than the proportionate ΔP. ☐
   (b) the proportionate change in demand is < than the proportionate ΔP. ☐
   (c) the proportionate change in demand = the proportionate ΔP. ☐
            (Tick the correct answer.)

6. In the following diagram which of the demand curves is elastic and inelastic. Give an example of a commodity which satisfies this description.

	Elastic/Inelastic	Example
D/C: $D_1 D_1$		
D/C: $D_2 D_2$		

7. In relation to price elasticity state the 'Summary Law' (linking price elasticity with total revenue).

   _____

   _____

8. Price elasticity of demand for normal goods is positive ☐ negative ☐ zero ☐

9. Income elasticity of demand for normal goods is positive ☐ negative ☐ zero ☐

10. The formula for calculating price elasticity of demand is:

   _____

   _____

   _____

11. Cross elasticity of demand for substitute goods will be positive/negative/zero. (Place a circle around your choice and give a one sentence explanation of your answer.)

_____

_____

12. Define a normal good: _____

_____

_____

13. A luxury good is _____

_____

_____

14. If income elasticity of demand for a good is negative, then it must be an inferior good. True/False

(Circle your choice and give a one sentence explanation of your answer.) _____

_____

_____

15. Income elasticity of demand for a good is 1.5 and sales in year 1 are 10,000 units. If the level of income is expected to rise by 10% in the following year, what level of sales is likely in year 2 ? _____

_____

_____

SECTION B

Keep your answers to the point (approx. 25 mins)

Q. 1

(a) Income elasticity of demand for good X is – 1.3
Income elasticity of demand for good Y is + 0.6
Which of the following classifications is most appropriate for each of the above goods:
(i) could not be a Giffen good; (ii) is certain to be a Giffen good; (iii) could possibly be a Giffen good?
Explain your answer.

(b) Given the E_D^P of three manufacturer's goods as follows, what price changes would you recommend to him to increase total revenue?
Good A: – 6.00; Good B: + 1.00; Good C: – 0.01.
Explain your answer

(c) Which of the following figures is likely to represent:
(i) Income elasticity of demand for potatoes:
(ii) Income elasticity of demand for fresh salmon;
(iii) Price elasticity of demand for sweets.
  – 3.2, – 0.1, zero, + 0.5, + 2.6? Explain each of your choices.

1. (a) What is income elasticity of demand? (15 marks) (defn, formula & signs)

   - it measures the responsiveness of demand to changes in income;
   - it is measured by: $\dfrac{\Delta Q}{\Delta Y} \times \dfrac{Y_1 + Y_2}{Q_1 + Q_2}$
   - for normal goods it is + ; and for inferior goods it is −.

   (b) Now you should be able to explain price elasticity of demand.

   (c) To determine the volume of profits a co. makes, we should compare total_____ with total _____.

   (d) Complete the following using the spaces provided: **(1990 Q.1)**

Route & E_D^P	Price Change	Effect on Q_D ↓	Effect on TR ↓	Effect on Costs ↓	What happens Profits? ↓
A: − 1.6	↑P				
	↓P				
B: − 1.0	↑P				
	↓P				
C: − 0.5	↑P				
	↓P				

   So, how would you change the   (i) Pa _____   (ii) Pb _____
   (iii) Pc _____   so as to maximise profits?

   (e) Cross elas. of demand between good A & B = + 2.3

   Cross elas. of demand between good A & C = + 0.4

   Cross elas. of demand between good A & D = − 0.7

   Cross elas. of demand between good A & E = − 1.5

   Recall: The cross elas. for substitute gds (if P butter ↑ then Q^D mar.) is _____ . The cross elas.
   for complementary gds is always _____ .

   Now, which of these goods are *complements* to good A? Goods: _____

   Why?   _____

   Which of them are the *closest substitute* for good A? _____

   Why? Because as the Pa ↑, the Q_D of good _____ ↑ by _____%

COSTS (1)

(1982 Q. 2)

(a) What are the conditions under which a profit maximising firm would be at equilibrium in: *[handwritten: mc is rising faster than mr]*

   1. The short run: (a) *[handwritten: MC = MR]*   (b) *[handwritten: AC is falling]*   (c) *[handwritten: Ar covers AVC]*

   2. The long run: (a) *[handwritten: MC = MR]*   (b) *[handwritten: Ar covers AC]* *[incl. normal profit]*   (c) *[handwritten: MC rising faster than mr]*

(b) The following costs are incurred by an entrepreneur in producing his *maximum output of 1 item per week.*
   Rent (lease of 6 months remains & option to renew lease for 3 more yrs): £50 per week *[VC]*; *wages*: £300 per week; *raw materials*: £250 per unit prod.; *Electricity*: £80 per week; *normal profit*: £100 per unit produced. *[FC annotations handwritten]*

   What is the *minimum price* at which the item can be sold if production is to continue?

   In the short run: _____ *[handwritten: 550]*

   In the long run: _____ *[handwritten: 780]*

   (Hint: look back at your answers to part (a) above.)

   ▶ See Higher Level Papers: 1992 Q. 1, 1989 Q. 3, 1990 Q. 1.

   [handwritten margin: Rent / Wages → VC / Raw m → VC / ESB / normal profit]

COST OF PRODUCTION

Answer all questions

1. Increasing returns to scale occur when:

   (a) The output is expanding _____ *[handwritten: Yes No Yes]*

   (b) Marginal cost is rising _____ *[handwritten: Yes No]*

   (c) Long-run average cost is falling *[handwritten: Yes]*

   Write 'Yes' or 'No' for each of (a), (b), and (c).

2. A firm is considered to be of optimum size when:

   (a) there are no fixed costs _____ *[handwritten: No]*

   (b) the firm is earning supernormal profit _____ *[handwritten: Yes]*

   (c) production is at a level where average costs are at a minimum _____ *[handwritten: Yes]*

   Write 'Yes' or 'No' for each of (a), (b), and (c).

3. If marginal costs are rising, then

   (a) average costs are rising.   (True)/False

   (b) a firm could not be at equilibrium.   (True)/False

   (c) normal profit is not being earned.   True/(False)

   (In each case place a circle around your answer.)

4. Write True or False for each of a, b, and c.

   (a) When average cost is at a minimum, marginal cost = average cost. *[handwritten: T]*

   (b) When average cost is constant, marginal cost = average cost. *[handwritten: F]*

   (c) Marginal cost exists only in the short run. *[handwritten: F]*

5. At what point in the following table do diminishing marginal returns set in?

No. of men employed	1	2	3	4	5
Total output, in units	10	25	42	59	75

   [handwritten beneath: 15 17 17 16]

   [handwritten answer: 4]

6. Normal profit is:

   (a) a cost of production.   (True)/False

   (b) the amount earned by each entrepreneur.   True/(False)

   (c) the amount of profit which is liable for tax.   True/(False)

   (In each case place a circle around your answer.)

7. During the short–run period is it true that each of the following cannot increase as the level of output is expanding?
   (a) Marginal cost   True/~~False~~
   (b) Average fixed cost   True/~~False~~
   (c) Average variable cost   True/False
   (In each case circle your answer.)
8. In order to increase his labour force from 10 to 11 an entrepreneur is obliged to raise the weekly wage rate from £100 to £105. What is the marginal cost of labour?

   _____ 155 _____

   _____

   _____

9. An external economy of scale arises when:
   (a) a firm grows so that it becomes economical to introduce a computerised accounting system.

                                                          True/~~False~~

   (b) specialised firms are set up to meet the needs of the industry.   ~~True~~/False
   (c) a supplier of raw materials can lower his prices through economies of scale.   ~~True~~/False
   (In each case place a circle around your answer.)

Q. 1

Output	Total Cost	Marginal Cost	Total Revenue	Marginal Revenue
0	25	—	–	–
1	55	30	58	–
2	82	27	100	42
3	107	27	126	26
4	131	24	150	24
5	152	21	168	18

   (a) Complete the above table.
   (b) What are the fixed costs of this firm?
   (c) At what level of output is profit *per unit* sold greatest? ①

Q. 2 1992
   (a) Assuming a competitive market, under what conditions would a profit maximising firm be at
       (i) long–run equilibrium; (ii) short–run equilibrium.   (30)
   (b) Max Flow Ltd incurred the following costs in producing their maximum output of two units per week:
       Rent £2,500 (per week). The lease has two years to run.
       Normal profit £400 (£200 per unit).
       Labour £500 (hired on a weekly basis).
       What is the minimum price at which each unit can be sold if production is to continue
       (i) in the short run?
       (ii) in the long run? Explain your answer.   (45)

PERFECT COMPETITION

1. List the assumptions of PC.

1. homogeneous
2. no one buyer > no one seller, no one seller.
3. no one seller
4. Buyer/seller act independently
5. Perfect competition
6. No barriers to entry/exit

2. Draw the S/R equilibrium for PC.

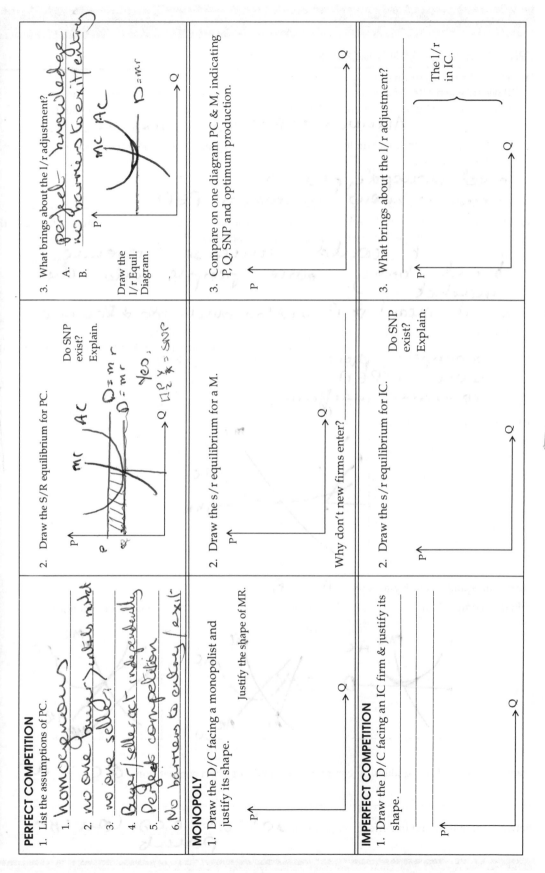

Do SNP exist? Explain.

$D = mr$
$D = mr$

yes, $\Pi \frac{\cancel{P} \times}{\cancel{Q}} = SNP$

3. What brings about the l/r adjustment?

A. perfect knowledge
B. no barriers to exit/entry

Draw the l/r Equil. Diagram.

$MC \ AC$
$D = mr$

MONOPOLY

1. Draw the D/C facing a monopolist and justify its shape.

Justify the shape of MR.

2. Draw the s/r equilibrium for a M.

Why don't new firms enter? _____

3. Compare on one diagram PC & M, indicating P, Q, SNP and optimum production.

IMPERFECT COMPETITION

1. Draw the D/C facing an IC firm & justify its shape. _____

2. Draw the s/r equilibrium for IC.

Do SNP exist? Explain.

3. What brings about the l/r adjustment? _____

The l/r in IC.

PRICE DISCRIMINATING MONOPOLIST (PDM)

(a) Define Price Discrimination:

It occurs when a firm charges sells the same goods at different ratios between price and marginal cost or selling the same goods to different consumers with different price elasticities of demand.

Give one example: _AIRLINES → BUSINESS CLASS etc_

Why is it possible for this firm to practise price discrimination? (Think of the conditions necessary for a PDM to operate.)

• need monopoly powers

• need to know customers PED

(b) A monopolistic firm which seeks to maximise its profit is at LR equil. If circumstances change so that this firm could engage in price discrimination – would it do so? Explain. (20)

Yes, provided: _it could increase revenue_ _& and bring more people into the market)_

No, if: _it meant ↓ P and too much so ↓ Revenue_

(c) The conditions necessary for a PDM are:

(i) _monopoly powers_

(ii) _know c's PED_

(iii) _consumer indifference_

(At what point does it decide to allocate its output to the export market?)

(d) Draw the l/r equilibrium diagram.

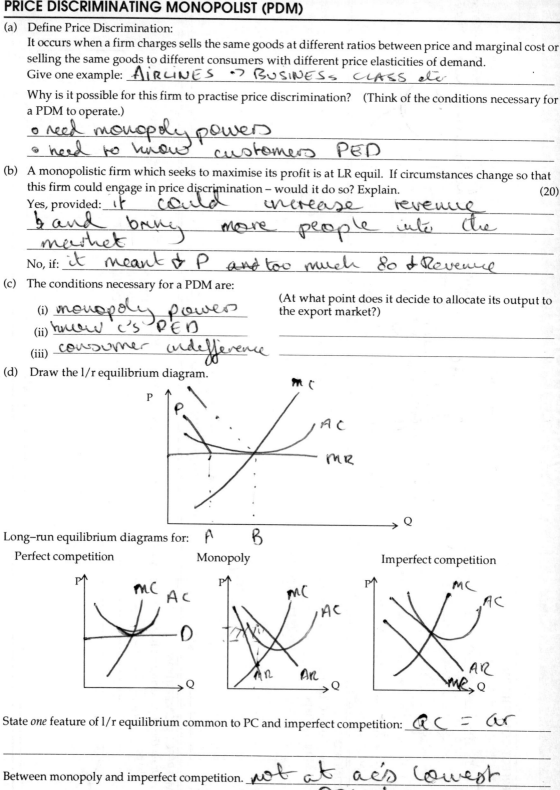

Long–run equilibrium diagrams for: A   B

Perfect competition   Monopoly   Imperfect competition

State *one* feature of l/r equilibrium common to PC and imperfect competition: _AC = AR_

Between monopoly and imperfect competition. _not at ac's lowest point_

OLIGOPOLY

(a) Define what is meant by an oligopolist market? _____
_____
_____

(b) When costs of production are falling oligopolists are more inclined to give out free gifts or engage in non–price competition than to reduce prices. Why? (40)
Two points required. One based on the idea of the kinked demand curve.

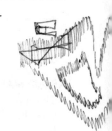

_____
_____

(c) What are cartels? _____

Give one example in Ireland: _____

(d) Are consumers better off with reduced prices or free gifts? _____
_____

(e) The Cournot Model (assume no costs of production): Show how equilibrium is arrived at.

Stage 1			Stage 2	Stage 3	Stage 4
P	Q	TR			
12	0	0			
11	3	33			
10	6	60			
9	9	81			
8	12	96			
7	15	105			
6	18	108			
5	21	105			
4	24	96			
3	27	81			
2	30	60			
1	33	33			
0	36	0			

Kinked D/C: Draw the equilibrium diagram which helps to explain *price rigidity*

P

Qty

COURNOT MODEL

Output in a *monopoly* is ½ that of a PC firm.

In an oligopoly with 2 *firms* output is $\frac{2}{3}$ of a PC firm.

In an oligopoly with 3 *firms* output is $\frac{3}{4}$ of a PC firm.

An oligopoly with 2 firms reaches equilibrium producing 12,000 units.* Show how this is reached.

Stage	Firm 1	Firm 2	Explanation
1.			
2.			
3.			
4.			
5.			

*Starting point!

MICROECONOMICS: FACTOR OF PRODUCTION MARKET

INTRODUCTION
1. Marginal physical productivity is: _____

   _____

2. Marginal revenue productivity is: _____

   _____

3. MRP = _____ × _____ (only in perfect competition MRP = MPP × _____).

4. Is marginal revenue productivity an appropriate criterion for setting wages in the public sector? Generally speaking, no. (To see why, go back to your answers in 1 and 2 above.) Why is this so?

   1. _____

   2. _____

5. Given your answer to 4 above, what other method(s) might be adopted?   (20)

   _____

   _____

   _____

LABOUR MARKET
1. The supply of labour to any economy depends on three factors:
   (a)   the total population
   (b)   _____   (c)_____
2. What factors determine the demand which a firm will make for labour?
   (The best way to answer this is to ask yourself when would a firm employ more workers.)

   (a) _____   (b) _____

   (c) _____   (d) _____

   (e) _____   (f) _____

3. What factors are relevant in determining the wages to be paid to a particular category of worker?
                                                                      (1987 Pass) (40)

   (Think of many different categories of workers – from teachers to pop stars – and ask what determines their pay.)

   (a) _____   (b) _____

   (c) _____   (d) _____

   (e) _____   (f) _____

CAPITAL MARKET
1983 Q. 6 (Hons)
(a) Distinguish between the classical & Keynesian theories of interest.   (45)

(b) On 1 Jan. 1980 I bought at its face value a £100 government bond which was paying 10% interest per annum. When there was a new issue of govt bonds paying 20% interest I sold my bond for its market value on 31 Dec. 1980. At what price was the bond sold? What would be my profit or loss on the entire transaction? What was the real interest rate of the bond if inflation during the year was 20%.   (30)

6TH ECONOMICS: THE LABOUR MARKET

SECTION A

1. A backward bending supply curve for labour means that: *and wage levels increase people well begin to substitute leisure for work*

2. What is meant by the term 'ratchet economy'? *When wages and price do not fall in an economy as demand falls.*

3. Define labour as a factor of production, *Any human activity which results in the creation of wealth*

4. What is economic rent? *Any surplus earned by a FOP over its transfer earnings*

5. State *two* means by which the government may attempt to improve the mobility of labour.
   Reduce barriers to entry for a trade
   Improve infrastructure

6. 'Wage drift' occurs when: *D_{LAB} above S_{LAB}, this leads to TU's increasing minimum wage prices.*

SECTION B (100 marks)

(a) What factors affect the supply of labour in an economy?
Draw the typical supply curve of labour & show the effect where the workers join a trade union. (10)

(b) What factors affect the quantity of labour demanded by an individual firm? (20)

(c) Are workers likely to earn an economic rent if the firm employing it sells its output in a perfectly competitive market? Explain your answer (20)

(d) Is it possible for workers to enjoy an economic rent if there is unemployment? Explain your answer. (10)

(e) List the main factors which account for people receiving different wage rates. (20)

(f) High wages cost jobs. Discuss the arguments for and against this statement. (20)

6TH ECONOMICS: THE FACTOR MARKET: CAPITAL/LAND/ENTERPRISE

SECTION A

1. Liquidity preference refers to: _____
   _____
   _____

2. State *two* developments which would cause a reduction in the marginal efficiency of capital.
   Drop in price Increase in price
   Drop in Increase in capital used

3. Give *two* examples of uninsurable risk which entrepreneurs bear.
   Loss of sales
   Bankruptcy

4. State *two* ways in which land (as a FOP) differs from the other FOP.
   Gift of nature
   Fixed in supply

5. If bond prices are expected to rise the speculative demand for money will increase. True/False (Circle your choice and give a one sentence explanation of your answers.)
   _____
   _____
   _____

6. Give *two* examples of circumstances as a result of which the demand for a variable FOP would not be reduced even though its price had increased.
   Price of good is a factor
   if productivity is rising

7. If a new national loan is issued at a higher rate of interest than that payable on existing loans, will the selling price of the existing loans
   (a) increase?   [ ]
   (b) decrease?   [✓]
   (c) remain unchanged?   [ ]

8. State *two* factors which are likely to affect the level of savings.
   Level of interest
   Level of income

9. Rent of ability is: _____
   _____
   _____

SECTION B

(a) Explain the way(s) in which a reduction in the rates of interest affects the Irish economy. (25)

(b) Distinguish between savings and investment. Is it desirable to have a high level of savings in the economy? Explain your answer. (25)

(c) Keynes set out *three* reasons to explain why people might like to hold their assets in the form of money. State them and the factors which affect them. (25)

(d) On 1 January 1990 I bought at its face value a £100 government bond which was paying 10% interest per annum. When there was a new issue of government bonds paying 5% interest I sold my bond for its market value on 31 December 1990. For what price was the bond sold? What would be my profit or loss on the entire transaction? What was the real rate of interest of the bond if inflation during the year was 2%? (25)

THE CAPITAL MARKET – WORKSHEET

1. Do the following represent 'investment' to the economy? Answer Yes or No in each case.
   (a) Buying a 10 yr old house ___*NO*___
   (b) Depositing money in a bank ___*YES NO*___
   (c) Buying shares in an existing company ___*YES*___
   (d) A company spending money on a new factory ___*YES*___

2. Liquidity preference refers to: ___*people wanting to keep money in liquid form, demand for money not dependent on r/i*___

3. What is the most important single factor which determines the following:
   (a) transaction M^D ___*Income*___
   (b) precautionary M^D ___*Income*___
   (c) speculative M^D? ___*R/i*___

4. If a new national loan is issued at a higher rate of interest than that payable on existing loans, will the selling price of existing loans:
   (tick the correct one)
   (a) increase? ☑
   (b) decrease? ☑
   (c) remain unchanged? ☐
   (d) depend on other circumstances? ☐

5. Is there an element of savings in each of the following?
   (a) Govt running a budget deficit? | *NO*
   (b) Purchase of RMs by a business? |
   (c) A person buying a new house by means of a building soc. mortgage? | *YES*
   (Write Yes or No for each.)

6. State *three* developments which would put upward pressure on Irish interest rates.
   A. ___*Increase in demand for money*___
   B. ___*Decrease in supply*___
   C. ___*ECB increasing r/i.*___

INTEREST RATES

Briefly state how a rise in r/i could affect each of the following. State *how* it could be affected and give a brief reason *why.*
   (a) Savings: ___*more valoable, you will get an ↑ return*___
   (b) Borrowing: ___*higher repayments less demand*___
   (c) Investment: ___*decrease, guaranteed ↑ return off savings*___
   (d) Level of inflation: ___*↓ inflation, less spending*___
   (e) Mortgage holders: ___*Higher repayments.*___
   (f) Imports: ___*go down, people spending less.*___
   (g) Servicing the national debt: ___*paying more*___
   (h) The value of our currency: ___*our interest rates become more attractive neverse*___

GOVERNMENT BONDS

- On 1 Jan. 1989 I bought at its face value a £100 govt bond paying 20% interest p.a.
- When there was a new issue of govt bonds paying 30%, I sold my bond for its market value on 31 Dec. 1989.
- The inflation rate during 1989 was 15%.

   (a) For what price did I sell my bond? ___*115*___
   (b) How much profit/loss did I make? ___*5*___
   (c) What was the real r/i on my bond? ___*5%*___

MACROECONOMICS – BUDGETING, TAXATION & NATIONAL DEBT

(a) Explain each of the following:

1. Current budget deficit: _____

_____

2. EBR: _____

_____

3. PSBR: _____

_____

4. National debt: _____

_____

5. Bal. of payments deficit: _____

_____

(b) If there was an increase of £25 m. in the curr. budget deficit, state, giving reasons, whether you would expect each of the other items to increase, decrease, or remain the same.

EBR: _____

PSBR: _____

Nat. debt: _____

BOP deficit: _____

(c) If the Irish govt decided to reduce the CBD, what course(s) of action might it adopt? Trace the likely econ. effects of the course(s) of action. (35)

Involves either changing *revenue* or *expenditure*. What are the possibilities and what would the overall effects be?

1. Taxation: _____

_____

2. Expenditure: _____

_____

3. Overall effects: _____

_____

(d) If there is an unexpected downturn in the level of economic activity, what effect would this have on the size of the CBD?

Tax: _____

_____

Expenditure: _____

_____

Are there any circumstances under which the government is justified in borrowing? (25)

Ans. _____

_____

_____

(e) Government fiscal policy causes a redistribution of income within the economy. State, giving reasons, if you consider this to be desirable. Set out the economic effects arising from this consequence of fiscal policy. (35)

(f) Trace the likely effects on the Irish economy if the govt reduces rates of income tax while leaving unchanged all other forms of taxation and government expenditure. (40)

MONEY & BANKING

(a) Explain the ways in which money can contribute to the smooth working of an economy. (25)
(It's just another way of asking the functions of money.)
State and, with one sentence, explain each.

1. _____

2. _____

3. _____

4. _____

(b) What qualities (or characteristics) are required of whatever is to be used as money? (20)

_____

_____

_____

_____

(c) M1 is: _____

_____

M3 is: _____

_____

(d) State for each of the following whether they are capable of ↑ the Ms.

1. Commercial banks: _____

2. Building societies: _____

3. Post Office Savings Bank: _____

(e) Is there any limit to the amount of purchasing power which banks can create?
Explain your answer. (25)

Yes there are. Set out 3 or 4 of these limitations.

1. _____

2. _____

3. _____

4. _____

(f) How would each of the following affect the ability of the banks to create purchasing power?

1. An increased use of 'plastic money': _____

2. A desire by banks to reduce their level of bad debts: _____

(g) Trace the likely economic effects if:

1. the supply of money was growing at a faster rate than a country's production of goods & services.
(Try to think of 2 separate effects.)

_____

_____

2. the supply of money was growing at a slower rate than a country's production of goods & services.

_____

_____

ECONOMICS: INFLATION & PRICES

SECTION A

1. Inflation is defined as: _____

   _____

   _____

2. Set out the *four* steps used in compiling a Composite Price Index.

   Step 1_____

   Step 2_____

   Step 3_____

   Step 4_____

3. An inflationary gap means:_____

   _____

   _____

4. What are the effects of inflation on:

   (a) People on fixed incomes? _____

   (b) Borrowers & savers? _____

   (c) Imports? _____

   (d) Exports?_____

   (e) Speculators? _____

5. State (and briefly explain) *three* contributory factors which have helped reduce Irish inflation rates.

   (a) _____

   (b) _____

   (c) _____

SECTION B

(a) If you wanted to know the rate of inflation: what index would you look up? (5)

(b) Explain how the Consumer Price Index is constructed. (30)

(c) Are changes in the above an accurate measurement of changes in the cost of living? Explain your answer. **(1990 Pass L. Cert.)** (30)

(d) Is it desirable to have a low rate of inflation? Discuss. **(1988 Pass L. Cert.)** (50)

ECONOMICS: POP. & EMPLOYMENT

SECTION A

1. Explain the term 'full employment'. _____

_____

_____

2. State *three* factors which have contributed to the decline in Ireland's population.

    (a) _____

    (b) _____

    (c) _____

3. What is the main source for arriving at the level of our unemployment?

    Briefly explain your answer. _____

    _____

    _____

    _____

4. Can you suggest from what sources we gather information on emigration from this country?

    (a) _____

    (b) _____

    (c) _____

5. What is meant by the term 'work-sharing'?

    _____

    _____

    _____

    Suggest *three* ways in which it may be achieved.

    (a) _____

    (b) _____

    (c) _____

6. What are the effects of emigration on:

    (a) Investment in education? _____

    (b) Dependency ratio? _____

    (c) Wage levels in Ireland? _____

SECTION B

(a) Distinguish between cyclical, frictional and institutional forms of unemployment. (15)

(b) Comment on the causes and the economic effects of the high unemployment rate in the Irish economy at present. (35)

(c) Suggest possible ways of reducing the Irish unemployment rate. (20)

1988

(a) Distinguish between Net Domestic Product, Net National Product, Gross National Product at Factor Cost & Gross National Product at Market Prices.

1988

(b) In respect of each of the following, state whether the development would affect

    (i)   our GNP,

    (ii) the standard of living in Ireland.

1. Growth of 'The Black Economy', i.e. people working and not declaring their income for tax purposes.

2. A man marries a woman whom he had previously employed as his housekeeper.

3. Foreign firms repatriate their profits. (50)

1984

(b) In year 1 National Income was £1,000 and the Consumer Price Index was 100.

In year 4 National Income was £3,122 and the Consumer Price Index was 140.

Express the National Income of year 4 at constant year 1 prices. (25)

1984

(c) 'Since teachers' salaries and non–contributory old age pensions are both paid for by taxes, neither should be included in the calculation of GNP.' Do you agree? Explain your answer. (35)

1983

(b) What effects would

    (i)   a general reduction in the working week, without any change in the level of production, and

    (ii) an increase in the rates of VAT have on (1) GNP at Market Prices, and (2) the general standard of living?

1987

(b) What is meant by GNP at current market prices?

What factors caused GNP at current market prices to increase over the past 5 years? (40)

1991.

(a) Why are *three* methods used to calculate the National Income? (15)

(b) Explain *two* of the methods mentioned above – briefly. (30)

(c) Is it possible to have an increase in the Gross National Product without an improvement in the general standard of living? Explain. (30)

ANSWERS

1985 and 1990

(a) Define 'National Income'. (15)

(b) In Ireland at present would you expect Gross National Product to be greater than, equal to, or less than Gross Domestic Product? Explain your answer. (20)

1990

(c) If you knew Gross National Product at Current Market Prices for 1980 and 1984, what other information would you consider relevant in attempting to assess changes in the average standard of living during the years in question? (40)

(a) National Income is: _____

_____

(b) I would expect Gross National Product to be _____ Gross Domestic Product because:

_____

_____

_____

_____

(c) Other information necessary to assess changes in the average standard of living would be:

1. _____

2. _____

3. _____

4. _____

5. _____

6. _____

1986

(a) Would you consider changes in:
(i) National Income; or
(ii) GNP at Factor Cost to be the better basis for assessing changes in the standard of living?
Explain your choice. (20)

(b) If everything else remained unchanged, what effect (if any) would the removal of food subsidies have on:
(i) the level of GNP at current market prices; and
(ii) the standard of living in the economy?
Explain your answer. (20)

(c) If an amount of money (say £10 million) which had previously been spent on domestically produced capital goods was spent, in the current year, on domestically produced consumption goods, what effect (if any) would this have on:
(i) the level of GNP; and
(ii) the standard of living, in the current year?
Would your answer be the same if you were considering the long-term outcome? (35)

(a) I would consider changes in_____ to be the better basis for assessing changes in the

standard of living, because _____

(b) Food subsidies removed:

	Level of GNP at Curr. Mkt Prices	Standard of Living
Effect on:		

(c) Effect of spending £10 m. on consumer gds rather than capital gds (both produced domestically):

	Level of GNP	Standard of Living
Current Year		
Long Term		

1988 and 1990

(a) Distinguish between Gross National Product and Gross Domestic Product. State, giving reasons, which of these you consider to be the better indicator of the standard of living in Ireland. (40)

(b) What factors affect our level of Gross National Product? (35)

ANSWERS

5. The following table shows the level of GNP, Consumption, Investment and Imports and Exports at the end of Period 1 and the level of Investment and Exports at the end of Period 2. Consumption and Imports depend on the level of GNP. (For the purpose of this question you may ignore the government sector.)

	GNP	Consump.	Invest.	Exports	Imports
Period 1	8,500	6,825	2,000	700	1,025
Period 2			2,100	800	

(a) If the average propensity to consume in Period 2 is 0.8 and the Multiplier is 2.5 calculate:
   (i)   the level of GNP at the end of Period 2.   (5)
   (ii) the level of consumption at the end of Period 2   (10)
   (iii) the level of imports at the end of Period 2.   (10)
   (iv) the marginal propensity to consume.   (10)
   (v) the marginal propensity to import.   (10)
(b) Assuming the growth in exports in Period 3 was 200, what level of Investment would be required to cut the balance of trade deficit to 190?   (15)
(c) What would the growth in savings be in Period 3 under the circumstances outlined in (b) above? (15)

1. Given

Period	GNP	=	C	+	I	+	X	–	M	Savings	(GNP-C)
1	8,500		6,825		2,000		700		1,025	1,675	(8500-6825)
2					2,100		800				
change											
3											

2. APC = 0.8 (so APS must be 1.00 – 0.8 = 0.2)
3. Multiplier = 2.5*
(a) Find
   (i) GNP, C, M in Period 2; (ii) MPC; (iii) MPM.

Steps
1. Injections between Periods 1 and 2: Inv. ↑ by £100 & X ↑ by £100. Total ↑ in injections = £200.
2. If Inj. ↑ by £200, then GNP ↑ by £200 × 2.5 = £500. (+ £8,500 = £9,000).
3. APC = 0.8, so C = £9,000 × 0.8 = £7,200.
4. Savings = £9,000 – £7,200 = £1,800.
5. Now £9,000 = £7,200 + £2,100 + £800 – M.
   So Ms = £9,000 – £7,200 – £2,100 – £800 = £1,100
The resulting position is:

Period	GNP	C	I	X	M	S
1	8,500	6,825	2,000	700	1,025	1,675 *
2	9,000	7,200	2,100	800	1,100	1,800
Change	500	375	100	100	75	125

Hence: MPC = $\dfrac{375}{500}$ = 0.75, and MPM = $\dfrac{75}{500}$ = 0.15

Check: Multiplier = $\dfrac{1}{1\text{-(MPC-MPM)}}$ = $\dfrac{1}{1-(0.75-0.15)}$ = $\dfrac{1}{1-0.6}$ = $\dfrac{1}{0.4}$ = 2.5*

(b)

Period	GNP	C	I	X	M	Savings
2	9,000	7,200	2,100	800	1,100	1,800
				+ 200 +	90	
3				1,000	1,190	

Step 1:

If bal. of trade is to be reduced to 190, then total imports in period 3 would equal 1,100 + 90 = 1,190.

Step 2:

So M can only ↑ by £90. If M ↑ by £90, how much must GNP have ↑ by?

Recall MPM = 0.15 ($3/_{20}$). So $1/_{20}$ of £90 = £30

So $20/_{20}$ = £30 × 20 = £600.

So GNP ↑ by £600 (+ £9,000) = £9,600.

Step 3:

£600 × 0.75 = ↑ in C = £450.

So C in Period 3 = £7,200 + £450 = £7,650.

Step 4:

Y – C = Savings, so £9,600 – £7,650 = £1,950.

Step 5:

What is investment?

£9,600 = £7,650 + I + £1,000 – £1,190.

So inv. = £9,600 – £7,650 – £1,000 + £1,190 = £2,140

Summary

Period	GNP	C	I	X	M	Savings
3	9,000	7,650	2,140	1,000	1,190	1,950

M. INTERNATIONAL TRADE

LAW OF ABSOLUTE ADVANTAGE

1. Output per worker

	Country	Beef		Tomatoes
			(kg. per week)	
	Ireland	400	or	600
	Holland	200	or	2400
Calculate total world output ▶				

Calculate the Opportunity costs:
IRE: B for T:
T for B:
HOLL: B for T:
T for B:

2. Calculate:
   (i)   Ireland's absolute advantage:_____
   (ii) Holland's absolute advantage:_____
   (iii) What should Ireland specialise in? _____
   (iv) What should Holland specialise in? _____

3. Specialisation takes place

	Country	Beef	Tomatoes
	Ireland		
	Holland		
Calculate total world output ▶			

Remember you are now calculating the output for 2 men specialising in each country.

4. Assume trade takes place
   (a) Suppose Ireland swops half of her output of _____ for Holland's _____
   (b) Assume an exchange rate of 6 kg beef for 6 kg tomatoes
   (c) So Ireland gives _____ kg _____ for _____ kg _____

       & Holland gives _____ kg _____ for _____ kg _____

5. Resulting position

Country	Beef	Tomatoes
Ireland		
Holland		
World Output		

6. Advantages of trade
   By looking at the results from specialisation and trade you should now be able to comment on the obvious advantages of trade.

   1. _____

   2. _____

LAW OF COMPARATIVE ADVANTAGE

Step

1. Output per worker

	Country	Beef		Tomatoes
			(kg per week)	
	Ireland	400	or	600
	Holland	200	or	2,400
Calculate total world output ▶				

Calculate the Opportunity costs:
IRE: B for T:
T for B:
HOLL: B for T:
T for B:

In world terms what is 1 unit of beef worth in terms of tomatoes?

2. Calculate

   (i)   Ireland's comparative adv/disadvantage:_____

   (ii) Holland's comparative adv/disadvantage:_____

   (iii) What should Holland specialise in? _____

   Why? _____

   (iv) What should Ireland specialise in? _____

   Why? _____

3. Specialisation takes place

	Country	Beef	Tomatoes	
	Ireland			Remember you are now calculating the
	Holland			output for 2 men specialising in each
Calculate total world output ▶				country.

   Now answer the following:

   (i)   Has production of beef ↑ or ↓?_____By what percentage?_____

   (ii) Has production of tomatoes ↑ or ↓? _____By what percentage?_____

   (iii) Using this information is the world better off or worse off? _____

4. Assume trade takes place.

   (i)   Look at point 1 above and the opportunity costs involved.

   (ii) Complete the following to calculate the possible terms of trade.

	Minimum amt of importer will accept _____	maximum amt of exporter will give _____
Ireland swops beef		
Holland swops tomatoes		

(iii) Assume it is 2 kg tomatoes for 1 kg beef, and that Ireland exchanges 400 kg beef for ____ kg tomatoes. Now complete the following:

Country	Beef	Tomatoes
Ireland		
Holland		

5. Advantages of trade

1. _____

2. _____

3. _____

1. _____ exports

    e.g. (a) _____

        (b) _____

add

2. _____ exports

    e.g. (a) _____

        (b) _____

        (c) _____

If total Ms > total Xs this is called a

_____

---

1. _____ imports =>

    e.g. (a) _____

        (b) _____

add

2. _____ exports

    e.g. (a) _____

        (b) _____

        (c) _____

If total Ms > total Xs this is called a

_____

Given this situation, what possible problems might occur within the economy?

THINK!

1. (Circular flow of income) _____

   _____

   _____

2. (Jobs) _____

   _____

3. (Value of IR£)_____

   _____

4. _____

   _____

   _____

Given these problems (caused by Ms exceeding Xs) can you suggest any remedies?

1. (Dealing with Ms) _____

   _____

   _____

2. (Dealing with Xs) _____

   _____

3. (Coping with why people can afford to buy so much Ms) _____

   _____

4. (Home produced goods)_____

   _____

5. (What could it do with the value of its currency?) _____

   _____

   _____

What are the main methods by which a country can reduce imports?

1. _____ 2. _____ 3. _____ 4. _____

Main advantage				
Main disadv.				

What is it?	

CAPITAL A/C

BOP Current A/C Surplus	or BOP Current A/C Deficit
plus (l/t Cap. Inflows)	*plus* (l/t Cap. Outflows)
A. _____	1. _____
B._____	2. _____
C. _____	
D. _____	
If we receive more cap. in one year then what, in Ireland, will rise?	If we pay out more cap. in one year, then what will fall?

1. The Current Account Balance
         plus   }   is called: the Balance of Autonomous Transactions
   Inflows of l/t Capital

2. Accommodating transactions.
   These accommodating transactions draw the Balance of Payments into balance in the accounting sense. If there was a deficit of £200 m. on our Balance of Autonomous Transactions, then our Official External Reserves would fall by this amount or foreign borrowing of £200 m. would be necessary or some combination of these two types of development to the value of £200 m. would ensue.

   There are certain ambiguities in some of the transactions on the Capital A/C Section as a result of which it is difficult to unambiguously classify each item as being either autonomous or accommodating. However, any official transaction in the Capital A/C Section, the purpose of which is to maintain the exchange rate between the domestic currency and a foreign currency (or currencies) at some desired level, may be unambiguously classified as an Accommodating Item.

3. Inter–relationships of Transactions
   There *can* be an inter–relationship between transactions which appear on the Balance of Trade and Autonomous Capital Transfers, e.g.
   (a) Funds transferred by a multinational co. to its Irish subsidiary:
       – this is a long–term capital inflow. However, the money could be used to buy foreign capital equipment: this appears as a physical import in the Balance of Trade.
   (b) A loan negotiated in a foreign country to buy capital equipment in that country:
       – again it's a l/t cap. inflow to buy a physical import (in the Bal. of Trade).
   (c) Foreign companies resident in Ireland exporting goods:
       – exporting gds has a beneficial effect on our Balance of Trade. However, they might then send back their profits to their home country (repatriation of profits). This is a l/t capital outflow.

1986 (Hons)

(b) The Industrial Development Authority (IDA) succeeded in encouraging a number of foreign firms to set up in Ireland. Describe the manner in which these firms affect our Balance of Payments. (40)

HISTORICAL VIEW OF EXCHANGE RATES

Complete the following chart, outlining the development of E/Rs

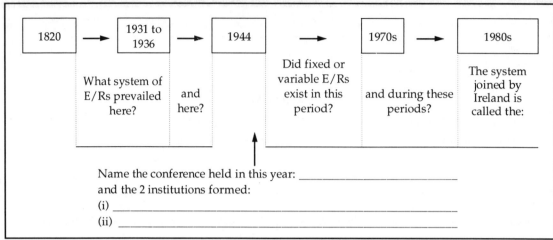

| 1820 | → | 1931 to 1936 | → | 1944 | → | 1970s | → | 1980s |

What system of E/Rs prevailed here? _____ and here? _____

Did fixed or variable E/Rs exist in this period? _____ and during these periods? _____

The system joined by Ireland is called the: _____

Name the conference held in this year: _____
and the 2 institutions formed:
(i) _____
(ii) _____

THE GOLD STANDARD

Main advantages of this system:

(a) encouraged _____ in foreign trade.

(b) Self–A _____ M _____

↓

illustrate this here.

| UK | | USA |

←—— Exports £10 m. Stg

Exports £7 m. Stg ——→

x ___ M by £___ m.   x ___ M by £___ m.

↓   ↓

BOP_____   BOP_____

Changes £3 m. into gold ⎫ ————————→
and sends to USA   ⎭

Does Money Supply   Does Money Supply
↓ or ↑ ?   ↓ or ↑ ?

Effects on prices? [ ]   [ ]

↓   ↓

Effects on exports? [ ]   [ ]

So by correcting the BOP problems the gold standard's main advantage was called the

Self–A_____ M _____.

State the *two* reasons for its abandonment.

1. _____

2. _____

THE STERLING AREA

1. State why it became so important?
    (a) _____
    (b) _____

2. Two groups of countries belonged to it?
    (a) _____ e.g. Australia/India.
    (b) _____ e.g. Japan.

3. To be a member of the Sterling Area you had to satisfy these 2 requirements:
    (i) _____
    (ii) _____

4. The economic advantages in being a member of the Sterling Area were:
    (a) Sterling was the most _____

    _____ in the world.

    (b) It was a _____ currency & so currencies aligned with it remained

    _____.

    (c) Countries had _____ to the

    _____ markets of London.

5. After 1939 many non–_____ members left because:
    (a) of the _____ of sterling, making

    it less _____.

    (b) trade between _____ countries

    became less _____.

The International Monetary Fund was established in 1944 at the Bretton Woods Conference.

Why was it established? _____

_____

In order for this aim to be achieved each member country had to_____

_____

and this was not allowed to change beyond +/– _____ %

What did each country contribute to the IMF? _____

This consisted of 75% in _____ and 25% in _____.

What did the country use the above for? _____

_____

_____

What was the advantage of this? _____

Besides the above, what else did the IMF insist on?_____

_____

Give examples of these measures:

(i)_____

(ii) _____

The system operated well until the 1970s. What happened? _____

_____

What system tried to establish a fixed exchange rate system in the 1980s? _____

INTERNATIONAL TRADE: REVISION QUESTIONS : MACROECONOMICS

Topic: consists of 3 areas:

(a) Reasons for international trade; problems with it; trade protection measures.

(b) Balance of payments: current & capital A/C; bal. of autonomous transactions; does BOP balance? BOP → deficit; problems & solutions; devaluation.

(c) Exchange rates.

A. REASONS FOR TRADE
Hons. 1983, 1985 & 1989/91 and Pass 1990

(a) Explain the Theory of Comparative Advantage and illustrate your answer with an example. (25)

(b) On what assumptions is the Theory of Comparative Advantage based? To what extent do these assumptions apply in the case of the Irish economy? (25)

Pass 1986

(a) Is international trade beneficial to the Irish economy? Explain your answer. (25)

Pass 1987

(b) Is there any economic justification for a government intervening in order to restrict international trade? Explain *one* means by which the government might restrict international trade if it wished to do so. (35)

B : BALANCE OF PAYMENTS

Hons 1986

(b) The Industrial Development Authority succeeded in encouraging a number of foreign firms to set up in Ireland. Describe the manner in which these firms affect our Balance of Payments. (40)

Pass 1985

(a) Give *two* examples of items which would appear on the Capital Section of the BOP. (20)

(b) Distinguish between the Balance of Trade and the Balance on Current Account, (and the Terms of Trade (Pass 1989)). (25)

C. EXCHANGE RATES

Pass 1986

(c) If sterling increased in value relative to the Irish Punt, what effect(s) would this have on the Irish economy? (35)

Hons 1988

(a) What factors affect the foreign exchange value of our currency? (20)

(b) State, giving reasons, if you would expect an increase in the foreign exchange value of our currency to improve or worsen our Balance of Trade. (& Pass 1989). (30)

Hons 1990

(c) Advs & disads of fixed v variable exchange rates.

SECTION A-TYPE QUESTIONS:

You should see for yourself that you know the answers to the following questions:

H 87/90:

Balance of Autonomous Transactions.

H 86:

formula for calculating the Terms of Trade.

H 84:

What is meant by exchange risk in international trade?

H 83/89:

If our TOT change from 103 to 98 then the price of our Xs relative to the price of our Ms has increased/decreased.

H 81:

1. State two effects if the govt imposes a quota on imports.

2. A common mkt is.

Pass 88:

1. A deficit on our Bal. of Trade occurs when.

2. Name *two* international economic institutions.

87:

devaluation means.

86:

as for 1988 (and Dumping).

85:

formula for Terms of Trade.

83/90:

1. The Balance of Payments is.

2. Devaluation is.

82/89:

Two examples of Invisible Imports (other than foreign holidays).

80:

1. What is meant by a Fixed Exchange Rate Policy?

2. State the infant industry argument for the imposition of tariffs on imports.

79:

What is meant by the terms of trade?

THE HISTORY OF ECONOMIC THOUGHT

Brief outline of topic:

Mercantilism	Classical Sch.	Neo–Keynesian
Physiocracy	Neoclassical	Keynes Monetarism

1. Place the following in chronological order (the figure 1 indicating the earliest).

Thomas Malthus	_____
John Maynard Keynes	_____
Alfred Marshall	_____
Karl Marx	_____
Milton Friedman	_____
Adam Smith	_____

2. Indicate the author of each of the following:

   (a) Inquiry into the Nature & Causes of the Wealth of Nations: _____

   (b) A Monetary History of the United States: _____

   (c) Das Kapital: _____

   (d) Essay on the Principles of Population: _____

   (e) General Theory of Employment, Interest & Money: _____

3. What economist(s) would you associate with each of the following::

   (a) Law of Comparative Costs? _____

   (b) Surplus Value of Production? _____

   (c) The Multiplier? _____

   (d) The Iron Law of Wages? _____

4. According to Keynesian theory:

   (a) The main factor influencing employment is _____

   (b) The main factor influencing investment is _____

5. Name *two* of the Fabian socialists:

   (a) _____   (b) _____

6. Indicate the economist(s) attached to the following Schools of Thought:

Mercantilism	Physiocracy	Classical	Neoclassical	Monetarist
1.	1.	1.	1.	1.
2.	2.	2.	2.	
		3.		
		4.		

7. State the *two* main ideas of each of the following Schools of Thought:

Mercantilism	1. _____ 2.
Physiocrats	1. _____ 2.

8. Explain Say's Law: _____

_____

_____

9. Which school believed in the idea of *laissez–faire*? _____

Briefly explain it: _____

_____

_____

_____

10. Using the following grid, indicate in brief form the main contribution(s) of each of the following economists:

Economist	Idea(s)
Adam Smith	1. _____ 2. _____ 3. _____ 4. _____
T. Malthus	1. _____ _____ 2. _____ _____
D. Ricardo	1. _____ 2. _____
Karl Marx	1. _____ 2. _____ 3. _____ 4. _____
Marshall (Neoclassical)	1. _____ 2. _____
J.M. Keynes	1. _____ 2. _____ 3. _____ 4. _____
M. Friedman	1. _____ 2. _____

1.

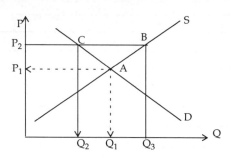

Figure 1

(a) In a free market what price would be established? _Qty₁_

(b) At P_2 the qty demanded = _is. low_

the qty supplied = _exceeds demand_

(c) Is there excess demand or supply? How much? _excess supply q₂ -q₃_

(d) In a free market with high prices, how would the market clear itself? _competition would come in @ lower prices, prices will fall to equilibrium_

(e) To prevent prices falling, what does the CAP do? _buy up excess supply_

(f) What qty of produce must be purchased to prevent prices falling? _excess over demand_

Who does this policy mainly benefit? _FARMERS_

Why? _They have a guaranteed price_

2. Name *three* main sources of finance which Ireland gets from EU funds.

(a) _Structural ESF_

(b) _ESCF_

(c) _Euro Inv. Bank_

3. Irish Industry & the EU

State the main advantage & disadvantage of EU membership for Irish industry.

Advantage	Disadvantage
Free market /no barriers	Increased competition
Bigger market	No protection
Attract non EEC countries	

4. Irish agriculture & the EU

(a) There are *five* main principles (or mechanisms) behind the CAP. Name these.

1. _Green pound_

2. _Intervention_

3. _Mechanisation_

4. _Guaranteed prices_

5. _Structural policy_

(b) State the main advantage & disadvantage of CAP to both the following groups.

Farmers	
Advantage	Disadvantage
Guaranteed prices Grants	↑ competition from other EU States

Consumers	
Advantage	Disadvantage
	higher food prices

(c) What are MCAs? _A tax on ag. exports and a subsidy on ag. imports._

ECONOMIC AIMS, POLICIES & CONFLICTS

1. Every govt has *five* main economic aims or objectives. State what you think to be the government's objectives at the moment.

   1. _____
   2. _____
   3. _____
   4. _____
   5. _____

2. To achieve these aims – or at least some of them – what policies does it pursue?
   (a) _____ policy. (b) _____ policy.
   Explain briefly what is meant by each type.

3. What type of policy did Milton Friedman favour?_____

   Explain it. _____
   _____
   _____

4. Returning to the govt's economic objectives in Q. 1 above, do you see any inherent conflicts in the govt trying to achieve all at the one time? For example, can it achieve a balanced budget and full employment? List *three* possible conflicts & explain why you think a conflict may arise.

A. _____

B. _____

C. _____

Section III:

Getting Ready for the Exam

1. A brief outline of the entire
   Micro & Macro course.

2. 100 revision questions on the course.

3. How to deal with the actual exam.

MAIN POINTS OF THE MICROECONOMICS COURSE

INTRODUCTORY ECONOMICS

1. *Economics* is a social science; allocation of scarce resources; resources which have alternative uses; to satisfy man's infinite needs and wants.
2. *Methods of analysis*:
   Deductive: Idea – logical reasoning – conclusion.
   Inductive: draw conclusions from historical facts.
3. *Definitions*: Wealth; Welfare; Capital; Income.
4. The *4 factors of production*: land, labour, capital and enterprise.
5. *Types of economic systems*: Centrally planned v Mixed Economies v Free Enterprise.
6. What factors should a firm consider when deciding where to locate its factory?
7. *Benefits and Costs of large-scale production*: economies and diseconomies of scale.

DEMAND, SUPPLY AND MARKETS

1. *Demand*: quantity demanded = f (P, Pog, Tastes, Income).
2. *Supply*: quantity supplied = F(P, Pog, costs of production, technology, costs of producing other goods, goals).
3. What causes a *shift* in a D/C and a S/C (a change in everything other than price) and a *movement along* a D/C or S/C (a change in price)?
4. *Ceteris paribus*: everything other than price remains unchanged.
5. *Equilibrium*: where Qd = Qs and there is no tendency to change from this.
6. *Government intervention* in markets: shortages – allocation on sellers' preferences; development of a black market situation.

UTILITY

1. *Assumptions re: Consumers' Behaviour*:
   (a) Acts rationally; (b) has limited income;
   (c) wishes to maximise his utility;
   (d) is subject to the Law of Diminishing Marginal Utility.
2. *Characteristics of an Economic Good*:
   (a) Scarce in relation to the demand for it;
   (b) must command a price;
   (c) must be transferable from one person to another;
   (d) must provide utility.
3. *Definitions*: Utility; Marginal Utility (the additional utility you gain from consuming an additional unit of a good).

Law of Diminishing Utility: as you consume extra units of a good, utility increases but at a decreasing rate, i.e. you get less extra satisfaction from each successive unit of a good consumed. Assumptions on which this law is based:
   (a) no elapse of time between successive units;
   (b) does not apply to addictive goods;
   (c) does not allow for changes in tastes or fashion;
   (d) it only applies after a certain minimum has been consumed (Origin).
4. *Equi-Marginal Principle of Consumer Behaviour*:
$$\frac{MUa}{Pa} = \frac{MUb}{Pb}$$
this helps to explain why a D/C slopes downwards from left to right,

e.g. in equilibrium $\frac{MUx}{Px} = \frac{MUy}{Py}$. Now if Px

decreases, then $\left(\frac{MUx}{Px}\right) > \left(\frac{MUy}{Py}\right)$.

Hence you could buy more of good X. As quantity demanded increases the MUx decreases. This continues until equilibrium is restored.
5. *Exceptions to the Law of Demand*: Snob goods; Shares on the Stock Exchange: Giffen goods.
6. *Definitions*: effective demand; joint demand; consumer surplus; consumer goods; consumer durables; capital goods.

ELASTICITY

PRICE ELASTICITY

1. *Definition*: responsiveness of quantity demanded to changes in price.
2. *Formula*: $\frac{\Delta Q}{\Delta P} \times \frac{P_1 + P_2}{Q_1 + Q_2}$
3. *Signs*: (Normal goods): – & (Giffen goods): +.
4. *Relationship between Price Elasticity and Total Revenue* (remember Costs): to increase total revenue, price should be charged in the following direction (but you must consider the effects on the costs of production).
   Price elastic goods: decrease prices.
   Price inelastic goods: increase prices.
   Unit elastic goods: leave prices unchanged.
5. *Factors affecting the value of price elasticity*:
   (a) number of substitutes available;
   (b) durability of the product;
   (c) amount of income spent on the good;
   (d) Is the good a luxury or a necessity?
   (e) Has the good many alternative uses?

INCOME ELASTICITY

1. *Definition*: responsiveness of quantity demanded to changes in income.

2. *Formula*: $\dfrac{\Delta Q}{\Delta Y} \times \dfrac{Y_1 + Y_2}{Q_1 + Q_2}$

3. *Signs*: For normal goods: +; for inferior goods: –

4. *Values*: Less than 1: inelastic; greater than 1: elastic.

5. *A Luxury Good*: has an income elasticity of demand which is greater than 1 and hence is income elastic.

CROSS ELASTICITY OF DEMAND

1. *Definition*: the responsiveness of quantity demanded of one good to changes in the prices of other goods.

2. *Signs*: Substitute goods: +; complementary goods: –

> *Remember*:
>
> when the price of a good changes it gives rise to *two* effects:
> • a substitution effect (which is always *positive*)
> • an income effect (which may be *positive* or *negative*).

COSTS

1. *Short run*: only one factor of production variable. *Long run*: all factors of production are variable.

2. *Total costs* = Fixed Costs + Variable Costs. (Can you give examples of each?)

Short-run Costs   Long-Run Costs

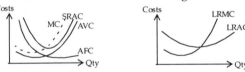

3. Why is the SRAC U-shaped; why is the LRAC L-shaped?
4. Explain the relationship between Marginal Cost and Average Total Costs.
5. State the Law of Diminishing Marginal Returns.

FACTORS OF PRODUCTION MARKETS

A. INTRODUCTION

1. *Derived demand*: where a factor is demanded, not for its utility, but for its contribution to the production process.

2. *Marginal Physical Product* (MPP): the extra output produced by the addition of an extra unit of input.

3. *Marginal Revenue Product* (MRP): the extra revenue received from the sale of the additional output produced.

4. $MRP = MPP \times MR$ (but in perfect competition MR = Price; so MRP = MPP $\times$ P).

5. *D/C for a factor of production* = MRP Curve

6. *Difficulty of measuring MRP*:
   (a) because the extra output produced might result from the addition of extra capital also, so it's difficult to disentangle both.
   (b) Not all factors produce output in the services sector.
   (c) In the public sector, where output is produced, it may not be sold in the market, so you cannot determine the MR.
   (d) Because of this, other things must be used to determine pay in this sector: pay comparability; qualifications; length of service etc.

B. LABOUR MARKET

1. *Labour*: is all human activity used in the production of wealth.
2. *Supply of labour* depends on: population size; wage rates; participation rates.
3. *Demand for labour*: is its MRP curve (see above).
4. *Demand for labour* by an individual firm depends on: marginal revenue productivity; tax on companies' profits; government subsidies; demand for the firm's output; availability of new technology; trade union involvement. (What's the effect of trade unions on the S/C for labour?)
5. *Reasons for wage differences*: trade union strength; skill; training; tradition; nature & conditions of job; monetary benefits; non-monetary benefits.
6. *Wage Drift*: when the D_{LAB} increases beyond the S_{LAB} available at the negotiated wage rate; in the short run, wage rates would increase above the negotiated rate and unions would re-negotiate a new rate. (When D_{LAB} falls through, the wage rates tend not to drop. This is called Ratchet Economy.)
7. *Definitions*:
   Transfer Earnings: the amount a factor can earn in the next best available employment.
   Economic Rent: anything which a factor earns above its supply price. (If this is short term only, it's called *Quasi Rent*.)

C. CAPITAL MARKET

1. *Definitions*:
   Capital: is man-made wealth used in the production of goods & services.
   Capital goods: goods used in the production of other goods, e.g. factories.
   Consumer goods: goods which people demand for the utility they provide.
   Consumer durables: consumer goods which have a long life span, e.g. a house.

2. *Why are Capital Goods demanded?*
   • for their contribution to output.
   • As they are employed, productivity increases and so does profitability.
   This increase in profitability is called the *Marginal Efficiency of Capital*: (MEC – this is the

MRP of capital *less* the costs of employing it).
- *Investment:* is the production of capital goods.
- *Capital Widening:* when extra capital leaves the capital/labour ratio unchanged.
- *Capital Deepening:*

3. *Savings:* is simply non-consumption.
   Who saves? Individuals (by not spending); businesses (who keep their profits); and the state (by running a budget surplus).
   Types of savings: compulsory, e.g. compulsory deductions from income;
   forced: where people can't get the goods they want.

4. *Factors affecting the Rate of Interest:*
   (a) the Bank Rate/MLR/Re-discount Rate;
   (b) the 'Pure' rate of interest (that payable on govt consuls);
   (c) The degree of lender's risk;
   (d) the length of time for repaying the loan;
   (e) the rate of inflation;
   (f) the demand for funds;
   (g) international factors; what is the German Bundesbank doing?

5. *Real Rate of Interest* = Nominal Rate – Inflation Rate.

6. *Effects of Changing Interest Rates:* If you're asked about this, consider:
   Savings; Borrowing; Investment; Mortgages; Imports; Spending; cost of servicing the National Debt; our currency value.

7. *Keynes's Liquidity Preference:* the desire of people to hold their wealth in money form.
   3 reasons:
   Transactionary – for daily expenses; depends on income.
   Precautionary – for irregular expenses; depends on income and rate of interest.
   Speculative – for profitable opportunities; depends on rates of interest.

D. LAND

1. *Definition:* that provided by nature for the construction of building and/or cultivation.
2. *Land is unique for two reasons:*
   - it's fixed in supply to the country (but not for individual purposes);
   - it has no cost to society as a whole. Hence all its earnings are economic rent.
3. *High prices cause high rents*, not high rents cause high prices.

E. ENTERPRISE

1. *Definition:* it is the controlling factor in the production process. It supplies the ideas and organises the other factors into production.
2. *Unique for:*
   (a) its the only factor that earns a loss;
   (b) its return is residual – it gets what is left over;
   (c) its returns can vary enormously – from SNPs to losses.

3. *Price:* is normal profit – included in the Average Cost Curve.
4. *Rent of Ability:* the extra profits which an entrepreneur earns because of his extra business acumen.
5. *Examples of uninsurable risks:*
   (a) demand for the firm's output might change;
   (b) risk of loss/act of God.
6. *Role of Profits* in a Free Enterprise Economy:
   - Normal profit must be earned or the firm will go out of business.
   - Profits/SNPs indicate to producers what goods and services consumers want; firms should enter the industry.
   - Profits/SNPs are the rewards to those firms which are most efficient.
   - A firm needs profits in order to expand.
   - When resources are scarce those firms with the highest profits can acquire, through paying higher prices, these scarce factors.

MACROECONOMICS: SUMMARY OF MAIN TOPICS

TOPIC 1: GOVT & ECONOMY

1. Reasons for & against govt intervention.
2. Methods for govt intervention.
3. Central Govt Finance, i.e. budgeting neutral, surplus & deficit budgeting.
4. The National Debt:
   (a) Reasons for ↑ ND:
       (i) productive investment
       (ii) social investment
       (iii) current budget deficit.
   (b) Problems for ND:
       (i) unequal distr. of wealth
       (ii) high cost of servicing debt
       (iii) loss of foreign exchange
       (iv) E/R movements.
5. Taxation:
   (a) Canons: Equity; Economy; Certainty; Convenience.
   (b) Regressive v Progressive taxes (VAT & PAYE).
   (c) Indirect v Direct taxes – differences.
   (d) Imposition & Incidence of Tax.

TOPIC 2: MONEY & BANKING

1. Functions of Money:
   (i) medium of exchange
   (ii) store of wealth
   (iii) measure of value
   (iv) standard for deferred payment.
2. Types of Money: coins, notes, cheques, credit cards.
3. Bank Credit in Ireland:
   (a) Power of Co. Banks to create money
   (b) Limitations on (a):
       (i) primary liquidity ratio
       (ii) secondary liquidity ratio
       (iii) Central Bank controls.
4. Central Bank:
   (a) Functions of Cen. Bk:
       (i) currency issue
       (ii) monetary policy
       (iii) bankers' bank
       (iv) manages external reserves
       (v) govt's bank.
   (b) Monetary Policy:
       (i) open market operations
       (ii) bank rate (MLR)
       (iii) special deposits
       (iv) advice & directives.
5. Associated & non-associated banks.
6. World Bank; IMF; EIB.

TOPIC 3: NATIONAL INCOME

1. Definition.
2. Methods of Measurement:
   (a) Income method
   (b) Expenditure method
   (c) Output method.
3. R/ship 'tween GNP @ Mkt Prices & Nat. Income.
4. GNP @ Current & Constant Prices.

5. Importance of National Income Statistics:
   (a) Economic growth
   (b) Employment
   (c) International comparisons
   (d) Role of govt in the economy
   (e) Distribution of wealth.
6. Limitations of N.I. stats:
   (a) Curr. & constant Ps
   (b) Distr. of wealth
   (c) Welfare – same as GNP?
   (d) Non-monetary servs.
7. Determination of National Income
   $$Y = C + I + G + (X - M)$$
   (a) C = f(Income levels; MPC (or MPS))
   (b) I = f(businessmen's expectations; r/i's)
   (c) G = f(political decisions @ budget time)
   (d) X= f(GNP in countries to whom we export)
   (e) M = f(income levels in Éire & MPM).
8. The Multiplier, i.e.

   $$\frac{1}{1 - MPC}$$ (closed economy no: X or M)

   or

   $$\frac{1}{1 - (MPC - MPM)}$$ (open economy, i.e. with X & M).

9. Circular Flow of Income:
   (a) Leakages: imports; savings; taxation (i.e. ↓ income in a country);
   (b) Injections: govt exp.; investment; exports (i.e. ↑ income in a country).
10. The Accelerator
    (i.e. an injection into the economy will lead to an increase in economic activity).

TOPIC 4: PRICES & INFLATION

1. Simple Price Index.
2. Composite Price Index:
   (a) choose a base year;
   (b) compile a SPI;
   (c) attach a weight;
   (d) multiply weight x (b) *Add*.
3. CPI
   (a) Importance:
       (i) use in nat. wage agreements
       (ii) gives inflation rate;
       (iii) international comparisons.
   (b) Disadvantages:
       (i) limited scope;
       (ii) no a/c of diffs in lifestyle;
       (iii) lags behind consumer trends.
4. Inflation
   (a) Causes:
       (i) demand-pull (ΣD too low => price rises);
       (ii) cost-push (cost of prod/n too high).
   (b) Problems caused by inflation:
       (i) savings discouraged;
       (ii) exports become dearer;
       (iii) imports become cheaper;
       (iv) poor sections of society suffer;
       (v) excessive wage increases;
       (vi) speculation encouraged;

      (vii) borrowing encouraged;
      (viii) confidence in currency is undermined.
5. Curbing Inflation
    A.   ↓ ΣD by:
        (a) ↓ C thro'
            (i)   ↑ taxes;
            (ii) restricting credit;
            (iii) incomes policy.
        (b) ↓ I → not likely. Why?
        (c) ↓ G thro'
            (i)   ↓ vol. of public servs;
            (ii) ↓ no of pubic employees;
            (iii) ↓ social welfare.
           Results in Unemployment/ ↓ Welfare /
           ↓ in Investment.
    B.   ↓ Costs of Production by:
        (a) Wage Restraint by:
            (i)   nat. wage agreements;
            (ii) price & incomes policy;
            (iii) statutory wage controls.
        (b) Other Costs, i.e. ↓ taxes; ↓ r/i's.
        (c) Productivity increases (see Notes)

TOPIC 5: POPULATION & EMPLOYMENT

1. World Pop. continues to increase.
    Implications:
    (a) extra food necessary;
    (b) UDCs least able to feed its people;
    (c) extra aid needed by UDCs by DCs;
    (d) income per head in UDCs declining;
    (e) lack of education & emply. in UDCs.
2. Pop. of Ireland: ↓ in Famine & continued due to emigration.
    Push-Factors:
    (a) famine;
    (b) overpop. in Ireland;
    (c) lack of indus/t employment;
    (d) political climate stale.
    Pull-Factors:
    (a) availability of employment;
    (b) real wage levels higher;
    (c) lack of social hindrances;
    (d) new communities abroad.
3. Effects of Emign on Economy:
    (a) ↑ in dependency ratio;
    (b) loss in no. of skilled workers;
    (c) ↓ mkt size => ↓ in investment opportunities;
    (d) high domestic wage levels;
    (e) edn & welfare 'wasted'.
4. Econ. Implications of ↓ Population:
    (a) mkt size ↓ resulting in falling business opportunities;
    (b) under-utilisation of resources, i.e. higher cost per head;
    (c) changing pattern of demand because of pop. structure;
    (d) labour mobility declines;
    (e) all 5 effects in (3) above if ↓ pop. is due to emig/n.
5. Recent Pop. Changes – see main notes.

6. Irish labour force trends:
    agr. 20%
    man. 33%
    servs 41%
    adm. 6%
7. Unemployment
    (a) Causes:
        (i)   economic recession;
        (ii) structural unempl.;
        (iii) frictional unempl.;
        (iv) seasonal/casual unempl.;
        (v)   transitional unempl.;
        (vi) inflation/rising costs;
        (vii) removal of protection.
    (b) Solutions:
        (i)   economic expansion (↑ C, I, G, X);
        (ii) regional policy for depressed areas;
        (iii) attract foreign investment;
        (iv) retraining (FÁS);
        (v)   import substitution.

TOPIC 6: ECON. AIMS, POLICIES & CONFLICTS

1. Econ. Aims
    (a) full employment;
    (b) stable prices;
    (c) bal. of payments equilibrium;
    (d) economic growth, i.e. ↑ GNP;
    (e) control govt borrowing.
2. Econ. Policies
    (a) Fiscal Policy: Δs in govt spending & revenue.
    (b) Monetary Policy: Δs in issue of currency.
    (c) Regional Policy: develop depressed areas in economy.
    (d) Monetarist Policy: limit govt spending hence no emply. is created. This ↓ in G also ↓ inflation & eventually ↑ employt.
3. Conflicts between (1) and (2)
    (a) Full Emp. & BOP Equil.:
        full emp. => large D. for gds & servs (incl. imports). This ↑ M => BOP equilibrium is difficult to achieve.
    (b) Full Emp. & Price Stability:
        with full emp. D is buoyant and thus demand-pull inflatn exists. Summarised in Phillips Curve and showing that with low unemply. high inflation will persist.
    (c) Econ. Growth & Price Stability:
        If ΣD > ΣS, then demand-pull inflation will always exist. Thus ΣS must also be controlled, otherwise econ. growth is accompanied with inflation.
    (d) Econ. Growth & BOP Equil.:
        With ↑ in ΣD => to ↑ in D for imports and thus BOP equilibrium becomes difficult.
    (e) Econ. Growth & Social Policy:
        The benefits of econ. growth may only apply to the better-off sections of society.
    (f) Econ. Growth & Regional Policy:
        Econ. growth and its benefits may be confined to certain areas of the country.

4. (a) Social Aims
     (i) to distribute wealth equitably;
     (ii) to control pollution.
   (b) Social Policies
     (i) to distribute wealth:
        taxation policy
        social welfare policy
        education policy
        health policy;
     (ii) to control pollution → legislation.
5. Social & Private Costs–see Notes.

TOPIC 7: EU

1. EU is a common market having:
   (a) free trade between members;
   (b) a common external tariff;
   (c) free movement of labour & capital.
2. CAP:
   (a) guaranteed prices;
   (b) intervention;
   (c) rationalisation in farm sizes;
   (d) mechanisation;
   (e) green pounds – see Notes.
3. Advs of EU to Irish Agriculture:
   (a) guaranteed prices;
   (b) higher prices (than prior to EU entry);
   (c) access to a larger market;
   (d) fall in dependence on UK market;
   (e) financial aid.
4. Disads of EU to Irish Agriculture:
   (a) MCAs;
   (b) higher input & material costs;
   (c) internal competition from other markets;
   (d) loss of control in decision-making.
   and to the consumer:
     (i) higher food prices;
     (ii) intervention (no ↓ in Ps);
     (iii) unemployment in agricult.
5. Effects of EU on Irish Industry:
   (a) Increased competition from member states.
   (b) Increased mkt for our industrial exports.
   (c) Financial aid from EU (grants, subsidies from EIB, ESF & ECSC).
   (d) Foreign investment by companies to get access to EU mkts.
6. Enlargement of EU.

TOPIC 8: INTERNATIONAL TRADE

1. Reasons for International Trade:
   (a) smallness of Irish population;
   (b) limited capability for large-scale prodn;
   (c) soil/climate unsuitable for prodn of crops;
   (d) limited supplies of minerals/energy;
   (e) capital too large for prodn of some goods;
   (f) allows for division of labour.

   | Absolute & Comparative Adv. |

2. Advantages of Free Trade.
3. Disadvantages:
   (a) preserve employment;
   (b) infant industry argument;
   (c) raise govt revenue;
   (d) correct a BOP deficit;
   (e) prevent 'low wage' competition.
4. Trade Protection Measures:
   embargoes; quotas; tariffs; subsidies.
5. Balance of Payments:
   (a) Definition;
   (b) Structure:
      Physical Xs – Physical Ms = BOT
         +   +   (fav. v unfav.)
      Invisible Xs Invisible Ms = BOP
                                 (Deficit or Surplus)
   (c) Problems of BOP deficit:
      currency weakness; income leakage;
      ↓ external reserves; ↑ foreign borrowing.
   (d) How to correct a BOP Deficit:
      ↓ Ms; ↑ Xs; devaluation*; deflation.

   *Devaluation: reducing the value of one curr. against other currs; aim is to make Xs cheaper & Ms dearer.

   Shortcomings:
   1. price elas. of demand for Xs (>1);
   2. price elas. of demand for Ms (>1);
   3. increase the Xs prices;
   4. wage increases;
   5. instability in E/Rs.

6. Exchange Rates
   (a) The Gold Standard:
     (i) curr. convertible into gold;
     (ii) reserves held in gold;
     (iii) M^S depended on gold.
     Advantages:
     (i) stable E/Rs;
     (ii) self-adj. mechanism.
     Disadvantages:
     (i) severe deflationary adj.;
     (ii) surplus countries didn't expand.
   (b) Determinants of a Country's E/R:
     (i) BOP posn, i.e. D_C & S_C to pay for Xs & Ms;
     (ii) speculation on foreign exch. mkts;
     (iii) level of domestic r/i;
     (iv) Central Bank intervention;
     (v) purchasing power parity theory.

(c) Types of E/Rs:

	Fixed	Variable
Advs	1. Stability in trade. 2. Encourages F/t	1. Provides an auto-matic mechanism for keeping the BOP in equil. 2. because of this govts don't have to ↓ demand for Ms & cause unemp.
Disads	1. To maintain a fixed E/R a govt must control a BOP by strict policies: (a) ↓ Ms. (b) Deflate economy, so ↑ unemployment.	1. Intro. uncertainty into inter. trade. 2. Speculation can lead to greater changes in a curr. value.

(d) The EMS (see notes).

TOPIC 9: ECONOMIC DEVELOPMENT

1. Classifications:
   Income per head; Output per person; % of pop. employed in agr. / ind. / servs; birth/death rate per 1,000; availability of health/edn services.

2. Problems /Characteristics of UDCs

1. Econ. imbalance. 2. Inadequate infra. 3. Shortage of capital. 4. Wealth inequality. 5. Imbal. pop. structure. 6. Imbal. occupational struc.	7. Low domestic demand. 8. Lack of education. 9. Miscellaneous prob/s: (housing, water etc.).

3. Steps to promote Econ. Devel.

1. Social environment. 2. Improve infrastruct. 3. Education. 4. Agr/al reform. 5. Urbanisation. 6. Improved infrastructure.	7. Advanced ed. facilities. 8. Sustained econ. growth thro ↑ D. 9. Devel. of tertiary sector.

4. Methods of Acquiring Capital

1. Earnings from X of a primary product. 2. Internal taxation (limited scope).	3. Foreign borrowing. 4. Foreign aid.

5. Benefits of Econ. Devel.

1. Improved living stds. 2. ↑ & imp. govt serv/s. 3. Social welfare benefits. 4. Self-sufficiency.	5. Increased empl. opportunities. 6. Quality of life improved. 7. Political stability is encouraged.

6. Costs of Econ. Devel.

1. Displacement of pop. 2. Disfiguration of landscape. 3. Pollution.	4. Unequal distr. of benefits. 5. Urbanisation. 6. Loss of values/ culture.

7. Rostow's Theory of Econ. Devel.

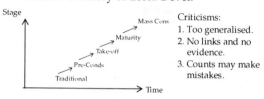

Criticisms:
1. Too generalised.
2. No links and no evidence.
3. Counts may make mistakes.

8. Sectors & Employment

Primary	Secondary	Tertiary
food & RMs	processing RM	distr. of gds/ serv/s

9. Defns:
   (a) Export-led growth (↑ Xs => ↑ GNP)
   (b) Capital/output ratio.

TOPIC 10: HISTORY OF ECON. THOUGHT

School	Main Idea(s)	Economists
Mercantilism	Wealth = Gold & Silver Self-sufficiency Trade protection	Thomas Mun Sir John Steuart
Physiocrats	Wealth = agriculture *Laissez-faire* Free competition	Quesnay Turgot (utility)
Classical school	*Laissez-faire* Free trade Perfect competition	Adam Smith David Ricardo (rent) Thomas Malthus (pop.) J.B. Say (Say's Law) J.S. Mill (wage-fund)
Neoclassical	Free enterprise Perfect comp. Cap./inv. essential	Marshall (utility, MRP, Mon.) Clark (MRP)
Socialism	3 classes Lab. th. of value Surplus value of prodn	Karl Marx
Keynesian	Liquidity pref. Multiplier ↑ Ge to ↑ ΣD	John Maynard Keynes

MICROECONOMICS: 1

INTRODUCTORY DEFINITIONS

1. Economics: social science; allocation of scarce resources among alternatives to satisfy man's infinite needs.
2. Methods of Analysis:
   Deductive: idea – logical reasoning → conclusion.
   Inductive: draw conclusions from historical facts.
3. Definitions: wealth; welfare; capital; income.
4. FOPs: land, labour, capital & enterprise.
5. Types of Economic Systems:
   free enterprise; centrally planned and mixed economies.
6. What factors should a firm consider when deciding where to locate a factory?
7. Large-scale production: E/S and D/S.

DEMAND, SUPPLY & MARKETS

1. Demand
   $$Q_N^D = f(P_N, P_{OG}, T, Y)$$
   Supply
   $$Q_N^S = f(P_N, P_{OG}, C_N, C_{OG}, T_N, G)$$
2. What causes a shift in a D/C and S/C?
3. What causes a movement along each?
4. *Ceteris paribus*: everything other than P_N remains constant.
5. Equilibrium: $Q_D = Q_S$, no tendency to change.
6. Govt intervention: shortages => allocation on sellers' preferences; devel. of a black mkt.

UTILITY

1. Assumptions re: consumer's behaviour:
   (a) acts rationally;
   (b) has limited income;
   (c) wishes to max. utility;
   (d) subject to LDMU.
2. Characteristics of an Economic Good:
   (a) scarce;
   (b) command a price;
   (c) transferable;
   (d) provides utility.
3. Definitions:
   • Utility: satisfaction from consuming a gd/service.
   • Mar. U: additional satisfaction from consuming an extra unit of a good.
   • LDMU: as you consume extra units of a good, utility increases but at a decreasing rate.
   Assumptions:
   (a) no elapse of time 'tween successive units;
   (b) doesn't apply to addictive goods;
   (c) doesn't allow for changes in tastes/fashion;
   (d) applies only after the Origin.

• Equi-Marginal Principle: $\dfrac{MU_X}{P_X} = \dfrac{MU_Y}{P_Y}$

↓

Explains why a D/C slopes downwards from left to right,

e.g. in equilibrium $\dfrac{MU_X}{P_X} = \dfrac{MU_Y}{P_Y}$. Now if $P_X\downarrow$,

then $\left(\dfrac{MU_X}{P_X}\right) > \left(\dfrac{MU_Y}{P_Y}\right)$. Hence buy more of

good X. As $Q_D \uparrow \rightarrow MU_X$ decreases. This continues until equilibrium is restored.
4. Exceptions to Law of Demand:
   Snob gds;
   Shares;
   Giffen gds.
5. Definitions: effective demand; joint demand; consumer surplus; consumer gds; consumer durables; capital gds.

ELASTICITY

Price

1. Responsiveness of Q_D to changes in price.
2. $\dfrac{\Delta Q}{\Delta P} \times \dfrac{P_1 + P_2}{Q_1 + Q_2}$
3. Signs: – (normal); + (Giffen).
4. Values: <1 (inelastic) = 1(unit) > 1(elastic).
5. R/ship between EP and Total Revenue (remember Costs!):
   Elastic: $\downarrow$ P; inelastic: $\uparrow$ P; unit elas.: P constant.
6. Factors affecting E_D^P:
   No. of subs available; durability of product; % of Y spent on good; necessity v luxury; no. of alternative uses (e.g. sugar).

Income

1. Responsiveness of Q_D to changes in income.
2. $\dfrac{\Delta Q}{\Delta Y} \times \dfrac{Y_1 + Y_2}{Q_1 + Q_2}$
3. Signs + (normal); – (inferior).
4. Values: <1 (inelastic); >1(elastic).
5. A luxury gd: + income elasticity & elastic in value.

Cross

1. Responsiveness of Q_D of gd X to changes in P_Y.
2. Signs: substitutes: +; complements: –

Remember: when the price of a good changes it gives rise to both a Substitution & Income Effect.

COSTS

- Short run: only 1 FOP is variable.
- Long run: all FOP are variable
- TC = FC + VC

SR Costs   LR Costs

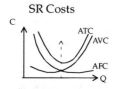

SRAC: U-shaped. Why?   LRAC: L-shaped. Why?

- R/ship between MC & AC:
  - If MC is above AC then AC is rising.
  - If MC is below AC then AC is falling.
  - If MC is equal to AC then AC is at a minimum.
- State the Law of Diminishing Marginal Returns.

ECONOMICS – REVISION MICROECONOMICS

1. A consumer is in equilibrium when _MU/P for each good is the same_.

2. The Law of Diminishing Marginal Utility states _that as more units of a good are consumed the MU will decrease_.

3. Quantity demanded depends on: _P_ , _Poc_ , _Pcomp_ , _Y_

4. A movement along a D/C is caused by _change in price_

5. A shift in a D/C is caused by _a change in Y, Pcomp_

6. Quantity supplied depends on: _P_ , _Poc_ , _T_ , _C, G, P_

7. A movement along a S/C is caused by _change in P_

8. A shift in a S/C is caused by _a change in Y, Poc, T, C, G, P_

9. Price Elasticity of Demand measures the _responsiveness of quantity demanded to a change in price_

10. For Normal goods E_D^P is usually Negative ☑ Positive ☐ Zero ☐

11. Goods which have a positive E_D^P are called _Giffen_ goods.

12. Good X: E_D^P = –3.2; Good Y: E_D^P = 0.1. Complete the following table:

	Good X	Good Y
E_D^P	–3.2	–0.1
Normal or	✓	✓
Elastic or Inelastic	Elastic	Inelastic
To ↑ TR, how to change price	drop	increase
Example	drop 10%, dq 32%	↑P by 10% d↓ 1%

13. Income Elasticity of Demand measures the _responsiveness of quantity to a change in income_

14. For Normal goods E_D^Y is usually: Negative ☐ Positive ☑ Zero ☐

15. Goods which have a negative E_D^Y are called _inferior_ goods.

16. Generally speaking _luxury_ type goods are income elastic and _necessity_ are income inelastic.

17. From the following figures: –3.2, –0.1, zero, +0.5, +2.6, which is likely to represent:

    (a) Income elas. of demand for potatoes? _+0.5_

    (b) Income elas. of demand for videos? _____

    (c) Price elas. of demand for sweets? _3.2_

18. Cross Elasticity of Demand of substitute goods is _positive_

    and for complementary goods is _negative_

19. Marginal Cost is _additional cost of producing an additional unit of output_

20. Complete: When (i) MC > AC, then AC is _rising_

    (ii) MC < AC, then AC is _falling_

    (iii) MC = AC, then AC is _lowest point_

21. If total costs are £100 when production falls to zero as a result of a contraction in demand, what is the level of fixed costs in the firm? £100

22. The SRAC is U-shaped because it slopes downwards due to *economies of scale* and upwards due to *law of diminishing marginal return*

23. The LRAC is composed of many SRAC curves and is U or L-shaped. It slopes downwards due to *economies of scale* and upwards due to *LDMR*. Give *two* examples of each.

   a) *specialisation of labour* b) *increased admin overheads*

   a) *Capital: cheaper to borrow* b) *slower decision making*

24. The SR Equilibrium conditions for a firm are:

   (a) *MC = MR*

   (b) *MC as it cuts mr from below*

   (c) *AVC covered*

25. In the LR what costs must be covered? *Average cost*

26. Supernormal profits are earned when *AR exceeds AC*

27. (a) The SRS/C for a firm in PC is _____ curve above _____ curve.

   (b) The LRS/C for a firm in PC is _____ curve above _____ curve.

28. The *two* main advantages of PC are:

   (a) *no wastage*

   (b) *lower prices*

29. A Monopoly is *when 1 company controls market.*

30. Compared with a firm in PC it produces a *smaller* output, which it sells at a *higher* price.

31. State the conditions necessary for a monopolist to engage in Price Discrimination:

   (a) *monopoly power*

   (b) *ability to seperate mkt.*

   (c) *lack of consumer knowledge*

   (d) *consumer indifference*

32. In Imperfect Competition there are *many* sellers, selling *similar goods* each trying to *differentiate* their *corner* of the market.

33. The main disadvantage of Imp. Comp. is that *inefficient use of resources heavy spending on advertising*

34. The 4 FOP are *land*, *labour*, *capital*, *entrepeneur*

35. The D/C for a FOP is its _____ curve.

36. Define Marginal Physical Productivity _____

   _____

   _____

37. MRP = _____ × _____ (in PC: MRP= _____ × _____)

38. Define Economic Rent _____

   _____

39. The S_{LAB} depends on

(a) _____

(b) _____

(c) _____

40. The D_{LAB} is: _____ curve.

41. State *five* reasons why wage rates differ;

(a) _____

(b) _____

(c) _____

(d) _____

(e) _____

42. (a) The *three* main factors determining the r/i are:

(i) _____

(ii) _____

(iii) _____

(b) The *three* minor factors are:

(i) _____

(ii) _____

(iii) _____

43. Keynes distinguished *three* reasons why a person demands money:

(a) _____

(b) _____

(c) _____

44. State *three* effects of changing r/i on the Irish economy.

(a) _____

(b) _____

(c) _____

45. What economist developed the idea of Economic Rent? _____

46. The factor 'enterprise' is unique for *two* reasons:

(a) _____

(b) _____

47. What effect will the intervention of a trade union have on the Supply curve for labour. (Draw it.)
Briefly describe what has happened.

WR

D = ?

Q

_____

_____

_____

48. In the spaces provided draw the long-run equilibrium diagram for the following types of market structure:

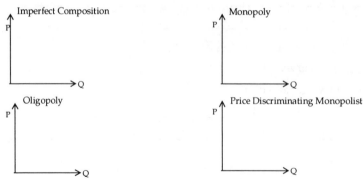

49. An oligopolistic industry with 2 firms produces 10,000 units in equilibrium. Show how it reaches equilibrium.
   (a) What output would a PC industry produce? _____
   (b) Show how equilibrium is achieved.

Stage	Firm A	Firm B	Explanation
1			
2			
3			
4			

50. When the price of a good changes it gives rise to *two* effects:

   (a) _____

   (b) _____

51. A firm is at optimum size when: _____

   _____

52. On 1 Jan. 1988 I buy a govt bond at its face value of £100 carrying 10% interest p.a. A new bond issue carrying 30% interest p.a. is issued during the year.

   (a) What price could I sell the bond for? _____

   (b) How much profit or loss would I make overall? _____

53. The Marginal Efficiency of Capital is:_____

   _____

54. Price Discrimination occurs when: _____

   _____

55. The substitution effect for a good is always_____

56. The income effect may be _____ or _____.

   If the good is normal the effect is_____.

   If the good is _____ the effect is _____.

57. Write out the formula for Price Elasticity of Demand._____

58. The *four* characteristics of an economic good are:

(a) _____

(b) _____

(c) _____

(d) _____

59. For what reason does the SRAC slope downwards? _____

For what reason does the SRAC slope upwards? _____

60. For what reason does the LRAC slope upwards? _____

Give *two* examples:

(a) _____

(b) _____

For what reason does the LRAC slope downwards? _____
Give *two* examples:

(a) _____

(b) _____

MACROECONOMICS

1. The *four* main functions of money are
   (a) _____
   (b) _____
   (c) _____
   (d) _____

2. The characteristics of that commodity which acts as money include:
   (a) _____
   (b) _____
   (c) _____
   (d) _____
   (e) _____

3. The *three* main types of money in use in Ireland are:
   (a) _____
   (b) _____
   (c) _____

4. The Cash Ratio is _____
   _____

5. The Secondary Liquidity Ratio is_____
   _____

6. The main functions of the Central Bank are:
   (a) _____
   (b) _____
   (c) _____
   (d) _____
   (e) _____

7. The *four* main instruments of its Monetary Policy are:
   (a) _____
   (b) _____
   (c) _____
   (d) _____

8. Complete the following ways to calculate National Income.

Keep it brief		Income	Output	Expenditure
		GDP @ factor cost	GDP @ factor cost	GDP @ mkt prices
	+/−			
=				

9. Complete:

$$\text{Net National Product @ Factor Cost}$$

$$+ \quad \underline{\hspace{4cm}}$$

$$= \text{Gross National Product @ Factor Cost}$$

$$+ \quad \underline{\hspace{3cm}} - \underline{\hspace{2cm}}$$

$$= \text{Gross National Product @ Market Prices}$$

10. Y = _____ + _____ + _____ + _____ − _____

11. A deflationary gap occurs when _____

_____

12. The MPC is _____

13. If MPC = 0.60, then MPS = _____

14. If MPC = 0.9 and MPM = 0.4, what is the MPC for domestic goods? _____

15. Complete the following to indicate the injections & leakages from a country's National Income.

16. The accelerator is _____

_____

17. The Law of Comparative Advantage states

_____

_____

18. The LOCA ignores the following:

(a) _____

(b) _____

(c) _____

(d) _____

19. Explain the 'Infant Industry' against free trade

_____

_____

20. The *four* main measures for trade protection are:

(a) _____

(b) _____

(c) _____

(d) _____

21. Complete the following:

Current Account

1. _____ – (a) _____ =
   e.g.   e.g.
              +   +

2. _____   (b)_____
   e.g.   e.g.

= BOP_____ BOP _____

22. State the *four* main problems caused by a BOP Deficit.

(a) _____

(b) _____

(c) _____

(d) _____

23. If imports are greater than exports, how can this be corrected?

(a) _____

(b) _____

(c) _____

(d) _____

24. Devaluation is_____

_____

25. The *two* reasons why the Gold Standard was abandoned are

(a) _____

(b) _____

26. The *five* main factors which determine a country's exchange rate are:

(a) _____

(b) _____

(c) _____

(d) _____

(e) _____

27. Central Fund charges are _____

_____

50. Outline *five* characteristics of an underdeveloped economy.

(a) _____

(b) _____

(c) _____

(d) _____

(e) _____

51. Name the economists associated with the following ideas:

(a) Law of Comparative Costs _____

(b) Surplus Value of Production _____

(c) The Multiplier_____

52. Indicate the authors of the following:

(a) *An inquiry into the Nature and Causes of Wealth of Nations*

(b) *Das Kapital*

(c) *Principles of Population and Effects on Society*

(d) *General Theory of Employment, Interest and Money*

53. State *one* name associated with *each* of the following theories:

(a) Mercantilism _____

(b) Physiocracy_____

(c) Classical Economics_____

(d) Neoclassical Economics_____

LEAVING CERTIFICATE ECONOMICS

<table>
<tr><td colspan="2" align="center">Higher & Ordinary Levels</td></tr>
<tr><td align="center">Layout</td><td align="center">Time</td></tr>
<tr>
<td>
Section A: 9 Qs: (100)
Section B: (300)
8 Qs: 75 m Qs
To do: Section A: 6 Qs
            Section B: 4 Qs
</td>
<td>
(i)   Reading Paper: 10 mins
(ii) Section A: 30 mins
(iii) Section B: each Q.: 28 mins

If time allows ans. an extra Q.
</td>
</tr>
</table>

1.	Look at the *marks*.
2.	Decide the number of *points required*.
3.	*State* the *point*.
4.	*Explain* the *point*.

WHEN YOU GET THE EXAM PAPER:

1. Read down through the *full* paper. Eliminate at once those questions you *can't* do.
2. The main mistake which most people make is choosing the wrong questions.
   It's important that you
   (a) attempt *all* questions in Section A, and
   (b) pick *your* 4 best questions in Section B (excluding National Income).
3. To choose your 4 best questions you should use the following procedure:
   (a) Go down through the questions and decide the maximum number of points that you think is required for each part of each question.
   (b) Now, how many of the points can you supply?
   (c) Those questions where you think you are giving the most should be answered and those where you supply the least avoided.
4. Once you've chosen your 4 questions, *don't* start changing the choice.
5. *Don't* include the question *Calculation-type National Income* in your 4 chosen questions. It should be attempted by *all* candidates as an extra question and it should be the *first* question attempted. Be sure to read this question very carefully.
6. Besides making an incorrect choice of questions the other major error is: *not answering the question specifically asked!* Be sure you know what the precise question asked is. Re-read it a few times. By jotting relevant points as you read the question, *it will help keep your attention focused on the precise question asked.*
7. Section A Questions: It is in your own interest to score maximum points here. Use the space provided to fully explain your answer. If asked about costs, draw the cost curves at the side. Then answer. Show all your calculations and workings.
8. Diagrams:
   (i) label axes;
   (ii) make them large;
   (iii) keep them simple.
9. Remember:
   (a) Marks→ Points→ State points→ Explain adequately
   (b) Correct *choice* of questions extremely important.
   (c) Answer: *Calculation-type National Income question* first.
   (d) Answer *four* remaining questions *fully*.
   (e) *Don't finish early.* (If you do, don't expect a decent grade.)

REVISION

(a) You should try to revise *all* the *Summaries* before the exam.

(b) For *Section A*: read the solutions to all Micro & Macro questions since 1977.

(c) Be sure to read the Summary on 'History of Economic Thought'.

(d) On the *night before*, and *morning* of the exam, read the 'Summary of Main Points' *plus* this page.

Section IV:

Solutions to Tests

1. Solutions to the more difficult tests (in Section 2).

2. Solutions to Section A questions from Leaving Cert.

   (1977–94 inclusive split between Microeconomics & Macroeconomics)

TEST: INTRODUCTORY ECONOMICS

Section A

1. A social science which studies human behaviour and how the world's scarce resources which have alternative uses are allocated to satisfy man's infinite needs and wants.
2. Moving from a general statement (e.g. all animals will die) to a particular statement using logical reasoning (e.g. a cat is an animal: so a cat will die).
3. Moving from a particular case to a general statement (see example: Introductory Definitions).
4. Land is anything supplied by nature which helps in the production of wealth. It is unique because:
   (a) it is fixed in supply; and
   (b) it has no cost of production to society as a whole.
5. That as increasing quantities of a variable FOP are applied to fixed quantities of another FOP, the returns per unit to the variable FOP will eventually diminish.
6. Is man-made wealth used in the production of goods & services.
7. Is the controlling factor in the production process. It organises the other FOP to produce a good/provide a service, and it bears the risk involved in production. It is unique because
   (a) its return is residual,
   (b) its returns can vary enormously,
   (c) it is the only FOP which can earn a loss.
8. Are the cost savings a firm benefits from as it grows in size (for examples, see Introductory Definitions).

Section B: All answered in the Notes.
Keep your answers to the point.

TEST: MARKETS, UTILITY & ELASTICITY (1)

1. (i) Must provide utility; (ii) is transferable; (iii) commands a price; and (iv) is scarce in relation to demand.
2. (a) $Q_D = f(P, P_{OG}, Y, T, E \text{ and } G)$
   (b) $Q_S = f(P, P_{OG}, T, C, G, D)$ (for explanations, see Demand & Supply).
3. The price at which demand equals supply and there is little tendency for the price to change.
4. (i) A drop in the consumer's income; (ii) a decline in the consumer's taste for the good.
5. (i) Beauty: it is not transferable; (ii) Raw sewerage: it does not provide utility.
6. As you consume additional units of a good the utility you get from each successive unit will eventually diminish.

7. False. It is *not* the MU for each good which is the same. Rather, it is the ratio of MU/P which is the same for all goods purchased.
8. . . . it gives rise to both a *Substitution effect* (and this is always *positive*, i.e. you will always buy *more* of the cheaper good) and an *Income effect* (this may be *positive* or *negative*). If the negative income effect is greater than the positive substitution effect, then this good is called a *Giffen* good.
9. PED measures the responsiveness of quantity demanded of a good to a change in its own price.
10. If PED is negative it means that as price increases: quantity demanded falls (and vice versa). If positive, then as price decreases the quantity demanded decreases, i.e. this is a Giffen good.

The formula for PED is: $\dfrac{\Delta Q}{\Delta P} \times \dfrac{P_1 + P_2}{Q_1 + Q_2}$

TEST: SUBSTITUTION & INCOME EFFECTS

1. $\dfrac{MU_A}{P_A} = \dfrac{MU_B}{P_B}$ i.e. $\dfrac{10}{\cdot 5} = \dfrac{20}{1}$
2. The Equi-Marginal Principle of Consumer Behaviour. This states that the consumer will spend his income in such a way that he will get the same marginal utility per penny spent.
3. Extra income is: 5 x 50p = £2.50.
4. $\dfrac{10}{\cdot 5} < \dfrac{20}{\cdot 5}$

   (i) Good B gives you the most MU per penny.
   (ii) So you should buy *more* of good B because you will get *more* MU per penny spent on Good B.
   (iii) So you should buy *less* of good A because you will get *less* MU per penny spent on good A.
   (iv) So the Q_D of good A *has fallen* and the Q_D of good B *has risen*.
5. This is called the *substitution* effect.
6. You will probably buy *more of both goods* (with your extra income). As your income increased, the Q_D of both increased.
7. This is called the *Income* effect.
8. If the extra income (£2.50) was taken in tax, then the only effect to take place is the *substitution* effect.
   The Q_D of A will *fall* and the Q_D of B will *rise*

9.

Summary	Substitution effect		Income effect	
	Q_D of A	Q_D of B	Q_D of A	Q_D of B
Price of B falls (extra income)	Falls	Rises	Rises	Rises
Price of B falls (no extra income)	Falls	Rises	No effect	No effect

TEST: MARKETS, UTILITY & ELASTICITY (2)

1. $Q_D = f(P, P_{OG}, Y, T, E \text{ and } G)$.
2. No. Because even though prices have increased, so have consumers' incomes and so they can increase their demand for goods/services.
3. Income £200; % spent 50%; so actual amount spent is £100.
   Income £400; % spent 40%; so actual amount spent is £160.
   So as income increased, quantity demanded increased. This is *not* an inferior good.
4.

Good	PED	YED
X	– 1.6: Normal	+ 2.21: Normal
Y	– 0.6: Normal	– 0.42: Inferior

   Neither of these goods are Giffen goods
5. A price change gives rise to 2 effects: *substitution & income*. Equi-Marginal Principle states that a consumer will allocate her income in such a way that she will get the same MU per penny spent. Because the price of A has fallen she now has 12 x 2p = 24p additional purchasing power.

We assume this additional 24p is taxed by the government. So she now gets most MU per penny spent from good A. So the Q_D of good A rises while the Q_D of good B falls until the ratios $\dfrac{MU_A}{P_A} = \dfrac{MU_B}{P_B}$

With the extra 24p purchasing power, she will now buy more of good A and more of good B. Not all goods will have the same income effect.

6. (See question 1 in Test: Markets, Utility & Elasticity (1).)
7. (i) Limited Income; (ii) Wishes to maximise total utility; (iii) Subject to the Law of Diminishing Marginal Utility; and (iv) Acts rationally.
8. $Q_S = f(P, P_{OG}, T, C, G \text{ and } D)$.
9. A movement along a S/C is caused by a change in the price of the good itself, while a shift in the S/C is caused by a change in any of the following: P_{OG}, T, C, G and D.
10. Quantity demanded equals Quantity Supplied at a price from which there is little tendency to change.
11. Good A: Price £8.00. Good B: Price £3.00. Good A will provide the consumer with most utility as he is prepared to spend over double the price of B on it. So to part with £8.00 he must be getting more utility.

TEST ELASTICITY (1)

	PED		YED		CED	
Definition	Measures the responsiveness of Q_D to changes in the price of the good.		Measures the responsiveness of Q_D to changes in the income of the consumer.		Measures the responsiveness of changes in the Q_D of one good (good X) to changes in prices of complementary/substitute goods (good Y).	
Formula	$\dfrac{\Delta Q}{\Delta P} \times \dfrac{P_1 + P_2}{Q_1 + Q_2}$		$\dfrac{\Delta Q}{\Delta Y} \times \dfrac{Y_1 + Y_2}{Q_1 + Q_2}$		$\dfrac{\Delta Q_X}{\Delta P_Y} \times \dfrac{P_{Y^1} + P_{Y^2}}{Q_{X^1} + Q_{X^2}}$	
Signs	Positive	Negative	Positive	Negative	Positive	Negative
	as P ↑: Q_D ↑ Giffen goods	P ↑: Q_D ↓ Normal goods	Y ↑: Q_D ↑ Normal goods	Y ↑: Q_D ↓ Inferior goods	P_{butter} ↑: $Q_{D\ margarine}$ ↑ Substitutes	P_{cars} ↑: $Q_{D\ petrol}$ ↓ Complements
>1 Values < 1 =1	(i) if P ↑ by 10%: Q_D ↓ by more than 10% (ii) if P↑ by 10%: Q_D ↓ by less than 10% (iii) if P↑ by 10%: Q_D ↓ by 10%		(i)if Y ↑ by 10%: Q_D ↑ by > 10% (ii) if Y ↑ by 10%: Q_D ↑ by <10%			
Factors which determine the value of a goods PED	1. No. of substitutes available. 2. Durability of the product. 3. Percentage of income spent on the good. 4. Is the good a necessity or luxury? 5. No. of alternative uses the good has. 6. Degree of importance of the good.		Luxury goods are: Income Elastic 1. YED = 1.5. Sales = 10,000. Income rises by 10%. So sales rise by 1.5 x 10 = 15% of 10,000 = 1,500. So sales rise to: 11,500.			
Price changes & their effects on total revenue	*For elastic goods:* To ↑ TR: ↓ Price. *For inelastic goods:* to ↑ TR: ↑ Price. *For unit elastic goods:* Any change in P will not change TR.		2. $\dfrac{\Delta Q}{\Delta P} \times \dfrac{P_1 + P_2}{Q_1 + Q_2} = \dfrac{-22}{0 \cdot 25} \times \dfrac{£1 + £1 \cdot 25}{100 + 78} = \dfrac{-22}{0 \cdot 25} \times \dfrac{£2 \cdot 25}{178} = -1.11$: Elastic. 3. Suppose Income = £10. She spends 50% = £5. Her income doubles to £20. She now spends 35% = £7.00. This good is *not* inferior as Y↑: Q_D rises from £5 to £7.			

TEST: ELASTICITY (2)

Section A

1. – 1.11: elastic (see solutions on Elasticity Test 1).
2. (C)
3. – 0.45 (i) because meat is normal and hence has a negative PED; and (ii) it's more an essential than a luxury and so would be inelastic (<1).
4. No.
5. (b)
6. $D_1 D_1$: elastic, e.g. video recorders ; $D_2 D_2$: inelastic, e.g. food.
7. For price elastic goods: decrease price to increase TR. For price inelastic goods: increase price to increase TR. For unit elastic goods: any change in price will not lead to a change in TR.
8. PED for normal goods is *negative*.
9. YED for normal goods is *positive*.
10. PED: $\dfrac{\Delta Q}{\Delta P} \times \dfrac{P_1 + P_2}{Q_1 + Q_2}$
11. CED for substitute goods is *positive*.
12. A normal good has a negative PED.
13. A luxury good is one which has a positive elastic YED.
14. True, because as $Y\uparrow$, Q_D for the good will fall.
15. 11,500 (see solutions on Elasticity Test 1).

Section B

(a) YED for Good X = –1.3. This good has a negative YED. Hence it is an inferior good. It has a negative income effect. If this negative income effect is greater than the positive substitution effect, then good X (iii) could possibly be a Giffen good.
YED for Good Y = + 0.6. This good has a positive YED. Hence it is a normal good. It has a positive income effect, i.e. as a consumer's income rises he will buy more of this good. This good Y (i) could not be a Giffen good.

(b) Good A: –6.00: Normal & Elastic: $\downarrow$ P and Q_D will $\uparrow$ by more than the $\downarrow$ in P, resulting in $\uparrow$ TR.
Good B: +1.00: Giffen & Unit Elastic: $\uparrow$ P and Q_D will $\uparrow$ by the same % $\uparrow$ as price. Hence TR will rise.
Good C: –0.01: Normal & Inelastic: $\uparrow$ P and Q_D will $\downarrow$ by less than the $\uparrow$ in P, resulting in $\uparrow$ TR.

(c) (i) YED for potatoes: potatoes are essential, hence income inelastic (<1). They are inferior, so have a – YED.
So YED for potatoes: –0.1.
(ii) YED for fresh salmon: fresh salmon is a luxury, hence income elastic (> 1). It is a normal good, so has a + YED. Likely value: + 2.6.
(iii) PED for sweets: sweets are a luxury, hence price elastic (>1). They are normal, so have a –PED. Likely value: –3.2.

TEST: ELASTICITY (3)

1. (c) To determine the volume of profits a co. makes we should compare total *revenue* with total *costs*.

(d)

Route & PED	Price Change	Effect on Q_D	Effect on TR	Effect on Costs	Effect on Profits
A –1.6	$\uparrow$P by 10%	Falls by 16%	Falls	$Q_D \downarrow$: Supply $\downarrow$: Costs $\downarrow$	Can't tell
	$\downarrow$ P by 10%	Rises by 16%	Rises	$Q_D \uparrow$: Supply $\uparrow$: Costs $\uparrow$	Can't tell
B –1.0	$\uparrow$ P by 10%	Falls by 10%	No change	$Q_D \downarrow$: Supply $\downarrow$: Costs $\downarrow$	Rises
	$\downarrow$ P by 10%	Rises by 10%	No change	$Q_D \uparrow$: Supply $\uparrow$: Costs $\uparrow$	Falls
C –0.5	$\uparrow$ P by 10%	Falls by 5%	Rises	$Q_D \downarrow$: Supply $\downarrow$: Costs $\downarrow$	Rises
	$\downarrow$ P by 10%	Rises by 5%	Falls	$Q_D \uparrow$: Supply $\uparrow$: Costs $\uparrow$	Falls

So, how would you change (i) P_A? Can't tell.
(ii) P_B? $\uparrow$ Price. (iii) P_C $\uparrow$ Price.

(e) The CED for substitute goods is *positive*. The CED for complementary goods is *negative*. So goods D and E are complements to good A, because each has a negative sign.
Goods B and C are substitutes to good A. Good B is the closest substitute because if the P_A increased by 10%, then the Q_D of B will rise by 23% (while that of C will only rise by 4%).

TEST: COSTS (1)

(a) (1) (a) MC = MR.
     (b) MC is rising.
     (c) AR covers AVC.
  (2) (a) MC = MR.
     (b) MC is rising.
     (c) AR covers AC.

(b) Fixed Costs: rent, £50; electricity, £80. Normal profit, £100. Variable costs: wages, £300; raw materials, £250.
  (i) Must cover variable costs: £300 + £250 = £550.
  (ii) Must cover *all* costs (including normal profit): £50 + £80 + £100 + £300 + £250 = £780.

TEST: COSTS OF PRODUCTION (2)

Section A

1. (a) No (b) Yes (c) Yes
2. Never more than one month.
3. (a) No (b) No (c) Yes
4. (a) True (b) False (c) False
5. (a) True (b) True (c) False
6. When the 5th man is employed as he adds only 16 units to total output.
7. (a) True (b) False (c) False
8. (a) False (b) True (c) False
9. 10 men @ £100 = £1,000. 11 men @ £105 = £1,155. So the MC of the 11th man is: £155.
10. (a) False (b) True (c) True

Section B

1. (a)

Output	Total Cost	Marginal Cost	Total Rev.	Mar. Rev.
0	25	25	-	-
1	55	30	58	58
2	82	27	100	42
3	107	25	126	26
4	131	24	150	24
5	152	21	168	18

  (b) Fixed Costs: £25
  (c) No. 2

2. (a) See solution to question in Test: Costs (1)
  (b) Max Flow Ltd
     Per Unit Cost

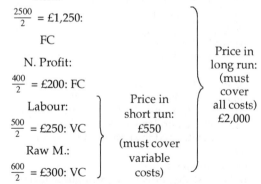

Rent:

$\frac{2500}{2}$ = £1,250:

FC

N. Profit:

$\frac{400}{2}$ = £200: FC

Labour:

$\frac{500}{2}$ = £250: VC

Raw M.:

$\frac{600}{2}$ = £300: VC

Price in short run: £550 (must cover variable costs)

Price in long run: (must cover all costs) £2,000

TEST: MARKET FORMS

Price Discriminating Monopolist

(a) Example: Telecom Éireann, ESB, Bus Éireann. These firms can engage in price discrimination because: (i) they have monopoly power; (ii) they can clearly separate their consumers and so can charge different consumers different prices for the same service.

(b) Yes, provided their profit increases and this will occur if the MR in the new market exceeds MR in its present market.
No, provided their profit decreases and this will occur if the MR in the new market is less than MR in its present market.

(c) (i) MC = MR; (ii) MC is rising; (iii) MC = MR (Home) = MR (Export). It will allocate its output in the export market when the MR in the home market falls below MR in the export market.

(d)

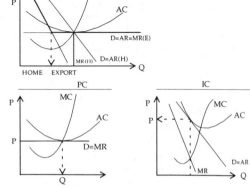

One feature of LR Equilibrium common to PC and IC: Neither firm will earn SNPs in the long run, i.e. AR = AC
and between Monopoly and IC:
Neither firm produces at the lowest point of AC.

TEST: OLIGOPOLY

(a) An *oligopolistic market* is one in which there are *few sellers* who are *interdependent* on each other. They produce *closely competing products* and take into account the *reactions of their competitors*.

(b) (1) For fear that their rivals will reduce their prices, resulting in a price war and less profits for all.
    (2) It is difficult to match the non-price competition measures of some firms.

(c) Cartels are firms within the industry who join together to control output and so force prices up, e.g. OPEC and the petrol companies in Ireland.

(d) Reduced Prices:
    1. because they now have extra purchasing power; and
    2. they can choose what to do with this extra income.

(e) Cournot Model

Stage 1			Stage 2			Stage 3			Stage 4		
P	Q	TR	P	Q	TR	P	Q	TR	P	Q	TR
12	0	0									
11	3	33									
10	6	60									
9	9	81				9	0	0			
8	12	96				8	3	24			
7	15	105				7	6	42	7	0	0
6	18	108	6	0	0	6	9	54	6	3	18
5	21	105	5	3	15	5	12	60	5	6	30
4	24	96	4	6	24	4	15	60	4	9	36
3	27	81	3	9	27	3	18	54	3	12	36
2	30	60	2	12	24	2	21	42	2	15	30
1	33	33	1	15	15	1	24	24	1	18	18
0	36	0	0	18	0	0	27	0	0	21	0

(f)

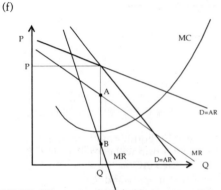

If MC changes to any level between points A and B, prices will *not* change.

Stage	Firm 1	Firm 2	Explanation
1	9,000		Demand = 18,000* A is a monopolist & will produce ½ of this.
2		4,500	Demand is 18,000 – 9,000 = 9,000. B will produce ½ of this.
3	6,750		Demand is 18,000 – 4,500 = 13,500. A will produce ½ of this.
4		5,625	Demand is 18,000 – 6,750 = 11,250. B will produce ½ of this.
		This will continue until equilibrium when both firms will produce 6,000 each.	
Equil.	6,000	6,000	

12,000 = 2/3 of output in PC. So 1/3 = 6,000 and 3/3 = 18,000, the output in PC.*

TEST: FACTOR OF PRODUCTION MARKET

1. MPP is the extra output produced when one additional unit of a FOP is employed.
2. MRP is the extra revenue earned when one additional unit of a FOP is employed.
3. MRP = MPP x MR
   (only in PC, MRP = MPP x P).
4. (a) Not all workers in the public sector produce output and so their MPP cannot be calculated.
   (b) Some public sector workers do produce output but it is not sold in the market. So MR cannot be calculated.
5. Pay comparability; qualifications; length of service; negotiations by trade union.

Labour Market

1. (b) Wage rate   (c) Participation rate.
2. (a) Workers' MRP   (b) Demand for the firm's output   (c) Payroll taxes   (d) Tax on companies' profits   (e) Subsidies on labour   (f) Price of capital   (g) Trade union membership.
3. (a) Workers' MRP   (b) Tradition   (c) Danger/risk of job   (d) Monetary & non-monetary benefits   (e) Training   (f) Skill.

Capital market

(b)	Money Return = Rate of Return
	on Old Bond on New Bond
	£10 = 20%
	£5 = 10%
	£50 = 100%

• Selling price = £50

• Buying price – (selling price + annual return)

£100 – (£50 + £10) = £40 (Loss)

• Real r/i = nominal rate – inflation rate = –10%.

TEST 2: 6TH YEAR: THE LABOUR MARKET

Section A
1. A backward bending S/C_{LAB} means that as W_R > the S_{LAB} > up to a point, but beyond this as W_R > further the S_{LAB} fl due to tax/leisure.
2. Full employment of the workforce is when all those willing to work are working at existing wage levels. (Ratchet Economy: see handout.)
3. Labour is all human activity used in the prod/n of wealth.
4. Economic rent: any payment to a FOP over its supply price.
5. Improving labour mobility: (a) re-training schemes; (b) relocation costs.
6. Wage drift occurs when the D_{LAB} rises beyond the min. negotiated W_R and wages must be > to attract extra workers.

Section B
(a) Factors affecting S_{LAB}: (i) population
(ii) wage rate (iii) participation rates.
What factors affect this?

Below W_X no labour will be supplied.

(b) Factors affecting the qty D_{LAB} by an individual firm:
• Productivity of the worker
• Taxation on co. profits
• Payroll taxes
• Govt subsidies
• Demand for firm's output
• New technology
• Trade unions.

(c) Are workers likely to earn E/R in a PC mkt? No.
(i) If workers earn E/R, the firm's costs are not as low as they should be. So with freedom of entry, new firms enter & squeeze out the firm; or
(ii) Under PC no SNP, so employees cannot get SNPs in form of E/R.

(d) Can workers get an E/R if there is unemployment?
Yes, due to activities of TUs or other rigidities in lab. mkt.
(e) Reasons for difference in wage rates
• MRP
• Training
• Tradition
• Conditions of the job
• Monetary benefits
• Non-monetary benefits

(f) See Handout.

TEST 2: 6TH YR: THE CAPITAL MARKET

Section A
1. Liquidity preference refers to the desire of people to hold their wealth in money form.
2. Two devels causing MEC to decline:
(a) > in the cost of capital gds or > r/i;
(b) fl in the price of the gd being sold.
3. Two uninsurable risks:
(a) Changes in tastes/fashion;
(b) Industrial disputes.
4. Two distinguishing characteristics of Land as a FOP:
(a) It is fixed in supply;
(b) It has no cost of prodn to society as a whole.
5. If bond prices are expected to >: effect on M_D^S: will fall as people will prefer to buy bonds now, so they do and the spec. M_D declines.
6. Two examples of devel. which would not cause the $D_{FOP}^{variable}$ to fl even tho' P >:
(a) If productivity >;
(b) If selling price of gd rose faster than FOP price >.
7. If a new Nat. Loan is given @ a higher r/i, the SP of existing loans will fall
8. Two factors affecting the level of savings:
(a) r/i;
(b) inflation rates.
9. Rent of ability is extra profits to entrepreneur because of extra business acumen.

Section B
(a) Effects of a fl in r/i on the Irish economy:
(i) Saving discouraged;
(ii) Investment encouraged;
(iii) Borrowing encouraged;
(iv) Easier availability of credit;
(v) > D for gds/servs;
(vi) Inflation pushed >;
(vii) More imports with BOP problems?
(viii) Currency difficulties?
(b) Savings: is non-consumption. Investment is the prodn of capital gds.
Desirability of having a high level of savings?
Yes, as they are a source of money for investment; or
No, as they are a leakage from the Circular Flow of Income: more difficult to > econ. growth. (Impact on imports & inflation)

(c) Keynes's Liquidity Preference
- Trans.: for daily expenses:
  depends on level of income;
  r/i has little effect.
- Precaut.:
  for something which may happen in future;
  depends on income & r/i.
- Spec.:
  to take adv. of profitable opportunities;
  depends on r/i.

(d) 1 Jan. 1990: £100 bond @ r/i = 10%. New bonds: 5%. Inflation: 2%
- Return on old bond: £10 = 5% (new r/i). 1% = £2, so 100% = £200.
- Mkt value = £200 + £10 (int.). Profit on bond = £110.
- Real r/i = 10% − 2% = +8%.

(b) Profit/Loss =	Buying Price	−	(Selling Price + Annual Return)
=	£100	−	(£67 + £20)
=	£100	−	£87
Loss =	£13		

(c) Real r/i	=	Nominal r/i	−	Inflation Rate
	=	20%	−	15%
	=	5%		

TEST: THE CAPITAL MARKET— WORKSHEET

1. (a) No (b) No (c) Yes (d) Yes.
2. The desire of people to keep their wealth in money/cash form.
3. (a) Income (b) Income (c) Interest rates.
4. (b) Decrease.
5. (a) No (b) No (c) Yes.
6. (a) Increased demand for money.
   (b) Inflation.
   (c) Increase in German interest rates.

Interest Rates

(a) Savings: increase; greater annual return.
(b) Borrowing: fall; cost has increased.
(c) Investment: falls if cost of borrowing has increased then borrowing is more expensive and so inv. falls.
(d) Inflation: falls; more savings, so less spending and also less borrowing, so spending falls.
(e) Mortgages: cost of repayment up.
(f) Imports: fall due to lower spending.
(g) Servicing Nat. Debt: rises.
(h) V. currency: possibly rise if hot/funk money attracted to Ireland.

Government Bonds

(a) Money Return on Old Bond	= Rate of Return on New Bond
(i) £20.00	= 30%
(ii) So £6.67	= 10%
(iii) and £67.00	= 100% : Selling Price of Bond

MACROECONOMICS

TEST: BUDGETING, TAXATION & NATIONAL DEBT

(a) *Definitions*: see Section 1 (Revision notes on this topic)

(b) *EBR*: will rise by £25 m. as the Current Budget Deficit is part of the EBR.

PSBR: will rise by £25 m. as it consists of the EBR.

National Debt: will rise by £25 m. because we must borrow this to finance the Current Budget Deficit.

BOP Deficit: will probably rise as spending has increased and some of this extra spending will be spent on imports, increasing the size of our BOP Deficit.

(c) 1. *Taxation*: increase direct or indirect tax. It is unlikely that income tax would be increased as it is already high. VAT is being 'harmonised' at present due to completion of the Single European Market. Hence the only likelihood for extra tax revenue is the introduction of new taxes.

2. *Expenditure*: reduce expenditure by
(i) reducing the no. of public sector employees (ii) introduce charges for services heretofore not charged for
(iii) reduce the level of current spending in education, health, social welfare etc.

3. *Overall effects*: any combination of the above would deflate the economy, resulting in higher unemployment.

(d) *Tax*: with higher unemployment income tax revenue would fall and also VAT/excise duty revenue would also fall.

Expenditure: with higher unemployment social welfare expenditure would rise.

Hence the overall effect would be an increase in the size of the Current Budget Deficit.

(e) *Yes*. If the borrowing results in a *self-liquidating debt*, i.e. the return generated exceeds the costs of loan repayment.

(f) *Yes*. Because it *helps the weaker sections of society*, e.g. people in receipt of social welfare & old age non-contributory pension recipients. Also high rates of VAT on cigarettes/alcohol might discourage the consumption of both, resulting in a healthier population.

The possible economic consequences:

1. It might lead to a disincentive to work (high social welfare compared to high taxes).

2. If VAT is high, inflation will result.

3. High taxes might encourage emigration from the country.

4. Such policy helps to increase economic welfare within the country.

(g) *Economic effects of reducing income tax rates*:

1. Tax revenue falls.

2. Greater incentive to work.

3. Trade unions may be willing to accept lower wage increases.

4. Hence the state may have a smaller public sector pay bill.

5. With lower tax there may be less incentive for people to emigrate.

6. People may now decide to leave the black economy and engage in the legitimate economy.

7. Because tax revenue is down the government may be forced to increase borrowing.

8. With higher disposable incomes, spending may increase leading to inflation and possibly more imports.

TEST: MONEY & BANKING

(a), (b) and (c): see Revision Notes in Section 1.

(d) 1. *Commercial Banks*: can increase the money supply because they can create approx. 10 times in credit what they receive in deposits. It can be calculated as follows:

$$\uparrow \text{Money Supply} = \uparrow \text{Cash Reserves} \times \frac{1}{\text{Banks Reserve Ratio}}$$

2. *Building Societies*: Now can as they now operate current accounts in a similar fashion to the banks and so can create credit in a similar fashion to the commercial banks.

3. *P.O. Savings Bank*: No. It does *not* give out loans. It simply acts as a safe place for depositing savings and earning interest.

(e) There is a limit to the amount of purchasing power a bank can create. These limits are:

1. The amount of cash deposits the bank has: more cash deposits mean increased credit creation ability.

2. The bank's reserve ratio: if this is lowered the bank can create more loans.

3. The availability of creditworthy customers: if uncommon, then less loans extended.

4. Central Bank guidelines, e.g. it may wish to restrict the availability of credit.

(f) 1. People are using less cash, so the banks have more cash deposits. Hence their ability to create credit is increased.

2. If a bank wishes to reduce its level of bad debts, it will be stricter on those to whom it gives loans. So it will probably distribute less loans.

(g) 1. (a) *Inflation*: prices will probably increase.
  (b) *Imports*: the increased demand for goods will be met by increased imports.
  (c) *Employment*: an increase in jobs in the long term.
2. (a) *Deflation*: a fall in prices
  (b) *Unemployment*: less goods/services being demanded, so less need for labour to produce it.
  (c) *Imports*: less demand for imports because of lower spending power.

TEST: INFLATION & PRICES

Section A

1. The continuous rise in the general price level as measured by the Consumer Price Index or the drop in the value of money.
2. Step 1: Choose a base year and let prices equal 100.
   Step 2: Calculate a Simple Price Index for each commodity, i.e. $\dfrac{\text{Pcurrent year}}{\text{Pbase year}} \times \dfrac{100}{1}$

   Step 3: Attach a 'weight' to each commodity.
   Step 4: Multiply the weight by the Simple Price Index for each commodity and add to get the result.
3. Means that the demand for goods & services exceeds the supply of goods and services and so prices will tend to rise.
4. (a) *People on fixed incomes*: their standard of living will decline.
   (b) *Borrowers*: will benefit as they will be paying a lower *real* rate of interest.
   Savers: will lose out as the interest rate they receive will be lower than the rate of inflation.
   (c) *Imports*: if import prices are lower than domestic prices, then imports will rise.
   (d) *Exports*: with inflation prices are rising and if higher than our competitors, our exports will not be as competitive abroad resulting in lower sales.
   (e) *Speculators*: will engage in buying any assets which protect against rising prices or a drop in the value of their investment. So speculation in property will be encouraged.
5. (a) Moderation in wage negotiation awards through PCW.
   (b) Lower costs of production, e.g. more competitive telephone charges.
   (c) Lower interest rates resulting in lower production costs.

Section B: All answered in the Revision Notes section on Inflation & Prices.

TEST: POPULATION & EMPLOYMENT

Section A

1. When all those willing to work are working at existing wage levels.
2. (a) Fall in our birth rate. (b) Fall in our fertility rate. (c) Rise in the marriage age.
3. The Live Register. This includes all those who are unemployed and receiving social welfare but are willing and available for work.
4. (a) Number of people applying for passports who give emigration as their reason for applying for a passport.
   (b) Number of people applying for visas, e.g. for the USA.
   (c) Number of people leaving Irish seaports and airports.
5. Where one or more people share their job and their income, resulting in an increased workforce.
6. (a) Lost to those countries to which Irish citizens emigrate.
   (b) Rises: a smaller working population looking after the remainder.
   (c) Tend to rise to keep skilled Irish workers from leaving also.

Section B: All answered in the Revision Notes section on Population & Employment.

SOLUTIONS TO THEORETICAL QUESTIONS: PASS L. CERT. NATIONAL INCOME

1988
(a)

Net Domestic product
+/– NFI from abroad
Net National product
+ Depreciation
Gross National product @ FC
+ Indirect taxes
– Subsidies
Gross National product @ MP

1988

(b)

Think of definition!

	GNP	Std of Living
Growth of Black Econ.	↓ because the incomes are not incl. in its calculation	↑ because people have higher incomes
Man marries his housekeeper	↓ as her income is no longer counted in GNP	No change (depends on level of Y & tax)
Firms repatriate their profits	if new: GNP falls if always existed: no effect	↓ as less incomes in the country

1984

(b) GNP = £1,000 when CPI = 100 in Yr 1
GNP = £3,122 when CPI = 140 in Yr 4
Find GNP in Yr 4 at constant Yr 1 prices.

$$\frac{3,200}{140} \times 100 = £2,230$$

(c) Should these be included in GNP?

   (i) Teachers' salaries: Yes because it's a return for supplying a FOP

  (ii) Non-Contr. pensions: No because they are simply a Transfer Payment.

1983

(b)

	GNP @ Mkt Prices	Std of Living
↓ in working week (with no Δ in production)	If no drop in wages then *no* Δ in GNP as same output prod.	↑ leisure time so ↑ standard of living
↑ VAT rates	↑ in GNP @ mkt prices	↓ std of living due to higher prices

1987

(b) Defn of GNP at Current Market Prices:

This is the total value of gds & servs produced in the economy at their selling prices.

What factors caused GNP to ↑ over the past 5 years?

- Inflation
- Changes in the level of taxes & subsidies
- Increases in wages (or payments to FOP)
- Increased demand for our goods
- Increased investment (thro' borrowing from abroad).

1991

(a) 1. So as to be more accurate, i.e. will you arrive at the same answer?

    2. The figures arrived at can be used as a cross-check on each other.

(b) See Revision Notes in Section 1 on National Income.

(c) Yes. Because:

  1. Population might increase resulting in a lower standard of living.

  2. Inflation may cause prices to rise resulting in a higher GNP but not necessarily a higher standard of living.

  3. While GNP may have increased it might be retained by a small section of the population — hence having little effect on the total population.

SOLUTIONS TO THEORETICAL QUESTIONS ON NATIONAL INCOME: 1985–90

1985

(a) Incomes which accrue to the permanent residents of a country from current economic activity in the prodn of gds and services or 'Income earned by Irish FOP'.

(b) GNP = GDP +/– Net factor income from the rest of the world.
GNP greater because:

  1. Foreign firms repatriating less profits.
  2. Emigrants' remittances.
  3. Interest repayment on foreign debt decreasing.

(c) 1. Inflation rate/cost of living index.
   2. Size of population.
   3. Distribution of GNP.
   4. Govt provision of services.
   5. Quality of life.
   6. Govt taxation policies.
   7. Increase in market orientation.

1986

(a) GNP at factor cost
   – Depreciation

  = NNP at factor cost (National Income)

The amount spent on depreciation is simply replacing old or worn-out capital, so it does not benefit the economy. It also reduces the amount spent on a day-to-day basis.   (20)
Depreciation is also hard to calculate so the answer is National Income.

(b) GNP at mkt prices: remove subsidies → P↑, so GNP @ mkt prices ↑.   (10)
Std of living: remove subsidies → cost of living ↑, so std of living ↓.   (10)

(c)

	Current Year	Long Term
GNP	No effect	*Falls* (lack of cap. gds)
Std of Living	*Rises*: people buying more consumer gds	*Falls*: because less capital gds to produce consumer gds

1988 & 1990

(a) GDP +/– Net Factor Income from rest of world = GNP. (15)
   GNP = better indicator of money available to people in Ireland (5), because:
   1. Repatriation of profits.
   2. Outflow of interest payments.
   3. Factor inflows, e.g. hiring of Aer Lingus plane; ESB consultancy services overseas.

(b) $Y = C + I + G + X - M$ (5)

   C: affected by incomes, pop. profile & pop. size.
   I: affected by rate of interest, technology; MRP–MC (i.e. marg. eff. of Capital).
   G: affected by fiscal policy.
   X: affected by competitiveness.
   M: affected by competitiveness.

Q. 5: National Income Question — Tricky!

1. Given

Period	GNP =	C +	I +	X	– M	Savings*
1	8,500	6,825	2,000	700	1,025	1,675**
2	9,000	7,200	2,100	800	1,100	1,800
change	500	375	100	100	75	125
3						

*(= GNP – C)   **(8,500 – 6,825)

2. APC = 0.8, so APS must be 1.00 – 0.8 = 0.2
3. Multiplier = 2.5*
Find (i) GNP, C, M in Period 2; (ii) MPC; (iii) MPM.

Steps

1. Injections between Periods 1 & 2: Inv. ↑ by £100 and X ↑ by £100. Total ↑ in injections = £200.
2. If Inj. ↑ by £200 then GNP ↑ by £200 x 2.5 = £500. (+ £8,500 = £9,000).
3. APC = 0.8. So C = £9,000 x 0.8 = £7,200.
4. Savings = £9,000 – £7,200 = £1,800.
5. Now £9,000 = £7,200 + £2,100 + 800 – M.
   so M_S =£9,000 – £7,200 – £2,100 – £800 = £1,100.
   The resulting position is:

Period	GNP =	C +	I +	X	– M	Savings*
1	8,500	6,825	2,000	700	1,025	1,675**
2	9,000	7,200	2,100	800	1,100	1,800
▶ change	500	375	100	100	75	125

Hence: $MPC = \dfrac{375}{500} = 0.75$ and $MPM = \dfrac{75}{500} = 0.15$

Check Multiplier $= \dfrac{1}{1 - (MPC - MPM)}$

$= \dfrac{1}{1 - (0.75 - 0.15)} = \dfrac{1}{1 - 0.6} = \dfrac{1}{0.4} = 2.5*$

(b)

Period	GNP =	C +	I +	X	– M	Savings
2	9,000	7,200	2,100	800	1,100	1,800
	600	450	40	+200	+90	150
3	9,600	7,650	2,140	1,000	1,190*	1,950

Step 1: If bal. of trade* is to be reduced to 190 then total imports in Period 3 would equal 1,100 + 90 = 1,190.

Step 2: So M can only ↑ by £90. If M ↑ by £90 how much must GNP have ↑ by?

Recall MPM = 0.15 (3/20). So 1/20 of £90 = £30, so 20/20 = £30 x 20 = £600.

So GNP ↑ by £600 (+ £9,000) = £9,600

Step 3: £600 x 0.75 = ↑ in C = £450. So C in Period 3 = £7,200 + £450 = £7,650.

Step 4: Y–C = Savings. So £9,600 – £7,650 = £1,950.

Step 5: What is investment? £9,600 = £7,650 + I + £1,000 – £1,190.

So Inv. = £9,600 – £7,650 – £1,000 + £1,190 = £2,140.

Summary:

Period	GNP =	C +	I +	X	– M	Savings
3	9,600	7,650	2,140	1,000	1,190	1,950

INTERNATIONAL TRADE — 1
LAW OF ABSOLUTE ADVANTAGE

Assumptions:

1. World consists of 2 countries.
2. There are only 2 products.
3. There are no free transport costs.
4. There is only 1 FOP — labour.
5. There is internal mobility of FOP.

Step 1.   Output per worker

Country	Beef	Tomatoes
	(kg per week)	
Ireland	400	600
Holland	200	2,400
Calculate total world prodn	600	3,000

*Calculate opportunity costs

Ireland: B for T: $\dfrac{600}{400}$: $1\frac{1}{2}$:1

T for B: $\dfrac{400}{600}$: $\frac{2}{3}$:1

Holland: B for T: $\dfrac{2,400}{200}$: 12:1

T for B: $\dfrac{200}{2,400}$: $\frac{1}{12}$:1

Step 2.   Calculate

(a) Ireland's absolute advantage: Beef: $\dfrac{400}{200}$ is 2:1
(b) Holland's absolute advantage:

Tomatoes: $\dfrac{2,400}{600}$ is 4:1

What should Ireland specialise in?   Beef.

What should Holland specialise in?   Tomatoes.

Step 3.   Specialisation takes place

Country	Beef	Tomatoes	
	(kg per week)		Output for 2 men specialising in each country
Ireland	800	–	
Holland	–	4,800	
Calculate: Total world output	800	4,800	Opp cost: 1B for 6 Ts*

Step 4.   Assume trade takes place

(a) Suppose Ireland swaps half of her output of beef for Holland's tomatoes
(b) Assume they exchange it as follows: 1 beef for 6 tomatoes*
(c) Then Ireland gives 400 kg beef for 2,400 kg tomatoes
and Holland gives 2,400 kg tomatoes for 400 kg beef.

Step 5.   Resulting position

	Beef	Tomatoes
Country	(kg per week)	
Ireland	400	2,400
Holland	400	2,400
Total world output	800	4,800

Step 6.   State the obvious advantages of specialisation & trade resulting from the above example:

1. Overall world prodn has increased.
2. Ireland has gained 1,800 kg tomatoes.
3. Holland has gained 200 kg beef.
4. Each country has a choice of goods.

LAW OF COMPARATIVE ADVANTAGE

Assumptions:

1. World consists of 2 countries.
2. There are only 2 products.
3. There are no free transport costs.
4. There is only 1 FOP — labour.
5. There is internal mobility of FOP.

Step 1.   Output per worker

	Beef	Tomatoes
Country	(kg per week)	
Ireland	400	600
Holland	800	2,400
Total world output	1,200	3,000

Calculate opportunity costs

Ireland: B for T: $\dfrac{600}{400}$: 1½ :1

T for B: $\dfrac{400}{600}$: ⅔ :1

Holland: B for T: $\dfrac{2,400}{800}$: 3:1

T for B: $\dfrac{800}{2,400}$: ⅓ :1

In 'world' terms what is 1 unit of beef worth in terms of tomatoes?

Ans.: 1 B for $\dfrac{300}{1,200}$ => $2\frac{1}{2}$ T.

Step 2.   Calculate:

(a)   Ireland's comparative disadvantage: (below)

beef: $\dfrac{400}{800}$ = 1 : 2; toms: $\dfrac{600}{2,400}$ = 1 : 4

(b)   Holland's comparative advantage:

beef: $\dfrac{800}{400}$ i.e. 2 : 1 toms: $\dfrac{2400}{600}$: 4

What should Holland specialise in?   Tomatoes.

What should Ireland specialise in?   Beef.

Why?   Least comparative disadvantage.

Step 3.   Specialisation takes place

Country	Beef	Tomatoes
	(kg per week)	
Ireland	800	–
Holland	–	4,800
Calculate: Total world output	800	4,800

Prodn of beef has ↓. By what %? $\dfrac{400}{1,200}$ i.e. 33%.

Prodn of toms has ↑. By what %? $\dfrac{1,800}{3,000}$ = 60%

Using this info. is the world better or worse off?

Yes. ↑ of 60% > ↓ of 33%. Also ↓ beef of 400 units is equivalent to 400 x 2½ = 900 tomatoes and has ↑ 1,800 units.

Step 4.   Assume trade takes place

(a)   Look at 1 above and the opportunity costs.
(b)   What will the terms of trade lie between? 1½ units and 3 units (see above *).
(c)   Assume it is 2 kg tomatoes for 1 kg beef and that Ireland exchanges 400 lb beef for 800 kg tomatoes.
(d)   Complete the following:

With trade	Beef	Tomatoes
Ireland	400	600
Holland	400	4,000

Step 5.   Comment on the advantages of International Trade.

1. Overall the world had become richer.
2. Each individual country has benefited.
3. Each country has a choice of goods.

HISTORICAL VIEW OF EXCHANGE RATES

Complete the following chart, outlining the development of E/Rs

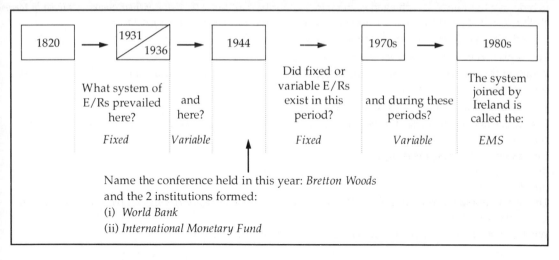

| 1820 | 1931 / 1936 | 1944 | 1970s | 1980s |

What system of E/Rs prevailed here? — *Fixed*

and here? — *Variable*

Did fixed or variable E/Rs exist in this period? — *Fixed*

and during these periods? — *Variable*

The system joined by Ireland is called the: *EMS*

Name the conference held in this year: *Bretton Woods*
and the 2 institutions formed:
(i) *World Bank*
(ii) *International Monetary Fund*

THE GOLD STANDARD

Main advantages of this system:

(a) encouraged *stability* in foreign trade.
(b) self-*Adjusting Mechanism*

illustrate this here:

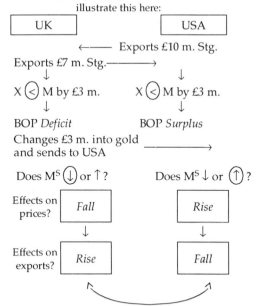

| UK | USA |

←——— Exports £10 m. Stg.

Exports £7 m. Stg.———→

X $\left(<\right)$ M by £3 m.

X $\left(<\right)$ M by £3 m.

BOP *Deficit*

BOP *Surplus*

Changes £3 m. into gold and sends to USA ————→

Does M^S $\left(\downarrow\right)$ or ↑?

Does M^S ↓ or $\left(\uparrow\right)$?

Effects on prices? — *Fall*

Rise

Effects on exports? — *Rise*

Fall

So by correcting the BOP problems the Gold Standard's main advantage was called the self-*Adjusting Mechanism*.

State the *two* reasons for its abandonment.

1. *Surplus countries do not like inflation.*

2. *Deficit countries do not like rising unemployment.*

THE STERLING AREA

1. State why it became so important?
   (a) *UK had extensive connections in trade.*
   (b) *London was the world's financial capital.*

2. Two groups of countries belonged to it?
   (a) *Commonwealth countries* e.g. Australia/India.
   (b) *Non-Commonwealth countries* e.g. Japan.

3. To be a member of the Sterling Area you had to satisfy these 2 requirements:
   (a) *Maintain fixed E/R with sterling*
   (b) *Hold high portion of reserves in sterling.*

4. The economic advantages in being a member of the Sterling Area were:
   (a) Sterling was the most *stable currency* in the world.
   (b) It was a *strong* currency & so currencies aligned with it remained *strong*.
   (c) Countries had *access* to the *financial* markets of London.

5. After 1939 many non-*Commonwealth* members left because:
   (a) of the *devaluation* of sterling, making it less *attractive.*
   (b) *Trade* between *Commonwealth* countries became less *important.*

The International Monetary Fund was established in 1944 at the Bretton Woods Conference.

Why was it established? *To restore stability to E/Rs and so encourage a growth in foreign trade.*

In order for this aim to be achieved each member country had to *set the value of their currencies fixed in terms of other currencies,* and this was not allowed to change beyond +/– 5% *in this fixed value.*

What did each country contribute to the IMF? *A quota of currency.*

This consisted of 75% in *its own currency* and 25% in *gold or US dollars.*

What did the country use the above for? *Members could withdraw it in the form of a loan when they found their currencies in difficulties.*

What was the advantage of this? *Currencies remained stable in value.*

Besides the above, what else did the IMF insist on? *The country must take corrective action to cure its BOP problems.*

Give examples of these measures:

(i)   *Credit squeeze,*
(ii) *Public spending cuts.*

The system operated well until the 1970s. What happened? *Some countries allowed their currencies to float against the US dollar.*

What system tried to establish a fixed exchange rate system in the 1980s? *EMS.*

TEST ON BALANCE OF PAYMENTS:

Current and Capital A/Cs: see Revision Notes in Section 1.

INTERNATIONAL TRADE: TEST

A. REASONS FOR TRADE

Hons 83 & 85

a) Table: Explanation of Table: see below for Table.

b) Assumptions: No Transport Costs; Constant Returns to Scale; Availability of alternative employment; Mobility of Factors; Distribution of Benefits: reference to Irish Economy.

Pass 86

b) Is international trade beneficial to the Irish economy? Explain your answer. (25)
   Yes:
   1. Enables us to consume gds which we cannot produce at home.
   2. Provides us with a market for production.
   3. Domestic production is subject to competition from imports.
   4. Lost employment.

Pass 87

b) Is there any economic justification for a government intervening in order to restrict international trade? Explain *one* means by which the government might restrict international trade if it wished to do so.
   Economic justifications:
   (i)   infant industry;
   (ii)   strategically important jobs;
   (iii)   prevent dumping;
   (iv)   maintain employment in a recession;
   (v)   prevent a trade imbalance;
   (vi)   enable an industry to decline gradually;
   (vii)   protect industry from cheap foreign labour.
   Economic means:
   tariffs /embargoes or exchange controls.

B. BALANCE OF PAYMENTS

Pass 85

a) *Two* examples of items appearing on the Capital section of the BOP:
   1. Foreign borrowing.
   2. Lending by banks or govt or industries.
   3. Transfers from EU institutions.
   4. Transfers affecting our external reserves.
   5. Repatriation of profits.

b)

Balance of Trade	BOP on Current A/C
Physical Xs – Physical Ms	Import & Export of Goods & Services

Hons 86

IDA attract more foreign firms
- Current a/c:
   1. It/they usually export, so money comes into Ireland; improves BOP.
   2. May import RMs → worsens our BOP.
   3. If they employ 'foreign' staff → outflow in invisible section.

- Capital a/c:
   1. May repatriate profits: worsens BOP.
   2. Because they invest in Ireland: improvement in our BOP.

C. EXCHANGE RATES

Pass 86

(c) If Sterling increased in value relative to the Irish Punt, what effect(s) would this have on the Irish economy?
   1. Cost of living increased in respect of consumption gds which we continue to import from the UK.
   2. Price of industrial imports from UK ↑ with subsequent ↑ in price of finished gds.
   3. Domestic producers more competitive against imports from UK. Irish goods more competitive or on UK mkts.
   4. Could affect interest rates.

Hons 88

(a) Supply of our Currency: visible & invisible Ms; repayments of capital; repatriation of profits; govt intervention; speculation.
   Demand for our Currency: visible & invisible xs; foreign investment in Ireland; emigrants' remittances; speculation; govt intervention.

(b) Xs: dearer – depends on E_D^P for Xs, some elastic/inelastic; industrial, agricultural gds; Invisibles.
   Ms cheaper – depends on E_D^P for Ms; competitiveness etc.

6TH ECONOMICS
INTERNATIONAL TRADE

1979

	Food	Mach.		
A	10	2	If A specialises in food, then 1 ton of food is worth 1/5 of a machine If A specialises in mach., then 1 machine is worth 5 tons of food.	Opportunity costs
B	16	8	If B specialises in food, then 1 ton of food is worth ½ of a machine. If B specialises in mach., then 1 machine is worth 2 tons of food.	
	26*	10*		

(a) 1. The LOCA states that where a country is more efficient in the production of all commodities, then it should specialise in the prodn of the commodity in which it has the greatest comparative adv., i.e. in which it is most efficient.

2. The LOCA applies in the above example. Why? Because B is most efficient in the prodn of both. It is 16/10 or 1.6 times more efficient in the prodn of food & 8/2 or 4 times more efficient in the prodn of mach. So *B sh. produce mach. and A sh. produce food* (in which it has the least comparative disadvantage).

3. With specialisation the results are:

	Food	Mach.	
A	20	0	In A, 2 men are now producing food, i.e. 10 x 2 (assuming the 2nd produces the same as the first man)
B	0	16	In B, 2 men are now producing mach., i.e. 8 x 2
	20	16	

4. Is trade justified? Yes. Why? Because in world terms* 1 machine is the equivalent of 2.6 tons of food. With specialisation output of food has ↓ by 6 tons. For the world to be at least in the same position as before, then the output of mach. must ↑ by at least 2 machines. Instead it has gone up by 6 machines. So the world is better off with specialisation.

(b) What would the possible terms of trade be?
1. A swaps food for machinery: for 1 ton of food sold it would want at least 1/5 of a machine, while the maximum B will give for each ton of food imported is ½ a machine. *To summarise:* 1 ton of food is worth between 1/5 and 1/2 a machine.

2. B swaps mach. for food: for 1 machine sold it would want 2 tons of food; while the maximum A will give for each machine imported is 5 tons of food. *To summarise:* 1 machine is worth between 2 and 5 tons of food.

(c) What factors other than comparative advantage might determine whether or not trade takes place?
1. Does free trade exist?
2. Would transport costs outweigh the advantages of specialisation?
3. Would labour be able to move from the production of one good into the prodn of the other?
4. Are alternative jobs available for the workers made unemployed?
5. Will the terms of trade be favourable for both countries?
6. What is the exchange rate between the currencies of both countries?

Devaluation

1987 Q. 3

1. Defn: it is the reduction in the foreign exchange value of our currency.
2. Example: originally IR£1 = $3, now IR£ = $2.
3. Aim:
   (a) to↑ P_M, and
   (b) ↓ P_X. How? Suppose Ire. exports cattle worth £1,000 and imports a mach. worth $3,000.
   Originally we receive $3,000 for exports and pay £1,000 for our imports
   Now we receive £1,000 x 2 = $2,000 for Xs and pay 3,000/2 = £1,500 for our imports.
   So: P_X ↓ and P_M ↑.

So to the answer. the effects of devaluation on:

Price Level	Will rise	(1) P_M will rise and we buy these, so CPI will rise; and (2) Price of imported raw materials will ↑, pushing up prices of gds/servs, and so price level rises.
Servicing the Nat. Debt	Will rise.	Because our curr. is now worth less in foreign curr. terms it will now take more IR£ to repay the foreign element of our nat. debt.
Money Wages in Ireland	Will rise.	As the cost of living has ↑, unions will try to negotiate a ↑ in wages so as to maintain their members' std of living. If granted, then money wages ↑.
Balance of Trade	Depends	P_X ↓, but if the PED for X is inelastic then we won't earn extra foreign currency. P_M ↑, but if the PED for M is inelastic then we will pay more for our imports. In this situation our BOT will get worse. PED for Xs and Ms must be > 1 (Marshall Lerner Condition).

THE HISTORY OF ECONOMIC THOUGHT

Brief outline of topic:

Mercantilism	Classical School		Neo–Keynesian
Physiocracy	Neoclassical	Keynes	Monetarism

1. Place the following in chronological order (the figure 1 indicating the earliest).

Thomas Malthus	2
John Maynard Keynes	5
Alfred Marshall	4
Karl Marx	3
Milton Friedman	6
Adam Smith	1

2. Indicate the author of each of the following:

(a) Inquiry into the Nature & Causes of the Wealth of Nations   *Adam Smith*

(b) A Monetary History of the United States   *M. Friedman*

(c) Das Kapital   *Karl Marx*

(d) Essay on the Principles of Population   *Malthus*

(e) General Theory of Employment, Interest & Money   *J. M. Keynes*

3. What economist(s) would you associate with each of the following?

(a) Law of Comparative Costs   *David Ricardo*

(b) 'Surplus Value of Production'   *Karl Marx*

(c) The Multiplier   *J. M. Keynes*

(d) The Iron Law of Wages   *Thomas Malthus*

4. According to Keynesian theory:
(a) The main factor influencing employment is   *Aggregate Demand*

(b) The main factor influencing investment is   *Businessmen's expectations*

5. Name two of the Fabian socialists:

(a) *H. G. Wells* (b) *Beatrice Webb*

6. Indicate the economist(s) attached to the following Schools of Thought:

Mercantilism	Physiocracy	Classical	Neoclassical	Monetarist
1. T. Mun	1. *Turgot*	1. *Smith*	1. *Marshall*	1. *Friedman*
2. *Sir J. Steuart*	2. *Quesnay*	2. *Malthus*	2. *Clark*	
		3. *Ricardo*		
		4. *Say*		

7. State the two main ideas of each of the following Schools of Thought:

Mercantilism	1. *Wealth consisted of gold & silver.* 2. *Countries should aim for a favourable trade balance.*
Physiocrats	1. *Agriculture was the only true source of wealth.* 2. *Laissez-faire; no govt interference.*

8. Explain 'Say's Law': *Economic crises and overproduction could not exist because production created demand.*

9. Which school believed in the idea of laissez–faire? *Classical School*

 Briefly explain it: *That there should be no govt interference in the economy — that matters should proceed without interference.*

10. Using the following grid indicate in *brief* form the main contribution(s) of each of the following economists::

Economist	Idea(s)
Adam Smith	1. *Division of labour* 2. *Labour theory of value.* 3. *Free competition.* 4. *Govt interference limited => Canons of taxation.*
T. Malthus	1. *Pop. growth ↑ faster than food supply.* 2. *Iron law of wages, i.e. just pay labour enough to survive. Otherwise pop. ↑ and wage rates fall.*
D. Ricardo	1. *Theory of economic rent (Factor Market).* 2. *Law of comparative adv. (Inter. Trade)*
Karl Marx	1. *Labour theory of value (it produces all the wealth).* 2. *Surplus value of production.* 3. *Profits invested in machines => ↑ unemployment.* 4. *Socialism would result from continuous class struggle.*
Marshall (Neoclassical)	1. *Utility theory of value.* 2. *Marginal revenue productivity.* 3. *Quasi-rent.*
J.M. Keynes	1. *Liquidity preference theory.* 2. *Income could be below full employment level.* 3. *Multiplier; MPC, MPM.* 4. *Savings need not equal investment.*
M. Friedman	1. *Monetarism, i.e. cut govt expenditure to ↓ inflation and boost demand, thereby ↑ jobs.*

1.

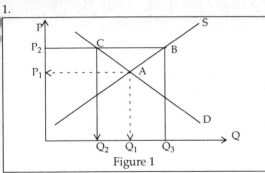

Figure 1

(a) In a free market what price would be established? *P_1*

(b) At P_2 the qty demanded = *Q_2*

the qty supplied = *Q_3*

(c) Is there excess demand or supply? *Supply*

How much? *$Q_2 Q_3$*

(d) In a free market with high prices, how would the market clear itself? *By allowing prices to fall, the Q_D ↑ and Q_S ↓.*

(e) To prevent prices falling, what does the CAP do? *Buys the surplus stock at P_2.*

(f) What qty of produce must be purchased to prevent prices falling? *$Q_2 Q_3$ BC*

Who does this policy mainly benefit?

EC farmers

Why? *Because it keeps prices high and hence their incomes are kept high.*

2. Name three main sources of finance which Ireland gets from EU funds.

(a) *European Social Fund*

(b) *European Regional Development Fund*

(c) *Euro. Inv. Bank*

3. Irish Industry & the EU

State the main advantage & disadvantage of EU membership for Irish industry.

Advantage	Disadvantage
Attracted non-EEC countries to locate their companies in Ire. and avoid the common external tariff.	*Irish industries now had to compete and hence some closed resulting in unemployment.*

4. Irish agriculture & the EU

(a) There are five main principles (or mechanisms) behind the CAP. Name these.
   (i) *Guaranteed Prices*
   (ii) *Intervention*
   (iii) *Mechanisation*
   (iv) *Structural Policy*
   (v) *'Green Pound' or MCAs.*

(b) State the main advantage & disadvantage of CAP to both the following groups.

Farmers	
Advantage	Disadvantage
↑ incomes or financial aid	*↑ competition from member states*
Consumers	
Advantage	Disadvantage
	higher food prices

(c) What are MCAs? *A tax on agricultural exports and a subsidy on agricultural imports.*

TEST: ECONOMIC AIMS, POLICIES & CONFLICTS

See Revision Notes in Section 1.

1977

FOP: Capital/Output Ratio is the qty of capital in money terms which is required in order to produce an extra unit of output in money terms.

FOP: Rent of Ability means a payment above transfer earnings to labour which persists in the l/r.

Mkt Forms: A profit-maximising firm is in equilibrium when:
1. MC = MR.
2. MC cuts MR from below.
3. S/R: covers AVC.
4. L/R: ATC.

FOP: National loan is issued @ higher r/i than that payable on existing loans, the selling price of existing loans will decrease

D + S: The substitution effect in relation to the cheaper good is always positive

Costs: Increasing returns to scale occur when:

(a) the Output is expanding: Yes.
(b) MC is rising: No.
(c) LRAC is falling: Yes.

1978

Mkt Forms: LR Equil in IC. Will firm earn SNP? No, because of freedom of entry. New firms come in and SNP are eliminated.

Mkt Forms: A firm which receives a govt subsidy: CIE, because of the social benefits attached to it.

Mkt Forms: If AR is ↑, MR must be

(a) increasing: Yes.
(b) at a maximum: No.
(c) equal to AR: No.
(d) greater than AR: Yes.

D + S: E_D^C for substitute goods is:
+: Yes. − : No, 0: No.

1979

Utility: Conditions for equilibrium: When ratio of MU to P is the same for all goods bought.

Elas.: E_D^Y is 1.5 & in Yr 1 Sales: 10,000. If Y↑ by 10%, what will sales be? If Y ↑ by 10%, Q_D will ↑ 15%, i.e. 1,500 units to 11,500.

Mkt Forms: LR S/C in PC: is the MC curve above ATC (in SR: MC above AVC).

Costs: Trader hires an assistant weekly, delivering milk he buys each morning. Deliveries are made in a van rented on a monthly basis. The SR period is:

(a) one day;
(b) never less than 1 wk;
(c) never more than 1 month.

D + S S/C shift to right:

(a) Existing E/S maintained: No.
(b) Improvement in prodn (Tn): Yes.
(c) ↑ D: No.

1980

FOP: A backward-bending S/C_{LAB} means that: As Wr ↑, S_{LAB} ↑ up to a point but for further W increases ↑ leisure will be substituted for an ↑ supply of labour.

Utility: Consumer in equilibrium buying 10 of A @ £2 ea. & 10 of B @ £6 ea. If MU_A is 5 units, what is MU of B? $\frac{5}{2} = \frac{x}{6}$ ∴ 30 = 2x ∴ x, i.e. MU_B = 15 units.

Mkt Forms: Barriers to entry into an industry:

1. Govt legislation;
2. Sole ownership of a patent;
3. Capital required too large.

Mkt Forms: Firm earning SNPs, MC is equal to

(a) AC: No.
(b) AR: No.
(c) MR: Yes.

1981

Elas.: E_D^C for substitute gds is positive, because if P_{butter} ↑ → $Q_{margarine}^D$ ↑.

Utility: Utility max. consumer is at equilibrium when: ratio of MU to P is the same for all gds purchased.

Costs: firm is of optimum size when:

(a) there are no FC: No.
(b) firm is earning SNP: No.
(c) AC @ a min.: Yes.

1982

FOP: Liquidity preference refers to: the desire of people to hold assets in a liquid form.

FOP: MRP must equal MPP x P. False. This only applies in PC. In other mkt forms P = MR. So MRP = MPP x MR.

Mkt Forms: LR Equilibrium for a firm:

(a) P = MR: PC only;
(b) AC @ a minimum: PC only;
(c) P > AC: Mon. only.

Mkt Forms: In Oligopoly:

(a) Firms will consider competitors' actions: True.
(b) Firm acting on its own cannot influence the level of sales: False.
(c) In SR on normal profit will be earned: False.

Costs: LDMR: As $\uparrow$ qtys of a variable FOP are combined with a fixed FOP, output $\uparrow$ but @ a diminishing rate.

Costs: if tax is levied on each unit of a good the effect on the firm's MC curve is: to shift it upwards.

1983

Mkt Forms: Price discrimination exists when a firm sells goods to different customers at a varying ratio between MC to Price.

Elas.: E_D^C for substitute goods is Positive

Costs: If MC are rising then,

(a) AC are rising: False;
(b) a firm could not be in equilibrium: False.
(c) normal profit is not being earned: False.

1984

FOP: Entrepreneur will employ Capital and Labour until the marginal productivity of each is equal. False.

He will employ each factor until the MC of it equals its MRP.

D + S: Consumer surplus is: the extra amount a consumer would be willing to pay for a good (rather than go without it) over the amount he actually pays for it.

MKT FORMS: In PC because of the competition it is only where MC is @ a minimum that a firm is in equil. False. LR Equil. in PC is where AC is @ a minimum, at which point AC is cut by a rising MC curve. Hence it could not be @ a minimum.

FOP: Two examples where the D for a variable FOP would not be reduced even though P $\uparrow$.

1. If selling price of good rose by a larger amt.
2. If productivity rose faster than the factor price increase.

D + S: Two circumstances which would cause a D/C to shift inwards towards the origin.

1. If P_{SUB} gd fell.
2. If P_{COM} gd rose.
3. If income fell.
4. If movement in taste against the good.

1985

Mkt. Forms: Homogeneous gds means: gds which consumers perceive as being the same/identical/perfect subs.

Mkt Forms: If MC > MR, then firm is not earning Normal Profit. False. Normal profit is earned when AC @ the level of output is not less than AR; AC could be less than AR even though MC exceeds MR.

FOP: If bond prices are expected to rise the Spec. D. for money will $\uparrow$. False. People would prefer to buy bonds now and thus they will prefer bonds to money, so Spec. D. money will decrease.

Mkt Forms: Why consider Oligopoly separately from IC? In O. there are few sellers, so indv. sellers will take into account the possible reactions of their competitors.

Mkt Forms: Two examples of Barriers to Entry:

1. Sole rights to RMs.
2. Economies of scale.
3. Patents.
4. Govt restrictions.

1986

Elas.: 100 items sold @ £1. If P $\uparrow$ to £1.25 sales drop to 78. Is demand elastic or inelastic?

$$\frac{22}{25} \times \frac{£2 \cdot 25}{178} = 1.11 \text{ Elastic}$$

FOP: In PC what r/ship exists between MRP & MPP? In PC, MRP = MPP x P.

Elas.: E_D^Y is – then a good is inferior. True because as Y $\uparrow \rightarrow Q_D$ falls. Then the good is inferior.

FOP: Two examples of Uninsurable Risks:

1. Loss of profits due to obsolete stock.
2. Bad management.

Costs: True/False

(a) When AC is @ a min., MC = AC: True.
(b) When AC is constant, MC = AC: True.
(c) MC applies only in the short run: No.

1987

FOP: Liquidity Preference refers to the desire of people to hold assets in a liquid form.

Elas.: A luxury good is a good for which E_D^Y is elastic

FOP: Employer trying to $\downarrow$ costs will employ FOP until MRP of each is equal. False

He will employ each factor until the MC = MRP.

FOP: Two developments which would cause a reduction in the Marginal Efficiency of Capital.

1. $\uparrow$ cost of capital gds
2. $\downarrow$ in price of good being sold.
3. $\uparrow$ in rate of interest.

FOP: Two ways in which land differs from other FOP:

1. Fixed in supply;
2. No cost of production.

1988

Mkt Forms: Limit pricing: Oligopolists setting prices at a level which limits competition or which makes entry of competitors more difficult.

FOP: MRP = MPP x MR. In PC, MRP = MPP x P.

Mkt Forms: MC > MR. False. Earning less max. profit says nothing about normal profit. (Must look at AR to find out about normal profit.)

Costs: Opportunity cost: False: The firm could have hired out the asset or the firm might have bought another asset.

Utility: Consumer equilibrium: when the ratio of MU to price is the same for all gds purchased, i.e. Equi-marginal Principle of Consumer Behaviour.

1989

Mkt Forms: A profit-maximising firm will be at equilibrium when:
1. MC = MR.
2. MC rising faster than MR.
3. S/r: covering AVC.
4. L/r: covering ATC.

FOP: Two uninsurable risks:
1. Demand for gds might change/competitive conditions change.
2. Risk of loss/financial-commercial risk.

Costs/Mkt. Forms: If the price of a good is falling the MR must be:
(i) less than price: Yes.
(ii) negative: No.
(iii) less than AC: No.

1990

Elasticity: An inferior good: has a negative income effect or as income increases, quantity demanded falls.

FOP: S/C of Labour to a firm is upward sloping. Give 2 reasons causing the S/C to shift to the right.
1. Increase labour force/reduction in income tax/other firms paying less.
2. More perks offered.

Utility: For a utility-maximising consumer to be in equilibrium, the MU of each good bought would be the same? False

It is the ratio of MU/P which is the same for all goods bought.

Costs: In order to earn SNP a firm must keep its costs to a minimum. False. To earn SNP then AR must exceed AC.

FOP: If bond prices are expected to rise, the speculative demand for money will increase. False.

People will prefer to hold bonds instead of cash and so the speculative demand for money will fall.

Costs: There is no opportunity cost to a firm in using an asset which it owns: False.

There is an opportunity cost in retaining it: they can sell it and earn some revenue.

Mkt Forms: A PC firm:
1. MC is at a minimum: No.
2. Price exceeds MR: No.
3. Economic rent is earned: No.

1991

FOP: Real interest rates are: those you receive on your investment once you've deducted the inflation rate from the nominal rate quoted.

FOP: Supply Price of a FOP is: that price at which a FOP is willing to supply itself to a particular use.

Mkt Forms: Price discrimination exists when a firm: sells the same goods to different customers at varying ratios between MC and price.

FOP: MRP must equal MPP x P in PC. True: because in PC each firm can sell additional output at the prevailing price. Hence MR = P in PC only.

Utility: Principal assumptions about a consumer's behaviour:
1. Limited income;
2. Subject to diminishing utility;
3. Acts rationally;
4. Tries to maximise utility.

1992

FOP: Liquidity Preference refers to: the desire of people to keep their wealth in cash form.

Mkt Forms: Consumer Surplus is: the difference between what a consumer is prepared to pay for a good and what he actually pays, rather than do without the good.

Mkt Forms: If MC = MR, then the firm is earning normal profit. False.

Normal profit is earned when AC = AR at the level of output produced. AC could be less than AR even though MC = MR.

FOP: The productivity of labour depends mainly on: the skill of each labour unit (which depends on training, skill, initiative etc.).

1993

Utility: The Law of Diminishing Marginal Utility states: that as a consumer consumes additional units of a good, his MU for each extra unit will eventually diminish.

FOP: A trade union as a monopoly supplier of labour means: that once the union has negotiated a minimum wage rate, no labour will be supplied below this wage rate.

FOP: Two uninsurable risks:
1. Change in tastes/fashion;
2. Industrial disputes;
3. Rising Costs.

Mkt Forms: Do firms in PC earn normal profit in the long run? Yes, because normal profit is included in AC and this must be covered in the long run.

1994

Mkt Forms: Consumer Surplus is: the difference between the highest price a consumer is willing to pay rather than do without it, and what the consumer is actually paying.

FOP: No opportunity cost to a firm using an asset it owns: False.

The asset could be sold (and the money invested) or rented out to earn extra income.

Mkt Forms: A profit-max. firm in PC will be in equilibrium in the short run when:
1. MC = MR;
2. MC cuts MR from below;
3. AR covers AVC.

Costs: The Law of Diminishing Returns states: when increasing quantities of a variable FOP are applied to fixed quantities of other FOP, eventually returns will decline.

1995

The Law of Equi Marginal Returns states: that a consumer will enjoy maximum satisfaction when the ratio of MU to price is the same for all different goods s/he consumes.

A perpendicular Supply Curve indicates: that the supply of a commodity is perfectly inelastic e.g. the supply of land to the country as a whole.

Give three reasons why profits are important in a free market system.

– normal profit is necessary for production in the L/R;
– it encourages entrepreneurs to take risks and establish a business;
– it allows businesses to finance expansion, research & development;
– it encourages investment;
– it allows the government to raise tax revenue.

A discriminating monopolist in order to earn maximum profits must produce that quantity of a good where MC = :

MC = MR (domestic) = MR (export).

List two forms or methods of collusion that firms operating in an oligopolistic market may practise:

– Limit pricing / Price collusion / Cartels
– Limiting the output produced
– Segmenting the market i.e. dividing the market between the firms.

1996

Economic Rent is defined as: the payment to an FOP over and above its supply price.

In perfect competition a firm will be in long run equilibrium when:
– MC = MR = AC = AR and
– AC is at a minimum point.

The Law of Diminishing Marginal Returns states: As more of a variable FOP is combined with fixed amounts of other FOPs the returns per unit to the variable FOP will eventually diminish.

To state that a trade union is a monopoly supplier of labour means that: they control the price of labour (wage rate) *or* the quantity of labour supplied to the market *but not both*.

1997

The Law of Diminishing Marginal Utility states: that as you consume additional units of a good the marginal utility gained from the last unit consumed will eventually diminish.

List three forms or methods of collusion which firms which are operating in an oligopolistic market may practise:

– Limit pricing / Price collusion / Cartels
– Limiting the output produced / Quota systems
– Segmenting the market i.e. dividing the market between the firms
– Refusal to supply firms who also buy from firms not in the cartel.

Define external economies of scale. Give TWO examples. These are the cost advantages to a firm when the industry in which it operates grows in size.

(i) better infrastructure
(ii) bulk purchasing of raw materials
(iii) development of subsidiary trades
(iv) development of separate research & development industries/units.

1998

What is Limit Pricing? Setting prices at a level which restricts competition / in an oligopoly market.

The Supply Price of a factor of production is: the minimum payment necessary to bring a factor of production into use and maintain it in that particular employment/use.

The MPP of a factor of production is: the increase in total output which occurs when one extra unit of a factor is employed.

State the two economic characteristics that land has:

(i) It is fixed in supply.
(ii) It has no cost of production / It is a free gift of nature / All its earnings are economic rent.
(iii) Land is a non-specific factor of production.

1978

Nat. Inc.: R/ship between GNP @ factor cost & national income: Nat. Income + Depreciation = GNP @ factor cost.

Tax: A Regressive tax is: falls most heavily on the lower income groups. Takes a higher % of income from lower income groups as Y decreases.

Govt: Name a product or firm which gets a govt subsidy & state why the govt considers it necessary.

CIE, because of the social service provided by CIE.

Int. Trade: Alteration in E/Rs: Yr 1 $1.83 = £1Stg. Yr 2 $1.85 = £1Stg. Has Sterling app./dep.?

Sterling has appreciated. It is now worth 2 cents more.

Econ. Aims: Two examples of Social Cost: vandalism, noise production, traffic congestion, pollution of atmosphere.

Econ. Aims: Two items of Infrastructure: roads, schools, hospitals etc.

1979

Nat Inc.: MPM means: the proportion of each additional unit of income spent on imported gds/servs.

Int. Trade: Two reasons why the value of the US$ on for. exch. mkts might not change even though all US workers got an increase in wage rates:

(i) ↑ productivity of American workers so unit costs of prodn are not increased.

(ii) American Central Bank intervenes to maintain exchange rates.

Banking: State effect on Ms of:

(a) ↑ in comm. banks' liquidity ratios: decrease.
(b) Buying govt bonds by Cen. Bank: increase.
(c) Increase in special deposits: decrease.

Econ. Aims: In a free enterprise economy the price paid for a good is always equal to:

(a) Social cost. No.
(b) Average cost of production. No.
(c) MC of production. No.

1980

Banking: PLR is: ratio of the holdings of a bank of notes and coins, plus balances with the Central Bank, to its current and deposit a/c liabilities.

EEC: A common market is:

(i) a free trade area;
(ii) a common external tariff;
(iii) free movement of lab. & cap.

Nat. Income: R/ship between GNP @ factor cost – Depreciation = National Income.

Inter Trade: Significance of an alteration in our TOT. from 105 to 103? TOT have deteriorated, i.e. for each unit of exports we can buy less units of imports.

Employ: Will the following ↑ or ↓ employment?

(a) ↑ 10% in productivity when money wages ↑ by 8%: increase.
(b) ↑ from 8.75% to 10% in employees' PRSI contr.: decrease.
(c) removal of emp. subsidies: decrease.

1981

Banking: Central Bank's Rediscount Rate means the r/i charged by the Cen. Bank for discounting first class bills of exchange or for acting as lender of last resort.

Nat. Inc.: If multiplier is 2 and MPC = 0.7, what is the MPM? $\frac{1}{1-(0.7-\text{MPM})}=2$, hence MPM = 0.2

Inter. Trade: What is the IMF? An institution set up to promote exchange rate agreements between countries and so encourage international trade.

Inter. Trade: Two possible effects of a quota on imports:

(i) Smaller qty of good on mkt;
(ii) Possible price increase.

Nat. Inc.: Two factors which affect savings:

1. Rates of interest;
2. Inflation rates;
3. Level of income.

Budgeting: A budget deficit is certain to ↑ GNP if:

(a) Govt spends money rather than invest it: No.
(b) Govt spends tax revenue abroad rather than @ home. No.
(c) Govt spends rather than saves: Yes.

1982

Tax: A Progressive tax is: one which takes into account a person's ability to pay and takes proportionately more from people on high incomes.

Nat. Inc.: If GNP at mkt prices is greater than GNP @ factor cost, then taxes exceed subsidies.

Budgeting: Estimates of Receipts & Expenditure of the govt shows: the estimated revenue & expenditure of each govt dept in the next fiscal year.

Intro: The deductive method of reasoning used in economics consists of: observing events and analysing the forces which cause them/reasoning from the general to the particular.

Inter. Trade: A Common Mkt is:

(i) where a free trade area exists;
(ii) a common external tariff is applied; and
(iii) free movement of labour and capital.

Banking: The Central Bank's Rediscount Rate is: r/i charged for discounting first class bills of exchange or acting as lender of last resort.

Int. Trade: If our TOT change from 103 to 98, then the P_X relative to P_M has increased/decreased, because one unit of Xs can now buy less units of imports.

Nat. Inc: GNP as a measure of welfare:

a) does not reflect inequalities in the distr. of income. True.
b) includes only the value of gds/servs actually bought and sold. True.

1984

Int. Trade: Exchange Risk in int. trade means: the danger that an exchange rate may change in the period between agreement on price and its payment.

Pop. & Empl.: Is Ireland underpop. or overpop? Overpopulated, as an ↑ in pop. => a↓ in GNP per head.

Econ. Aims: Example of one private benefit and one social benefit from second level educ.

Private: easier to get a job; entry to 3rd level; increased earning capacity.

Social: productivity of workforce increased; reduced vandalism.

Tax: Would an ↑ income tax allowance of £300 be of equal benefit to a man paying £10,000 tax or paying £50?

No, because the marginal rate of the big earner is higher than that of the lower earner.

1985

Banking: M/3 means: currency + (inter-bank balances) or current a/cs and deposit a/cs in associated & non-associated banks.

Econ. Aims: If a private co. constructs a toll bridge, are there any social benefits (a benefit which you don't have to pay for)?

Yes: less traffic pollution; better traffic flow.

Banking: Two courses of action which the Central Bank might take to reduce the money supply:

1. ↑ liquidity ratios;
2. ↑ bank rate;

3. Sell in open mkt operations;
4. Call in special deposits.

1986

Budg.: A neutral budget is: where current govt expenditure = current govt revenue. It is neither inflationary nor deflationary.

Banking: A Funding Operation by the Central Bank means: selling s/t loans instead of m/t or l/t loans so as to ↓ cash reserves and ↓ credit.

Nat. Inc.: If MPC = 0.7 and MPM = 0.2, by how much do imports rise if there is an injection of £1,000 into the economy?

$$\text{Mul.} = \frac{1}{1-(0.7-0.2)} = 2. \uparrow \text{GNP} = £1,000 \times 2 =$$

£2,000. 0·2 of this is spent: £400 on imports.

Int. Trade: The formula for calculating the 'terms of

$$\text{trade'} = \frac{\text{Index of Export Prices}}{\text{Index of Import Prices}}$$

1987

Intro: Supply-side policies/economics refers to: policies designed to increase the level of economic activity by making markets more efficient.

Int. Trade: Balance of Autonomous Transactions refers to: bal. on Curr. a/c + l/t Capital Inflows.

Int. Trade: A common market exists between countries when:

(i) a free trade area exists;
(ii) a common external tariff is applied;
(iii) free movement of labour and capital.

General: If the level of econ. activity is falling, state if this adds to or lessens the level of econ. activity:

(i) the multiplier process. Lessens.
(ii) payment of unemp. benefits. Adds to.

1988

Banking: Short-term Credit Facility (STF): borrowing by the commercial banks from the Central Bank at a penal rate of interest set by Central Bank.

Intro.: The deductive method of reasoning: observing events and analysing the forces which cause them, or reasoning from the general to the particular, or looking at the effects and finding the causes.

Int. Trade: Capital a/c section of the BOP: transfers from EC institutions; repatriation of profits; foreign borrowing/lending by banks or govt.

Budgeting: Automatic Stabiliser: taxation, social welfare benefits.

1989

Econ. Growth: Econ. development: where an ↑ in the GNP (or std of living) in the economy involves a change in the structure of society.

Budgeting: PSBR: borrowing of the entire public sector, i.e. central govt, local authorities and state-sponsored bodies.

Int. Trade: Fav. movement in terms of trade means: that the price of imports has fallen relative to the price of exports (or vice versa), or a given volume of exports will buy a greater volume of imports.

Nat. Income: GNP @ Factor Cost ± Net Factor Income from the rest of world = GDP @ Factor Cost.

Econ. Aims: Private benefit of 2nd level education: improved earning ability of individual.

Social benefit of 2nd level education: less vandalism; quality of labour force improves.

Banking: Funding: selling s/t loans instead of m/t or l/t loans so as to ↓ cash reserves and ↓ credit.

1990

Budgeting: A neutral budget means: neither inflates/deflates the economy.

Int. Trade: Balance of Autonomous Transactions refers to: Balance on Current a/c of BOP & long-term capital inflows.

1991

Budgeting: The effective incidence of a tax is: who ends up paying the tax. The impact of a tax is where the tax is levied. Whether the incidence is the same depends on the relative price elasticities of supply & demand.

Budgeting: The PSBR is: borrowing by the Exchequer plus borrowing by state agencies and local authorities.

Banking: Funding means: the Central Bank is lengthening the time profile of the debt. It is exchanging short-term loans (or loans almost mature) for long-term loans.

Econ. Growth: The Accelerator Principle is: where an increase in demand for consumer goods results in a more than proportionate increase in the demand for capital goods.

1992

Banking: The Central Bank Re-discount Rate means: the interest rate charged by the Central Bank when it acts as lender of last resort, i.e. for re-discounting first class bills of exchange.

Population: A country is overpopulated when: a rise in population leads to a decrease in the GNP per head.

Int. Trade: The Capital a/c of the BOP is: an account of a country's inflow & outflow of capital which give rise to a consequent net increase/decrease in the external reserves of a country.

Econ. Thought: The Labour Theory of Value is: the value of an item is equal to the quantity of labour which produced it.

NAT. Income: The MPS is: the proportion of each additional unit of income which is saved.

1993

Budgeting: A progressive tax is one which takes proportionately more from higher income groups, i.e. as incomes rise: tax rises.

Population: Overpopulation occurs when an increase in population leads to a decrease in GNP per head of pop.

Econ. Growth: Social Costs are: the costs to society as a whole of using/producing a product, e.g. pollution, noise.

Nat. Income: MPS = 0.26. MPT = 0.24 & MPM = 0.4. If injection of IR£1 m. occurs, find increase in GNP.

$$\frac{1}{(1 - MPC) + MPM + MPT} = \frac{1}{0 \cdot 26 + 0 \cdot 4 + 0 \cdot 24}$$

$$= \frac{1}{0 \cdot 9} = 1 \cdot 1$$

Budgeting: The tax wedge is: the difference between take-home pay and the cost of this person's employment.

1994

Budgeting: The effective incidence of a tax means: the person who suffers the burden of the tax.

Banking: Broad Money Supply means: Currency & Deposit & Current account balances in the associated banks *plus* Deposit & Current a/c balances in the non-associated banks *less* Inter Bank Balances.

Nat. Income: Relationship between GNP at Factor Cost & National Income: GNP – Depreciation = NNP.

Budgeting: A neutral budget means: it neither inflates nor deflates the economy.

Econ. Thought: Malthus's Theory on Food Supply & Population: population increases geometrically while food supply increases arithmetically.

1995

The Primary Liquidity ratio is defined as: The ratio of cash to total deposits which the banks are obliged to (must) maintain by the Central Bank to meet the cash demands of their depositors.

The PSBR is: Borrowing by the state to fund the EBR and Local Authority borrowing and Semi-state bodies.

The difference between GNP @ FC and GDP @ FC is: GDP @ FC +/- Net Factor Income from the Rest of the World = GNP @ FC.

The tax wedge is defined as: The difference between the after tax income which the employee receives and the cost to the employer of employing that employee.

1996

The principal function of the National Management Treasury Agency is: the management of the national debt i.e. to arrange for loans at the cheapest rate of interest and to replace existing dear loans with cheaper new loans.

The tax wedge is defined as: The difference between the after tax income which the employee receives and the cost to the employer of employing that employee.

Assuming that the Irish Economy, MPS = 0.26, MPT = 0.24 and MPM = 0.4, by how much would national income increase if there were an injection of £10 million into the economy?

$$\text{Multiplier} = \frac{1}{1 - (0.74 - 0.4 - 0.26)} = \frac{1}{0.92}$$

$$= 1.09 \times £10m = £11m.$$

Name a source other than the Live Register from which the unemployment figures may be taken: Labour Force Survey.

State two contributions in economic thought of either the monetarists or the supply side economists.

(1) An increase in money supply will cause inflation.
(2) Reduce state involvement/privatisation.
(3) Supply side policies in place of demand management.
(4) Reduce income tax.
(5) Control monopolies.
(6) Reduce the power of Trade Unions.

1997

The 'black economy' is defined as: 'all that economic activity which is not recorded and is not included in the national income accounts'.

The difference between Gross National Product at factor cost and Gross Domestic Product at factor cost is: GNP @ factor cost +/- Net Factor Income from the Rest of the World = GDP at factor cost.

A country is said to have an optimum population when: it has the level of population at which output per person is at a maximum, given the existing economic resources, or constant returns to labour given the existing economic resources.

Define Social Costs. Give two examples.
This is the price/cost which society has to pay for the existence of a particular product.

(i)   pollution – air, water
(ii) noise nuisance
(iii) traffic jams.

The Purchasing Power Parity Theory states: That in the absence of non-price barriers to international trade/in a free market the price of a good should be the same in all markets that have an exchange rate mechanism between them.

State three contributions to economic thought of the monetarist economists:

(1) favoured monetary policy rather than fiscal policy
(2) reduction in money supply will reduce inflation
(3) free trade – minimum government interference
(4) support privatisation.

1998

The PSBR is: EBR (CBD + Capital borrowing) & Semi State and Local Authority borrowing.

The PLR is defined as: The ratio of cash & balances to total deposits which the commercial banks are obliged to maintain by the Central Bank.

Define demand pull inflation: Increase in the level of demand without a corresponding increase in supply thereby causing prices to rise. Aggregate Demand greater than Aggregate Supply.

The tax wedge is defined as: the difference between what it costs an employer to employ a person and that employee's net pay after deductions of tax, PRSI and levies.

A country is said to be overpopulated in the economic sense when: it has too many people in relation to the other production resources.

An Roinn Oideachais

LEAVING CERTIFICATE EXAMINATION, 1997

ECONOMICS - HIGHER LEVEL

SECTION A (100 marks)

Answer any <u>six</u> of the following:-

1. The Law of Diminishing Marginal Utility states

    _____

    _____

    _____

    (16 marks)

2. The 'black economy' is defined as

    _____

    _____

    _____

    (16 marks)

3. The difference between Gross National Product at factor cost and Gross Domestic Product at factor cost is

    _____

    _____

    _____

    (16 marks)

4. List three forms or methods of collusion which firms which are operating in an oligopolistic market may practise.

    _____

    _____

    _____

    (16 marks)

5. A country is said to have an optimum population when

    _____

    _____

    _____

    (16 marks)

. Define external economies of scale. Give **two** examples.

_____

_____

_____

(17 marks)

. Define social costs. Give **two** examples.

_____

_____

_____

(17 marks)

. The Purchasing Power Parity Theory states

_____

_____

_____

(17 marks)

. State **three** contributions to economic thought of the monetarist economists.

_____

_____

_____

_____

(17 marks)

ECONOMICS - HIGHER LEVEL
(400 MARKS)

THURSDAY, 26th JUNE 1997 - MORNING, 9.30 - 12.00

Answer not more than <u>six</u> questions from Section A and <u>four</u> questions from Section B.
Credit will be given for clear, precise, relevant answering and for orderly presentation of material.

SECTION A (100 marks)

The questions in this section are on a separate sheet which also provides space for your answers.
The completed sheet is to be returned with your answer books at the end of the examination.

SECTION B (300 marks)

Not more than <u>four</u> questions to be answered. All questions carry equal marks (i.e. 75).

Note the sub-divisions in the questions.

1.   (a)   Outline the main factors that affect the supply of a good or service.   (25 marks)

   (b)   (i)   Give **one** reason that will cause a movement along a demand curve.

      (ii)   Give **five** reasons that will cause a shift in a demand curve.   (25 marks)

   (c)   There is a small number of types of goods to which the Law of Demand does not apply.
      Discuss briefly **three** of these types of goods.   (25 marks)

                                                                                                [75 marks]

2.   (a)   Explain with the aid of a diagram, the long run equilibrium position of a firm
      operating in perfect competition.   (25 marks)

   (b)   Outline the assumptions governing perfect competition.   (25 marks)

   (c)   (i)   Why does perfect competition benefit consumers?

      (ii)   Why does perfect competition benefit the economy?

      (iii)   A firm operating in perfect competition is said to be a 'price taker'. Explain briefly.   (25 marks)

                                                                                                [75 marks]

3. (a) The unemployment figures that are taken from the Labour Force Survey are significantly lower than those taken from the Live Register. Which do you think gives a more accurate picture of the true level of unemployment? Briefly explain. (20 marks)

(b) List and briefly explain **four** factors that affect the demand for labour by a particular firm. (20 marks)

(c) Outline **three** factors that explain wage differences for different occupations. (20 marks)

(d) State **two** factors that determine the efficiency of labour. (15 marks)

[75 marks]

4. (a) Define:

(i) The Law of Comparative Advantage.

(ii) The Terms of Trade. (20 marks)

(b) Explain, with the aid of an example, the Law of Comparative Advantage. (25 marks)

(c) Discuss the reasons why the Irish economy engages in international trade. (30 marks)

[75 marks]

5. (a) Define the Broad Money Supply (M3). (15 marks)

(b) Explain, with the aid of an example, how the commercial banks can create credit (money). (30 marks)

(c) Outline the functions of the Central Bank. (30 marks)

[75 marks]

6. (a) List **two** factors that influence consumer spending in the economy and briefly explain how they do so. (20 marks)

(b) List **four** factors that influence the level of investment by entrepreneurs in an economy, adding a brief explanation in each case. (30 marks)

(c) Outline, with the aid of a diagram, how changes in the level of investment affect the level of National Income. (25 marks)

[75 marks]

7. **(a)** Outline **three** reasons why the government borrows money and increases the National Debt.

(20 marks)

(b) In 1995 the balance outstanding on the National Debt was £30,209 million.

Outline the negative economic consequences or problems caused by the National Debt. (30 marks)

(c) State **three** means by which the Irish government might attempt to reduce significantly the National Debt and outline briefly the likely economic effects of each of these measures. (25 marks)

[75 marks]

8. **(a)** Name **five** semi-state companies that have been privatised in recent years. (15 marks)

(b) Set out arguments for and arguments against the privatisation of semi-state companies.

(40 marks)

(c) Do you think that privatisation of these companies would benefit

(i) the consumer

(ii) the taxpayer

Briefly explain your answer in each case. (20 marks)

[75 marks]

ECONOMICS - HIGHER LEVEL

SECTION A (100 marks)

Answer any **six** of the following:

1. The Public Sector Borrowing Requirement is

   (16 marks)

2. What is Limit Pricing?

   (16 marks)

3. The Primary Liquidity Ratio is defined as

   (16 marks)

4. The supply price of a factor of production is

   (16 marks)

5. Define demand pull inflation.

   (16 marks)

6. The tax wedge is defined as

_____

_____

_____

(17 marks)

7. The Marginal Physical Productivity of a factor of production is

_____

_____

_____

(17 marks)

8. A country is said to be overpopulated in the economic sense when

_____

_____

_____

(17 marks)

9. State the two economic characteristics that land has.

_____

_____

_____

(17 marks)

ECONOMICS - HIGHER LEVEL
(400 MARKS)

THURSDAY, 25th JUNE 1998 - MORNING, 9.30 - 12.00

Answer not more than **six** questions from Section A and **four** questions from Section B.
Credit will be given for clear, precise, relevant answering and for orderly presentation of material

SECTION A (100 marks)

The questions in this section are on a separate sheet which also provides space for your answers.
The completed sheet is to be returned with your answer books at the end of the examination.

SECTION B (300 marks)

Not more than **four** questions to be answered. All questions carry equal marks (i.e. 75).

Note the sub-divisions in the questions.

1. (a) Explain with the aid of a diagram, the long run equilibrium position of a firm which
    is operating in monopoly.   (25 marks)

    (b) How does monopoly lead to an inefficient use of resources?   (15 marks)

    (c) Define price discrimination. Give **three** examples.   (15 marks)

    (d) What are the conditions that must exist to enable price discrimination to be practised?   (20 marks)
    [75 marks]

2. (a) Define **each** of the following and in each case give the formula by which it is measured.
    (i)   Gross Elasticity of Demand
    (ii) Income Elasticity of Demand.   (20 marks)

    (b) If a consumer spends £20 per week on petrol when its price is 60p per litre, and continues to spend
    £20 per week on it when its price is increased to 62p per litre, what is the consumer's price elasticity
    of demand for petrol (in respect of this price change)?   (20 marks)

    (c) Briefly explain how a knowledge of elasticities is useful to
    (i)   A producer of goods who is considering increasing production.
    (ii) The government when it is considering if it should increase indirect tax on a commodity.
    (iii) A monopolist when she is deciding to fix the price for the good which she is selling.
    (35 marks)
    [75 marks]

3. **(a)** State **three** reasons why the unemployment figures taken from the Labour Force Survey are a much more accurate measurement of the true level of unemployment than those taken from the Live Register. (15 marks)

   (b) Economists generally include the following among the reasons for the rather high unemployment rate in Ireland:

   (i) The Irish labour market is inflexible and over-regulated.

   (ii) The difference between take-home pay for an unskilled or semi-skilled worker and the value of the monetary and non-monetary social welfare unemployment benefits available to him is too narrow.

   Discuss each of the above briefly. (30 marks)

   (c) Outline some changes in government policies which might result in higher employment in Ireland.
   (30 marks)
   [75 marks]

4. **(a)** Define **each** of the following:-

   (i) Direct taxation.

   (ii) Indirect taxation.

   (iii) Tax avoidance.

   (iv) Tax evasion. (25 marks)

   (b) Outline **four** adverse economic effects of high levels of direct taxation. (25 marks)

   (c) Suggest **four** means by which the government might reduce direct taxation. (25 marks)
   [75 marks]

5. **(a)** Define: **(i)** Savings

   (ii) Investment. (15 marks)

   (b) List and explain the factors affecting:

   (i) The level of savings.

   (ii) The level of investment by entrepreneurs in the Irish economy at present. (35 marks)

   (c) Suggest some means by which the Irish government might encourage an increased level of investment in the Irish economy. (25 marks)
   [75 marks]

6. **(a)** The Maastricht Treaty sets down a number of economic conditions for member-states of the European Union which wish to participate in monetary union (including the single Euro currency) by 1999.

State **five** of these conditions. In the case of each of the conditions that you have stated, does Ireland fulfil that condition at present. (25 marks)

(b) Outline some of the likely economic effects if Ireland joins the single currency. (25 marks)

(c) What might the likely economic effects be for the Irish economy if Ireland joins but sterling remains outside the single currency. (25 marks)

[75 marks]

7. **(a)** Define 'National Income'. (10 marks)

(b) Define **each** of the following:-
(i) Gross Domestic Product at Factor Cost.
(ii) Gross National Product at Factor Cost.
(iii) Gross National Product at Market Prices. (20 marks)

(c) In Ireland at present would you expect GNP to be greater than, equal to, or less than GDP. Briefly explain your answer. (15 marks)

(d) **(i)** It has been estimated that in the Irish economy,
MPM = 0.4, MPT = 0.24 and MPS = 0.26.
Calculate the value of the multiplier.
(ii) Ireland is a small, very open economy. What would be the likely economic consequences if the government were to raise the level of aggregate demand by using expansionary fiscal and monetary policies. (30 marks)

[75 marks]

8. **(a)** Define the entrepreneur as a factor of production. (10 marks)

(b) Give **two** reasons why the factor of production, enterprise, is unique. (10 marks)

(c) What are the non-insurable risks that an entrepreneur faces in business? (20 marks)

(d) Consider the importance of
(i) Entrepreneurs
(ii) Profits
in a free market economic system. (35 marks)

[75 marks]

ECONOMICS - ORDINARY LEVEL

SECTION A (100 marks)

Answer any <u>six</u> of the following:-

1. What is meant by a direct tax? Give <u>ONE</u> example.

(16 marks)

2. Give <u>TWO</u> examples of current spending by central government.

   (i) _____

   (ii) _____

(16 marks)

3. What is meant by the term **'inflation'**?

(16 marks)

4. A manufacturing firm's costs may be divided into fixed costs and variable costs. Explain what is meant by <u>**FIXED COSTS**</u> and give <u>ONE</u> example of fixed costs.

   EXAMPLE: [ ]

   OR

   Explain what is meant by <u>**VARIABLE COSTS**</u> and give <u>ONE</u> example of variable costs.

   EXAMPLE: [ ]

(16 marks)

5. An increasing number of people are availing of third level education. State **ONE** advantage of this development to the economy in general.

_____

_____

_____

(16 marks)

6. National Income $\gamma = C + I + G + X - M$

$C = £1,200$ m; $I = £300$ m; $G = £400$ m; $X = £40$ m and $M = £30$ m

Calculate, using the above figures, the level of national income.

(Show all your workings)

_____

_____

_____

(17 marks)

7. Complete the following sentence:

Price Elasticity of Demand (P.E.D.) measures:

the percentage change in_____ for a good caused by a percentage

change in the_____ of the good.

For normal goods, price elasticity of demand is_____

(17 marks)

8. State **any three** of the main aims of Government Economic Policy.

(i)   _____

(ii)   _____

(iii) _____

(17 marks)

9. Recent media reports suggest that many individuals are involved in the black economy. What is meant by the term: the **'black economy'**.

_____

_____

_____

(17 marks)

ECONOMICS - ORDINARY LEVEL
(400 MARKS)

THURSDAY, 26 June - 9.30 - 12.00

Answer not more than **SIX** questions from Section A and **FOUR** questions from Section B. Credit will be given for clear, precise answering and orderly presentation of material.

SECTION A (100 marks)

The questions in this section are on a separate sheet which also provides space for your answers. The completed sheet is to be returned with your answer books at the end of the examination.

SECTION B (300 marks)

Not more than **FOUR** questions to be answered. All questions carry equal marks (i.e. 75)

Note the sub-divisions in the questions.

1. The diagram below represents the long run equilibrium position of a firm in **Perfect Competition**.

Marginal Cost

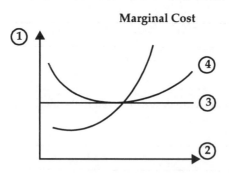

(a) (i) Copy the diagram into your answerbook and clearly label each of the lines numbered, 1 to 4.   (8 marks)

     (ii) Show on your diagram:
           • the output the firm will produce.
           • the average cost of producing this output.
           • the price it will charge for this output.
           • whether the firm is earning normal profit or super normal profit.   (17 marks)

(b) One of the assumptions/characteristics of perfect competition is that all the goods sold are homogeneous goods.

    (i) Explain what is meant by the term: 'homogeneous goods'.

    (ii) Should a firm in perfect competition advertise its goods?
        Explain your answer clearly.   **(20 marks)**

(c) Consider the example of a firm in Ireland which is involved in the supermarket trade. These firms regularly advertise.

Outline **one** advantage and **one** disadvantage of advertising in the case of any **two** of the following:

    (i)   the supermarket itself.

    (ii)   a consumer who uses the supermarket.

    (iii)   the economy in general.   **(30 marks)**

                                                          [75 marks]

2. A manufacturing firm combines labour with the other factors of production to produce a product.
It then sells this product on the market and receives the revenue.

(a) Name the **other** factors of production referred to above.   **(15 marks)**

(b) State and explain briefly **two** reasons which would encourage a manufacturing firm to employ additional workers.   **(20 marks)**

(c) Most workers, when the wage rate per hour increases, are willing to work more hours. But there are some workers who prefer to work less hours as the wage rate per hour increases. Suggest **one** reason why a worker might choose to do this?   **(10 marks)**

(d) All workers do not receive the same rate per hour worked. A skilled person may earn many times as much as what an unskilled worker earns.
State and explain briefly, **three** reasons why there are different wage rates paid for different jobs.   **(30 marks)**

                                                          [75 marks]

3. The diagram below represents **demand** and **supply** in a market.

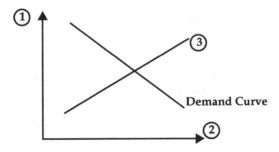

(a) **(i)** Copy the above diagram into your answer book and clearly label the lines, 1 to 3.

    (ii) Show on your diagram:
      • the price charged for the goods on this market.
      • the quantity sold on this market.   **(25 marks)**

(b) Suppose the demand curve in the above diagram moves out to the right as shown below:

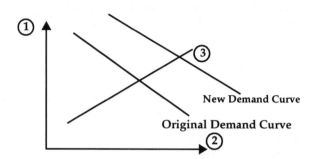

New Demand Curve

Original Demand Curve

      (i)   State (or show) what has happened to the price charged and the quantity sold;
                                       (10 marks)

      (ii)   State and explain **two** reasons why this might happen i.e. why a consumer
             would demand more of a commodity.   (15 marks)

(c)   During 1996 the demand for beef by Irish consumers declined.
      (i)   State and explain **one** reason for this decline.
      (ii)   State and explain **one** effect which this decline in demand for beef may have on beef
            producers in Ireland.
      (iii)   State and explain **one** measure which the European Union could take to help Irish beef
            producers.   (25 marks)

                                                        [75 marks]

4.   **(a)** The estimated government current budget for 1996 was as follows:

Government current income:	£12,434 m	Government current expenditure:	£12,516 m

Answer the following questions:

      (i)   What is the amount of the difference in the two figures given, and what is the economic term
           used to describe this difference?

      (ii) How does the government finance this difference?

      (iii) Give **two** examples of government current income.   (20 marks)

    (b) The government collects considerable amounts of revenue in taxes each year.
        State **two** uses to which this tax revenue is put.   (10 marks)

    (c) Explain the effect which a reduction in the rates of income tax in Ireland would have on **any two** of
        the following:
        (i)   the government's current budget;
        (ii)   the level of employment in Ireland;
        (iii)   the level of emigration from Ireland.   (20 marks)

(d) Three examples of indirect taxes in Ireland are:

Value Added Tax, Excise Duty and Custom (import) Duty.

     (i)   Explain briefly but clearly any **two** of the above taxes.

     (ii)   State and explain **one** reason why the government chooses regularly to increase the rate of VAT/Excise Duty on commodities such as cigarettes and alcohol and not on foodstuffs.

                                      (25 marks)

                                   [75 marks]

---

5. Membership of the European Union has resulted in many benefits to Ireland's small open economy.

    (a) **(i)**   Name **three** members of the European Union, other than Ireland.

         (ii)   What is meant by the term: 'open economy'.   (20 marks)

    (b) State and explain **three** benefits of membership of the European Union to Ireland.   (30 marks)

    (c)

        In period 1: | IR£1 = 10 Deutschmark | In period 2: | IR£1 = 5 Deutschmark |

The Irish punt has gone down in value relative to the German Deutschmark. Discuss the possible effects that this fall in the value of the Irish punt will have on:

     (i)   Ireland's **exports** to Germany.

     (ii)   Ireland's **imports** from Germany.   (25 marks)

                                   [75 marks]

---

6. **(a)** Money is defined as anything which is accepted in payment of a debt.

        State **two** items which are accepted as money in a modern economy.   (10 marks)

    (b) The four functions of money in an economy are:
- It acts as a medium of exchange.
- It acts as a measure of wealth.
- It acts as a store of wealth.
- It acts as a standard of deferred payment.

        Explain what is meant by any **two** of the above functions.   (20 marks)

    (c) **(i)**   State **any two** of the functions of the Central Bank.

         (ii)   Write brief notes on **each** of these functions.   (30 marks)

(d) Suppose the supply of money in an economy is greater than the supply of goods and services in that economy.

Explain the effects which this may have on **either**:

(i)   Prices for goods and services in that economy;

or

(ii)   The amount of goods imported into that economy.   (15 marks)

[75 marks]

7. **(a)** Explain what is meant by the term 'Full Employment'.   (15 marks)

    (b) The number of people unemployed in Ireland has been falling recently.

(i)   State and explain **two** possible reasons for this.

(ii)   State and explain **two** benefits of this to the Irish economy.   (30 marks)

    (c) In recent years the number of people emigrating from Ireland has declined.

(i)   State and explain **two** reasons for the high levels of emigration from Ireland in the past.

(ii)   State and explain **two** reasons why the numbers emigrating has declined.   (30 marks)

[75 marks]

8. **(a)** Many underdeveloped countries (UDC's, sometimes referred to as the Third World) are experiencing economic problems at the moment.

(i)   State **four** problems which UDC's are currently experiencing.

(ii)   Write brief notes on any **one** of these.   (30 marks)

    (b) The governments of these countries could take various measures to deal with those problems.

(i)   State **three** of these measures.

(ii)   Write brief notes on any **two** of these measures.   (25 marks)

    (c) Consider an underdeveloped country which is beginning to develop its infrastructure (such as improvements in land, transport, communications, education, health, housing etc.).

•   State and explain **two** advantages of these improvements to the citizens of the country.

or

•   State and explain **two** disadvantages of these improvements to the citizens of the country.   (20 marks)

[75 marks]

LEAVING CERTIFICATE EXAMINATION, 1998

ECONOMICS - ORDINARY LEVEL

SECTION A (100 marks)

Answer any <u>six</u> of the following:-

1. In the case of **THREE** of the following what do the initials stand for?
   (i)   EBR: _____
   (ii) IMF: _____
   (iii) ECU: _____
   (iv) WTO: _____
   (16 marks)

2. Savings, in economics, simply means not spending all or part of your income. State **TWO** factors which may affect a person's level of savings.
   (i)   _____
   (ii) _____
   (16 marks)

3. Complete the following sentences:
   Economics is a _____ science. It studies how scarce _____ are best
   distributed to satisfy our infinite_____ and _____ .
   (16 marks)

4. State and explain **ONE** method by which a government might restrict free international trade.
   _____
   _____
   _____
   (16 marks)

5. Name one of the two sources from which the numbers of people unemployed in Ireland are taken.
   _____
   _____
   (16 marks)

6. When a demand curve shifts outwards from the origin (i.e. out to the right) more of the commodity will be demanded by the consumer. State and explain **ONE** factor which may cause a demand curve to shift out to the right.
   _____
   _____
   _____
   (17 marks)

7. What is meant by an indirect tax?

_____

_____

Give two examples of indirect taxes.

(i) _____ (ii) _____

(17 marks)

8. State **TWO** of the functions of money.

(i) _____

(ii) _____

(17 marks)

9. A student who completes his/her Leaving Certificate in June enters a third level college in September. Suggest **ONE** possible 'opportunity cost' of this course of action to the student.

_____

_____

_____

(17 marks)

ECONOMICS - ORDINARY LEVEL
(400 MARKS)

THURSDAY 25 JUNE - 9.30 - 12.00

Answer not more than **SIX** questions from Section A and **FOUR** questions from Section B. Credit will be given for clear, precise answering and orderly presentation of material.

SECTION A (100 marks)

The questions in this section are on a separate sheet which also provides space for your answers. The completed sheet is to be returned with your answer books at the end of the examination.

SECTION B (300 marks)

Not more than **FOUR** questions to be answered. All questions carry equal marks (i.e. 75).

Note the sub-divisions in the questions.

1. The diagram below represents the long run equilibrium position of a firm in **Imperfect Competition**.

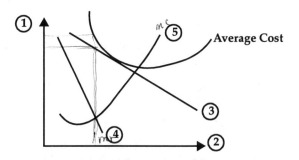

(a) (i) Copy the diagram into your answerbook and clearly label each of the lines numbered, 1 to 5. (10 marks)

(ii) Show on your diagram:
- the output the firm will produce.
- the average cost of producing this output.
- the price it will charge for this output.
- whether the firm is earning normal profit or supernormal profit. (20 marks)

(b) (i) State **FOUR** distinguishing characteristics/assumptions of an Imperfectly Competitive market structure.

(ii) Write brief notes on any **THREE** of these. (25 marks)

(c) The firm shown in the above diagram does not produce at the lowest point of the average cost.

   (i)   Suggest one reason why this may be the case.
   (ii)   Are the resources being efficiently used? Explain briefly.   (20 marks)

                                                                               [75 marks]

2. The Law of Diminishing Marginal Utility states 'that as we consume more of a good or service the extra utility we get from consuming each extra unit will eventually fall'.

   (a)   Suggest **TWO** commodities which people consume which may not result in the fall of their marginal utility.
          Explain your answers briefly.   (20 marks)

   (b) (i) Complete the following Table

Number of oranges consumed	1	2	3	4	5
Total utility in utils.	12	29	47	58	66
Marginal Utility, in utils (for each extra orange consumed)	12			11	

   (ii) At what point does Diminishing Marginal Utility set in?
   (iii) Explain your answer, briefly.   (25 marks)

   (c)   The following diagram represents the Supply of Irish Potatoes and the Demand for Irish Potatoes in Irish supermarkets.

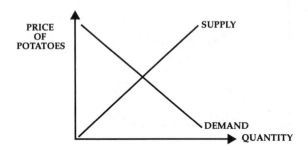

   Explain the effects which **EACH** of the following may have on
                              EITHER
                      the Supply of Irish Potatoes
                              OR
                      the Demand for Irish Potatoes

   (i)   a successful advertising campaign in favour of Irish potatoes is introduced;
   (ii)   a tariff on imported potatoes is removed;
   (iii)   bad weather disrupts the production of Irish potatoes.

   Explain your answers clearly. You may use diagrams if you wish.   (30 marks)

                                                                               [75 marks]

3. (a) An entrepreneur requires factors of production to produce commodities. One of these factors of production is **'enterprise'**.

      (i)   Name the other **THREE** factors of production.

      (ii) Explain what is meant by **'enterprise'**. (20 marks)

   (b) The factor of production enterprise is different from the other factors of production. State and explain **TWO** reasons why this is so. (20 marks)

   (c) Entrepreneurs are important to the growth of an economy.

      (i)   State and explain **TWO** reasons why entrepreneurs are so important to the Irish economy.

      (ii) State and explain **TWO** ways by which the Irish government could encourage more individuals to become entrepreneurs . (35 marks)

                                                                       [75 marks]

4. (a) Some semi-state companies have been privatised.

      (i)   Explain what is meant by the term 'privatisation'.

      (ii) Give **ONE** example of a company that has been privatised.

      (iii) Give **TWO** reasons why the government has privatised some semi-state companies. (25 marks)

   (b) State **ONE** possible effect which privatisation may have on **ANY TWO** of the following:

     •   the taxpayers in the economy;
     •   the employees within the state companies;
     •   the consumers of the company's good or service. (25 marks)

   (c) The rate of income tax has been falling recently in Ireland.

     Answer **ANY TWO** of the following:

      (i)   Will this development encourage people to work?

      (ii) How might this development affect the demand for goods and services in the economy?

      (iii) How might this development affect the level of inflation in Ireland?

     Explain your answers clearly. (25 marks)

                                                                       [75 marks]

5. (a) (i)   Explain what is meant by visible/physical exports.

           Give **TWO** examples of visible exports.

      (ii) Explain what is meant by invisible exports.

           Give **TWO** examples of invisible exports. (25 marks)

   (b) The industrial Development Authority has been successful in attracting more foreign companies into Ireland.

     Discuss the effect(s) of this development on **ANY TWO** of the following:

      (i)   the level of employment in Ireland;

      (ii) the balance of payments;

      (iii) the level of government current revenue (or government current expenditure).

     Explain your answers clearly. (30 marks)

   (c) State and explain **TWO** reasons why - in your opinion - foreign companies find Ireland an attractive location for their operations. (20 marks)

                                                                       [75 marks]

6. (a) The National Income of a country is the total of the incomes received by each of the four factors of production in that country in a given year.
   (i) Name the **THREE** ways which are used to calculate National Income.
   (ii) Give **ONE** reason why all these three methods are used, instead of one. (20 marks)

   (b) The Gross National Product of a country at market prices is defined as 'the value of all the goods and services produced in a country valued at the prices paid for them by consumers in the market'

   Explain the effect which each of the following will have on GNP at market prices:
   (i) a rise in the level of Value Added Tax;
   (ii) the payment of food subsidies to Irish producers. (20 marks)

   (c) Given: National Income = C + I + G +X - M
   C = £1,200m; I = £500m; G = £300m; X = £40m and M = £30m.
   (i) Explain what each of the above symbols/letters stands for.
   (ii) Calculate, using the figures provided, the level of national income.
   Show all your workings. (15 marks)

   (d) Ireland's Gross National Product has been rising in recent years.
   State and explain **TWO** advantages of this development to the economy. (20 marks)

   [75 marks]

7. (a) (i) List **FOUR** of the main economic aims of the government.
   (ii) Write brief notes on **ANY THREE** of these aims. (25 marks)

   (b) The government has certain policies available to it to help it achieve its aims. Among these are:
   - Fiscal Policy
   - Monetary Policy
   - Prices and Income Policy.

   Explain what is meant by **ANY TWO** of the above policies. (30 marks)

   (c) The government is paying the fees for students who attend third level colleges in Ireland.
   (i) State **ONE** economic advantage and **ONE** economic disadvantage of this policy.
   (ii) Write brief notes on each of your answers in (i) above. (20 marks)

   [75 marks]

8. (a) The number of people living in the Irish Republic is counted regularly. This is usually done once every five years
   What is this called? (10 marks)

   (b) Many economists have commented on Ireland's 'greying population'. They are referring to that fact that Ireland's population is getting older.
   State and explain **TWO** consequences of this development for the Irish economy. (20 marks)

(c) Rev. Thomas Malthus considered the problems of population and food supply.

Answer **ANY TWO** of the following:

(i) What did he say concerning population and food supply?

(ii) What did he say concerning population and wage rates?

(iii) To which school of economic thought did he belong? (20 marks)

(d) One of the advantages to workers of membership of the European Union is the increased mobility of labour.

(i) State **ONE** way in which EU membership has improved the mobility of labour.

(ii) It is understood that some unemployed people refuse an offer of an unskilled job. State **TWO** reasons why they might refuse such a job. (25 marks)

[75 marks]